Europe 1492

Europe 1492

Portrait of a Continent Five Hundred Years Ago

Franco Cardini

Facts On File
New York • Oxford

Opposite the frontispiece: Detail of Battle of Lapiths and Centaurs, *by Michelangelo Buonarroti. The artist's biographer, Ascanio Condivi, says that the work was completed on the death of Lorenzo the Magnificent (April 1492) and that it represents "the rape of Deianeira [the wife of Heracles] and the battle of the centaurs." The theme is obscure to moderns, but what is shown is probably the rape of Hippodameia by the centaur Eurytion, an episode from Ovid's* Metamorphoses. *Michelangelo was then 18; at 13 he had been placed as an apprentice in the Florentine workshop of Domenico and Davide Ghirlandaio against the will of his parents, since to his father and uncles it seemed "shameful" to have art in their house. The young Michelangelo then spent two years in the Medici household, visiting the Medici garden at San Marco with its "various statues and ornate figures." It was here that he began his carer as a sculptor.*

Europe 1492
Portrait of a Continent Five Hundred Years Ago

Copyright © 1989 by Anaya Editoriale s.r.l. / Fenice 2000 s.r.l., Milan

Facts On File books are available at special discounts when purchased in bulk quantities for businesses, associations, institutions, or sales promotion. Please contact the Special Sales Department of our New York office at 212/683-2244 (dial 800/322-8755 except in NY, AK, or HI).

Created and produced by Fenice 2000

Editorial director Lorenzo Camusso
Editing and photographic research Luca Selmi, Cecilia Lazzeri, Jordanit Ascoli
Original art Marco Giardina
Managing editor Orietta Colombai
Production Renzo Biffi
Translation Jay Hyams
Typesetting Fotocompograf s.r.l. Milan
Printing Amilcare Pizzi S.p.A., Cinisello Balsamo (Milan)

Library of Congress Cataloging-in-Publication Data

Cardini, Franco.
Europe 1492: portrait of a continent five hundred years ago / Franco Cardini.
   p. cm.
  Bibliography: p.
  Includes index.
  ISBN 0-8160-2188-0: $ 50.00
  1. Fifteenth century. I. Title.
D203.C37 1989
909'.4--dc19

British Library Cataloguing in Publication Data

Cardini, Franco
Europe 1492: a portrait of a continent 500 years ago.
  1. Europe, 1453-1517
  I. Title
  940.2'1

  ISBN 1-0-81602-188-0

Printed in Italy

10 9 8 7 6 5 4 3 2 1

Contents

Half a Millennium Ago

*Between the Mediterranean and the ocean, Europe is an indented peninsula, rich in ports and landings. By the end of the 15th century, all the coastal areas were being intensely navigated. All that was lacking was the incentive to confront the open sea. The engraving above (*Battle of Ten Naked Men*), by Antonio del Pollaiuolo (ca. 1470), is representative of the humanistic atmosphere of the period.*

ourteen ninety-two. Five hundred years ago, yet the date remains vividly engraved on our historical memory and our collective imagination. In 1492, the peoples of the Old World were roused as extraordinary news flew from Santiago de Compostela to the Vistula, the Bosphorus, and all across Europe. Even now, at a distance of five hundred years, we look back with wonder at that fateful year 1492.

A warm evening on October 11–12, somewhere in the Atlantic Ocean: a little to the east of the island of Guanahani (Watling), the island that would later be called San Salvador, in the magical and tricky waters of the Bahamas. Earlier that day, sailors aboard a little three-ship fleet from

Spain under the command of a Genoese seafarer had gathered from the water indications of land: reeds, pieces of carved wood, and a branch with berries. They had been at sea for more than a month. At about ten o'clock that night, from the quarterdeck of the *Santa Maria*, Christopher Columbus and another sailor saw a dim, quivering light in the distance. The light seemed to be moving, as the admiral would later write, *como una candelilla de cera che se alzava y levantava* ("like a little wax candle rising and falling"). Some scholars have objected that at a distance of about 27 nautical miles — roughly 30 miles, or the distance the ships must then have been from shore — it would have been extremely

difficult to make out such lights. Others have demonstrated, however, that the lights would have been visible, and the most plausible theory is that Columbus was seeing the bonfires lit by the natives to keep fleas out of their cabins.

The lights eventually went out, but Columbus stayed on course, heading for where he had last seen them. Finally, at two in the morning, Rodrigo de Triana, the lookout on the lead ship, the *Pinta*, saw white cliffs in the moonlight and signaled the flagship. The *Santa Maria* caught up and verified the landfall. Columbus sang out to Martín Alonso, the captain of the *Pinta*, "You *did* find land! Five thousand maravedis for you as a bonus!"

The events of that famous night of October 11–12, 1492, have been greatly discussed and even a little embroidered. It has been pointed out that if, a few days earlier, the admiral had not abandoned the westward course for one heading west-southwest, following the flight of "a great multitude of birds," the ships would have entered the Gulf Current and might have landed in Florida or Virginia instead, vastly changing the course of history. Scholars try to avoid speculation, but the temptation exists. It has been noted, however, that there is something mysterious — some have even dared to say fated — in that discovery of the coast of San Salvador: the sailors led on by the flight of birds, the pieces of carved wood floating on the water like a message in a bottle, the light quivering "*como una candelilla.*" The year 1492 was a year of omens.

"I remember that it was the fifth of April MCCCCLXXXXII," the Florentine chronicler Bartolomeo Masi recalled, "around the third hour of night, when a darkness of weather came, water and wind, and six thunderbolts fell together; and they struck the lantern in the cupola of Santa Maria del Fiore [in Florence], which ruined

8

The artist known as the Master of Saint Gudula worked in Brussels around 1480. In this detail from Virgin with Mary Magdalen and a Devout Woman, *the background is depicted through a window that looks out onto a garden and an enchanting view of the sea. Two gentlemen and a lady contemplate the ships on the unruffled waters of the port basin, beyond the crenellated wall. At this time, Italian painting was learning*

to master the representation of perspective and the depiction of unlimited space. This era would also see the discovery of vast new geographical areas. It is tempting to underline this similarity.

A similarly segmented window illuminates the picture by Rogier van der Weyden of Saint Luke Drawing the Virgin. *(There are three almost identical versions in existence, and there is considerable dispute as to which is the original and which are contemporary copies; the detail reproduced here is from the Munich version, end of the 15th century.) A man and a woman turn to look at the small waves that the wind stirs up on the waters of the estuary, the city on the bank, the quays of the port, the little figures that move along the streets between the houses, and the road that goes along the edge of the rocks where knights pass by. Light clouds drift across the sky. We can imagine that the man and woman are waiting for someone's return. It is certain that other men and women waited like this at Palos for those who had left on an unusual sea voyage.*

9

many statues in the church and outside.... When this dark weather came, it was said that it was Lorenzo di Piero di Cosimo de' Medici who had let loose a spirit that he was said to have kept mounted in a ring; it was said that he had freed and let go this spirit, and it was at that point that this event

happened. And it was said that he had kept that spirit in that ring for many years; and because he was very sick at that time, he had freed it."

Bartolomeo Masi thus conjured up a time, in the collective memory of his city

and in his own personal memory, that historians would later see as the "passage" from the Middle Ages to the modern age. What could be more symbolic than that Lorenzo the Magnificent, a Solomon with a savvy nose for business, should, on the eve of his death, free from a ring the demon that, in the imagination of his fellow citizens, had been his companion and had helped him accumulate his family's vast fortune and guide the state? It seems that, in reality, Lorenzo was not as capable a politician — or wizard — as he seemed (or as his contemporary historian Francesco Guicciardini made him out to have been), and without doubt, he was not at all a capable administrator of his financial fortune. Nevertheless, this liberated demon can be taken as a symbol for the passage from the "Christian" Middle Ages to the "Faustian" modern age. These were times that rushed ahead on their own momentum, that seemed determined to forge a new future.

Ten months before the admiral's arrival on the dunes of San Salvador and four months before the departure from this earth of the Magnificent, something else of importance had happened: On January 2, 1492, the Catholic rulers Isabella of Castile and Ferdinand of Aragon made their formal entrance into the Alhambra of Granada, the last Muslim palace in Europe. (While 48 years earlier, at the other end of the continent, the age-old palace of the Byzantine emperors, the world's foremost Christian monarchs, had become an Ottoman seraglio.) "Only God is the true conqueror," cautioned Arab writings decorating the walls and ceilings of the splendid residence of Granada. The western crusade had met with complete success, and Christ now prepared — with the admiral — to cross the ocean. A few weeks later, on March 31, the Catholic kings signed an edict expelling the Jews from Spain: many converted, others fled. This was the final step in a long process that began with the destruction of Jerusalem

The British Isles were ruled by the hereditary monarchies of England and Scotland. The English crown also controlled the city of Calais in France and part of Ireland.

The borders of the Holy Roman Empire did not always coincide with political realities: For example, Silesia and Moravia were ruled by the king of Hungary, and the Swiss confederation was independent.

In Scandinavia, the crowns of Denmark and Norway were uniteds. Denmark then included part of what is today southern Sweden.

Four hereditary monarchies ruled the Iberian peninsula: Portugal, Navarre, Castile, and Aragon. Portugal possessed Tangier and Ceuta in Africa. Beginning in 1479, Castile and Aragon were under the same rule.

In France, the English had been driven out (except for Calais) and Burgundy had collapsed. The crown had thus acquired important lands, including Burgundy (1477), Provence (1481), Brittany (1491), and Orléans (1498).

In theory, a large part of Italy was ruled by the Holy Roman Empire, but the peninsula was also home to five important political powers: the republic of Venice, the Papal States of the Church, the Aragon kingdom of Naples, Milan, and Florence.

10

The political arrangement of Europe at the end of the 15th century. Latin was still the universal language for religion, law, diplomacy, and communication among scholars of all disciplines. The European peoples had formed their national identities to a greater or lesser extent, but the political subdivisions, which were still changing, were often far from reflecting these identities.

Sketched in the style of a mariner's pilot book, with radiating lines that correspond to compass directions and small figures of the pope, emperor, and various kings, Europe is presented here with age-old inaccuracies. This map dates from about 50 years after the end of the century. Spain is represented by a figure of Philip II, who became king in 1556.

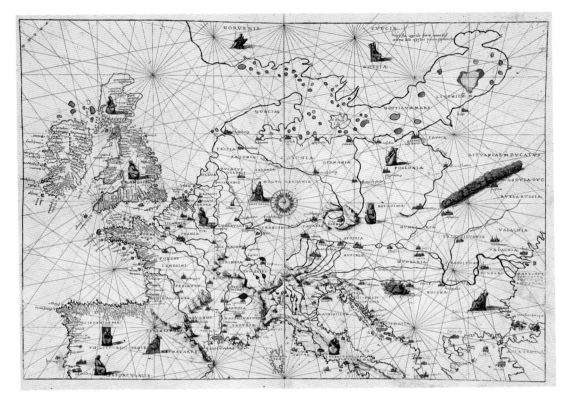

by Titus (A.D. 70), and it ushered in a new age of systematic persecutions, which would eventually lead to the ghettoes, the pogroms, and the desolation of the extermination camps. In this sense, too, one might say that the modern age began in 1492.

While the age was still medieval, it held out portents of the future. The man with that period's most ingenious mind, the one most forward looking—who, indeed, imagined, invented, planned, and sketched the future — was then 40 years old. Leonardo da Vinci was installed at the court of Lodovico Sforza, for whom he designed equestrian statues, cannons, and theatrical machines. A 27-year-old Augustinian monk at the Dutch monastery of Steyn, enthralled by the classics, would soon leave the monastery because of a lack of vocation: Erasmus was about to become the leading scholar of the age. A few years younger was the offspring of a rather illustrious but quite penniless Florentine family, the 23-year-old Niccolò Machiavelli, who, in 1494, would quietly enter the chancellery of his city to begin an unremarkable bureaucratic career. He would later write *The Prince* and become for Elizabethan England the caricature of Italian villainy.

In Florence, the Medici court was in a crisis following the death of Lorenzo the Magnificent. Gone were the days when that court had patronized the humanist scholars Marsilio Ficino and Giovanni Pico della Mirandola. But the house of Piero, Lorenzo's inept son, still patronized both mature artists and promising young talent, among them Michelangelo Buonarroti, adept at wielding the chisel, with a sullen character and a face disfigured by the blow of a fist that had broken his nose. Michelangelo was 17: One year older was the son of a captain of the duke of Ferrara, Lodovico Ariosto, who was studying law but had a stronger inclination for literature: His *Orlando furioso* was first published in 1516 and became an instant classic of romance literature. In Urbino, Raphael Santi, son of the mediocre court painter Giovan-

ni Santi, was nine years old, as was a Saxon boy, Martin, son of a miner named Luther.

These circumstances seem extraordinary. The existence in Europe at the same time of so many geniuses makes us raise those old but not yet exhausted — and even less resolved — historical questions about the coincidences, the imponderables, the "whys" that in one way or another seem to preside over human events.

On the political front as well, 15th-century Europe was home to intrigue, drama, and larger-than-life personalities. A few days after Columbus's departure for what he believed would be Asia, a conclave of cardinals elected as pope Cardinal Rodrigo Borgia, a man rich in goods, worldly energy, lovers, and children. He became Alexander VI, perhaps the most controversial pope of Christendom; a few years later he would arbitrate between Spain and Portugal on their respective areas of influence and expansion in the Atlantic Ocean

and the New World. In France, 22-two-year-old Charles VIII — after being momentarily assured of the union of the duchy of Brittany to his crown, due to his marriage with the duchess Anne — was preparing for the invasion of Naples, thus initiating a conflict with the leader of the Holy Roman Empire, Maximilian of Hapsburg; the Tudor king of England, Henry VII; and the Catholic kings of Spain, Ferdinand and Isabella. The redefinition of Europe's political relationships would follow, years of tension and conflict, first in the Italian peninsula, then in all of western Europe. The Europe of absolute monarchs was at hand, even if they had not yet taken off the cloaks of feudal lords.

What follows here is a vivid portrait of Europe in 1492, the image of a continent drawn at the waning of what would soon become the Old World, and the dawn of the New.

11

Europe:
A Name,
A Political
Reality

Empires lost,
empires founded

You are without doubt the greatest sovereign in the world. You lack but one thing: baptism. Accept a little water, and you will become ruler of all these cowards who wear sacred crowns and sit on blessed thrones. Become my new Constantine: I will be for you a new Sylvester. Convert, and together we will found, from my Rome and from Constantinople, which by now is yours, a new universal order."

These words, addressed to the sultan Mohammed II, were written around 1461 by the humanist Enea Silvio Piccolomini, who had reigned three years on the throne of Peter under the name Pope Pius II. It is very unlikely that his epistle, written in elegant and sharp Latin, ever reached the shores of the Bosphorus: In reality, it was meant to be a bitter and sarcastic *excitatorium* ("incitement") directed to the western princes who had revealed themselves fainthearted and incapable of checking the Turkish peril.

Two years earlier, the pope had tried to unite them in a congress in Italy at Mantua, with the aim of planning a new crusade, but found himself facing the disarming reality that was Europe at that time. The legation of the Holy Roman Emperor Frederick III had shown interest only in making sure that any possible anti-Ottoman undertaking would not benefit his primary Balkan-Danubian enemy, the Hungarian Matthias Corvinus. The duke of Milan and the king of France had glared at each other, each eager to support his own candidate for succession to the throne of Naples, respectively, Ferrante of Aragon and Louis of Anjou. The Florentines and Venetians stalled, looking for ways to fulfill the papal requests — which they could not ignore — yet at the same time avoid displeasing the sultan, from whom they hoped to obtain both commercial and political favors. Only the "Great Prince of the West," Philip III (the Good), duke of Burgundy, had unequivocally supported the pope's planned crusade,

All, or almost all, the sovereigns of Europe at the end of the 15th century are united in prayer before Saint George in this unusual anonymous miniature from a prayerbook, painted around 1493. Pictured are the emperor Frederick III of the Hapsburgs; his son Maximilian, king of the Romans, who would succeed him in 1493; Ferdinand II, ruler of a recently united Spain; England's Henry VII, first of the Tudors, whose marriage to Elizabeth, daughter of Edward IV, had ended the Wars of the Roses. Philip the Handsome, son of Maximilian and Mary of Burgundy, represents a prosperous and dynamic state that did not yet exist as a separate entity, Burgundy. The figure set apart is the young Charles VIII, king of France.

hoping to reap from it chivalric glory and
political and religious prestige — all the
essentials, that is, for gaining uncontested
leadership of Europe.

The congress at Mantua ended without
accomplishing its goals; the "Letter to Mohammed," which in the mind of the pontiff
should have been a call to action, passed
almost unnoticed in the chancelleries of the
western sovereigns. Europe was still governed by the political theory of *res publica
christianorum* ("Christian republic") which
gave leadership to the pope and the emperor,
but in fact the continent was moving towards
becoming in principle what it had already
been for a long time in practice: a mosaic of
princes and republics, each intent on doing
that which, a few decades later, the skeptical
Florentine thinker Niccolò Machiavelli
would define as its own "particular." Those
princes, those republics, were willing at the
most to join together in leagues and tolerate,
in the name of the ancient *auctoritat* ("authority"), rule by the pope or the emperor.
But the diplomatic structure on which a
league or alliance stood was formed of
fragile ethics and mutual consent. It would   15

Philip the Good, duke of Burgundy, surrounded by his court, receives the Chroniques de Hainault *from Jean Wauqelin, a Flemish miniature attributed to Rogier van der Weyden. Of fragile health, Philip became duke at 23 after the murder of his father, John the Fearless (nephew of the king of France, killed by order of his cousin, duke Louis d'Orléans, the leader of the Armagnac). Philip was coldly energetic and astutely pertinacious: During the Hundred Years War he was allied first with the English and then with the king of France. At the height of his fortunes he was reputed to be the most powerful ruler in Christendom. In the miniature he wears the collar of the Order of the Golden Fleece, which he instituted on the occasion of his third marriage. The young man to the duke's left is his son, the future Charles the Bold.*

not be difficult for it to collapse if communal interests in some way conflicted with private desires.

In this sense, the late 15th century saw the dawn of modern Europe, with its continental wars and political intrigues. But practice often precedes the attitudes which support it. The people of the 15th century may have acted like "moderns," but they thought like "medievals." This break in the unity of the Christian world was, in theory, unacceptable. The failure of the pope or Holy Roman Emperor to lead a united Europe had led to a vacuum of power. And since in politics, like nature, any vacuum is immediately filled, into this one flowed the schemes and ambitions of other rulers.

What would the future of Europe have been had good fortune smiled on the plans and nationalistic schemes of the dukes of Burgundy?

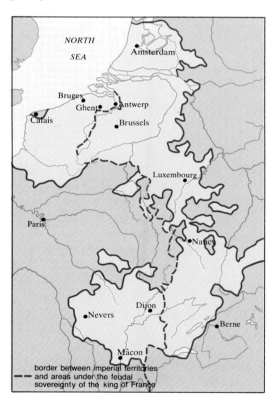

Charles the Bold presides over the chapter of the Order of the Golden Fleece in this Flemish miniature from the 15th century. The golden fleece was a symbolic reminder of the legend of Jason, but the Greek hero had been perjured. The classical theme lent itself to allusions of Burgundy's political attitude to France, so the scholars of the court tended to interpret the symbol of the order as the fleece of Gideon. The

Bible describes how Gideon asked God for a sign: "I will place a wool fleece on the threshingfloor; and if there is dew on the fleece alone, and it is dry on all the ground, I shall know that you will save Israel by my hand" (Judges 6:37). Gideon's fleece was also considered an allegory for the conception of the Virgin.

Burgundy, or rather, the territory governed by the duke of Burgundy in the 15th century. The first large-scale federalistic experiment in Europe, it extended from the North Sea to the Alps, including Amsterdam, Liège, Brussels, Bruges, Ghent, Dijon, Mâcon, Amiens, Nancy, and lands belonging to the French throne and to the empire. Built up by Philip the Good, it ended with the death of his son, Charles the Bold.

In 1447, Philip the Good — French prince of the house of Valois, vassal of the king of France for the duchy of Burgundy and the counties of Flanders and Artois, but also lord, under various titles, of many imperial lands, such as Brabant, Hainault, Luxembourg, and Franche-Comté — had refused the royal crown offered him by Frederick III (who himself, only five years later in 1452, assumed the crown of the Holy Roman Emperor in Rome). Philip did not hide his ambitions, however, and proceeded to build the foundation of what could be defined as the first great experiment in European federalism: He organized a state that, divided into various governing bodies respectful of local traditions and local liberties, extended from Amsterdam and Rotterdam to Dijon and Mâcon and from Amiens to Nancy. The son born of his marriage to Isabella of Portugal, Charles the Bold, carried these ambitions further. Charles dreamed of uniting his states in a single territory and pursued his goal with a severity unknown to his father. His ferocity can be seen in the destruction of Dinant in 1466, the capture of Liège in 1467, and the violent repression of the revolt that took place in that city the following year. It appears in the acquisition of the landgrave of upper Alsace, sold to him in 1469 by Sigismund, duke of Austria, and the conquest in 1473 of the duchy of Gelderland.

Charles was a man of boundless dreams, hoping to gain the imperial crown of the west, perhaps even that of the east, following a crusade that would have liberated Constantinople. In the meantime, he aimed at carving out a state, well knit if not united, wedged between France and Germany that would have revived the 9th-century kingdom of Lotharingia, which had stretched from the North Sea to the Mediterranean. But even with the strong support of England, Savoy, Venice, and Milan, he could not overcome the hostility of the king of France and the Swiss. The Swiss defeated

Opposite: A detail from the Madonna with Chancellor Rolin, by Jan van Eyck. The Burgundian landscape and city in the background have, at different times, been identified with Maastricht (perhaps the painter's birthplace), Liège, Utrecht, Lyons, Geneva, and Autun, but it is probably an idealized setting. To compose it, the artist drew on several different sketches he had made during the course of his travels. Nicolas Rolin was head of the council with which Philip the Good surrounded himself (he appears on the duke's right in the miniature from the Chroniques de Hainault on page 16). Van Eyck was taken on by Philip in 1425 as "valet de chambre" and as court painter with all the implicit "honneurs, prérogatives, franchises, libertéz, droits, prouffis et émoluments."

This mobile arrow launcher (balista quadrirotis), drawn by two armored horses, appears in a codex of the 15th century; it definitely never saw the battlefield. Served by a crew of only two men, it is claimed to be of great use in combat because *ut omni latere in hoste sagittas impellat* ("it fires arrows on the enemy from all sides"). At this time, war machines became enormously creative (including those designed by Leonardo).

This was partly due to suggestions gained from rereading classical texts, but in fact war was being revolutionized by the use of firearms and in particular by artillery, which proved itself effective in sieges.

BALISTA QVADRIROTIS.

Ex emplum baliste qdrirotis.

Xemplum baliste· cuius fa
brica ante oculos positam sbulis
pictura testatur· Subiecta nanq;
rotarum quatuor facilitas duo
bus subiunctis et armatis equis
ad usus hanc bellicos trahit· Cui
tanta e utilitas pro artis industria
ut omni latere i hostes sagittas i
pellat sagittarii libertatem et
manus imitata· habet foramina
per quatuor partes· quibus pro

commoditate rerum circumducta
et flexa· facillime ad oes impetu
parata consistat· que quidem
a fronte coclee machina et depo
nitur celerius et erigitur suble
uata· Sed huius temo in qua
uis partem necessitas uocet cita
et facili conuersione deflexus eri
gitur· Sciendum e autem quod
hoc baliste genus duorum opera
uirorum sagittas ex se non ut

20

"Of mortal things there is nothing more uncertain than the events of war, nothing more unforeseeable; nothing that goes further beyond the minds of men. Victory does not depend either on numbers or on force." This opinion was expressed by the Florentine chancellor Coluccio Salutati, speaking in his official role on behalf of the intentions of the signory. Although he expresses himself in elevated terms, he is in fact describing only the opportuneness of contingency; war was fought in a way suitable to the age. At the top right, the sack of a conquered city in a miniature from the Chroniques, by Jean Froissart, ca 1460; at bottom, a conflict between warriors in armor armed with lances in a 15th-century painting.

him in 1476, at Grandson and Morat, and he fell in battle on January 5, 1477, during a futile attempt to retake Nancy. His corpse, half eaten by wolves, was found two days later.

For a time, it seemed that a century of carefully planned, hard-won gains on the part of the house of Burgundy had been lost. While Ghent was in revolt, the Estates-General took advantage of the opportunity and obtained from Charles's daughter and heiress, the duchess Mary, a "Great Privilege" that destroyed any central power. At the same time, Louis XI of France seized Burgundy and set his sights on Artois and Hainault. Then Flanders, which had a long tradition of revolt against the French crown, reacted against the prospect of falling once again under French domination. From Ghent to Lille, the consensus held that it would be better to remain faithful to Mary, who was now married to Maximilian, son of the Hapsburg emperor Frederick. The French invasion was stopped in August 1479 at Guinegate. Following the death of Mary in March 1482, the Estates-General appointed Maximilian as regent and guardian of their son, Philip the Handsome.

Above: Having disembarked from their ships and set up their luxurious tents (for the commanders) outside its walls, an army prepares for a siege. This is another miniature from the Chroniques, *by Jean Froissart, ca. 1460. Top: Conflict between English and French knights and archers in Normandy (1417) during the Hundred Years War, a miniature from the late 15th century from the* Chronique d'Angleterre, *by Jean de Wavrin.*

Andrea Navagero said of the campaign by Ferdinand of Spain for the conquest of Granada (1492) that it "was a noble war, there was not yet much artillery ...and it was much easier to prove oneself courageous ...every day they were within arm's reach, and every day they did some great deed."

The peace signed with France at Arras in 1482 was tenuous. Towards the end of the 15th century, the Flemish region, like Italy, seemed destined to be, sooner or later, the scene of a European dispute. But in Italy, the "system" of balance (in large part invented *a posteriori* by the historian Guicciardini) seemed to work, whereas Flanders was restless. Maximilian's artillery and mercenaries were unwelcome, and there was constant agitation between 1484 and 1488, first in the Flemish cities, then in those of the Brabant. Then, in 1488, any hope for unity seemed to be shattered: Maximilian was a prisoner at Bruges, French troops owned the countryside, and the people were in revolt, wanting to throw off the Hapsburg yoke and apparently content to return to 21

Charles VIII, appeared content, at least for the moment, with his northeastern borders (and turned his thoughts to Naples and the Mediterranean).

Maximilian was not convinced. After the Italian campaign of the energetic and adventurous king of France, Maximilian quickly drew up an alliance with the Catholic kings of Spain, who seemed to him to

The crossbow

This painting by Carpaccio is one of the large canvases of the *Legend of Saint Ursula.* Drawing the bow of a crossbow was a very difficult operation. Beginning in the 15th century in Germany, Switzerland, France, and England, heavy crossbows, particularly those used in hunting large animals, were supplied with an ingenious mechanism that used cranks and racks to draw the bow. Although a longbow could be fired more quickly, a crossbow fired a heavier arrow with a greater initial velocity; it was a truly lethal weapon. The Second Lateran Council (1139) argued the legality of the crossbow's use in war and sanctioned its use only against infidels. However, Christian princes, when assembling armies to battle other Christian princes, enlisted divisions of mercenary crossbowmen (those from Gascon and Genoa were considered the best).

the old domination under the shadow of the golden fleur-de-lis.

Then, again, the unexpected happened: Antwerp, the citadel of the new mercantile wealth and true heir of the wealthy Bruges, remained faithful to the son of the duchess

22

Mary and to his father and regent. On October 12, 1492 — the same day on which Columbus stepped ashore at San Salvador — the rebellious city of Ghent capitulated. A few months later, with the peace of Senlis (May 1493), the young king of France,

Opposite: Naval forces for use in war. A fleet of round-ended ships (a galley is within sight), anchored off the coast; from Passages faiz oultre mer par le Francois contre les Turcqs, *by Sebastien Mamerots. The event illustrated took place in 1396, although the French artist's illustration was made approximately a century later. War, however, was changing. From the Italian point of view, the awareness of this came*

with Charles VIII at Naples: "Until 1494 wars were long, the days were not bloody, and the ways of taking land by storm were both slow and difficult; and although artillery was already in use, it was used with so little skill that it did not offend very much" (from the History of Italy, *by the Florentine Francesco Guicciardini).*

A ffin qͥl ne se͂ble
que par enuie
ennuy ou fau͛lte
dauoir assez beu

ystoire doustre mer Je naye de
ause la conqueste de consta
tinople faicte par les fracois
ie la toucheray mais en tres
bꝛief en ces pͭits passages aus

par ce q͛lle fut faicte par ͭ͡hi
ens sur ͭ͡hiens. En la cite de
Jadres assegiee ou procham
precedent article arꝛiuerēt
mahieu de mont morency
et plusieurs autres seignez
et pelerins francois. Et en
telle mesmes cite bꝛut par
deuers les pelerins Alexis

Lance, halberd, artillery

A chronicle from Perugia recounts that in 1364 the commune had 500 hand cannons made for use against the English mercenaries led by John Hawkwood. Such hand cannons—small bombards that could be carried by hand—are the ancestors of personal firearms. The oldest record of these weapons may be a Forlì chronicle from 1281. Firing these weapons involved igniting gunpowder with a red-hot iron or piece of charcoal held with tongs. It was necessary to have a lit firebox or oven nearby, so use of these weapons on open ground was practically impossible. It was only during the last three decades of the 16th century that personal firearms began to effectively replace steel—that is, bladed—weapons. The Perugia chronicle states that the hand cannons had the power to pierce armor, a thought that must have had an ominous ring for the knight dressed in his impressive metal suit. However, the decline in armored cavalry was tied to various phenomena, including social as well as military changes; firearms merely delivered the final blow.

During the first phase of the Hundred Years War, the French knights were consistently defeated by English longbows. At Agincourt (1415) 5,000 French knights were killed, most of them victims of

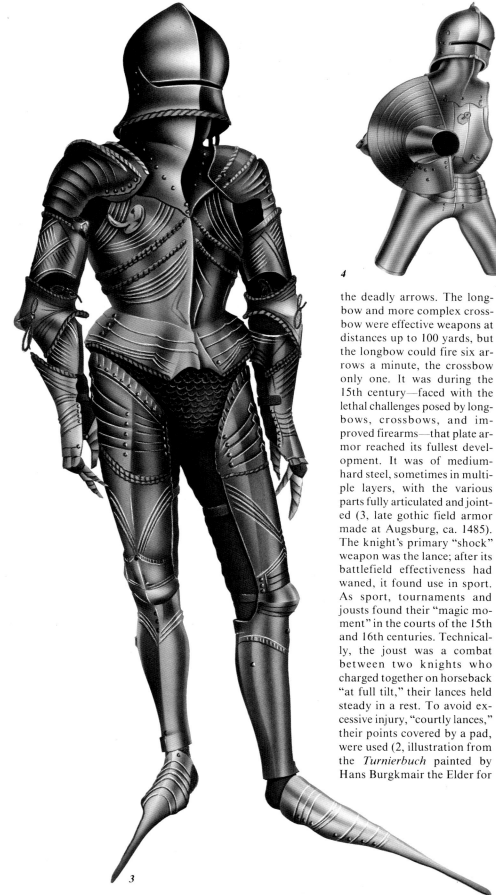

4

the deadly arrows. The longbow and more complex crossbow were effective weapons at distances up to 100 yards, but the longbow could fire six arrows a minute, the crossbow only one. It was during the 15th century—faced with the lethal challenges posed by longbows, crossbows, and improved firearms—that plate armor reached its fullest development. It was of medium-hard steel, sometimes in multiple layers, with the various parts fully articulated and jointed (3, late gothic field armor made at Augsburg, ca. 1485). The knight's primary "shock" weapon was the lance; after its battlefield effectiveness had waned, it found use in sport. As sport, tournaments and jousts found their "magic moment" in the courts of the 15th and 16th centuries. Technically, the joust was a combat between two knights who charged together on horseback "at full tilt," their lances held steady in a rest. To avoid excessive injury, "courtly lances," their points covered by a pad, were used (2, illustration from the *Turnierbuch* painted by Hans Burgkmair the Elder for

1

2

24

3

the Hapsburg emperor Maximilian, a great jousting enthusiast; 4, Maximilian's jousting armor, made at Innsbruck, ca. 1490). To further reduce the danger, the participants were separated by a wall (2). The moment of impact of the knights' charge was electrifying, and it further enhanced the excitement of the tournament, which also depended largely upon ritual for its dramatic effect: formal ceremonies, audiences with ladies, presentation of the knights in their gaudy clothes, fancily caparisoned horses (1, also from the *Turnierbuch*).

On the battlefield, infantry armed with polearms could resist the attack of mounted knights if they remained in compact ranks. The militiamen from the Swiss cantons, deployed in rectangular formations ranging from 20 to 70 men deep, defeated the Haps-

caliber pieces showed their value much earlier than small portable firearms. Powerful cannons soon made the walls of castles useless. On the battlefield, also, artillery proved its effectiveness: At Formigny in Normandy (1450), the French artillery master had two culverins brought to bear on the flank of the English archers and routed them. Without the support of their archers, the English met a bloody defeat. Culverins (from the Latin *coluber*, meaning "snake") were artillery pieces one-quarter to one-third longer than bombards or cannons of the same caliber (6, 7, two Burgundian culverins made of iron, from the middle of the 15th century, both mounted on wheeled carriages). The first artillery pieces, made of bronze or iron, had fixed carriages (8, cannon reconstructed based on a draw-

ing from the final decade of the 14th century). The explosion of the charge knocked them over, and they had to be laboriously righted. Mounting the cannon on a carriage with two or four wheels, which made it easier to transport, helped resolve this difficulty: The recoil rolled the gun back on its carriage, and it could more easily be put back into action.

From the beginning, artillery showed itself most useful in sieges, and only later did cannons become mobile enough to play a dominant role on the battlefield (5, iron mortar from the 15th century; 9, large-caliber bombard built in Flanders, from the middle of the 15th century). Calais was probably the first city to experience assault by artillery (1347). Edward III of England employed about 20 pieces of artillery, and the city surren-

5

dered after 11 months. Many of the projectiles fired by the cannons hit their target, but, according to a contemporary chronicler, "thanks to divine intervention, no one was hurt, not a single man, woman, or child." The projectiles in use were round rocks: They cost less than iron balls and weighed less, which meant that

they could be better propelled by the weaker gunpowder of the time. A century later (1453), Mohammed II arrayed 13 large bombards and another 56 smaller cannons around Constantinople. Each of the bombards, cast by a Hungarian master gunsmith, had to be dragged by 60 oxen and pushed into place by 200 men.

6

7

8

9

burg knights at Sempach (1386) and then the Burgundian chivalry of Charles the Bold at Grandson (1476) and Morat (1476). The deadly weapon at the heart of the Swiss tactical formation was the halberd, a union of the lance and the ax; thus it was both a thrusting and a slashing weapon. The use of the halberd began to decline in the face of portable firearms, but at the end of the 14th and beginning of the 15th centuries, the Swiss infantry dominated the field of battle and were often employed as mercenaries.

The first phase of the Hundred Years War was characterized by the longbow; the second was won by the French and revealed the military importance of artillery. Large-

which were comprised of principalities of various sizes, feudal dominions, both lay and ecclesiastical, and free cities.

Thus the brightest crown in Christendom was, in effect, also one of the weakest. It was weak, first of all, because it was elective and thus necessarily subject to the ongoing tension between those who, having acquired the crown, sought to hand it down to their heirs and those who, though possessing the legal power to bestow the crown, had neither the prestige nor sufficient force to take it themselves and at every new election raised the price of their vote. Since the college of electors was in reality composed of powerful men from the German kingdom, it was an unstable body with uncertain outlines. In 1356, the emperor Charles IV of the dynasty of the counts of Luxembourg — his father had obtained the crown of Bohemia by way of marriage —

be well-suited to keeping his unruly neighbor at bay. In 1496, Maximilian's 18-year-old son, Philip the Handsome, married Joanna, daughter of Ferdinand and Isabella of Spain. The marriage was brief — Philip survived barely another decade — but it resulted in the birth, on February 24, 1500, of a son. For many decades that child of an Austro-Burgundian father and a Spanish mother, a pale boy with the weak Hapsburg jaw, united the destinies of Germany, the Low Countries, a large part of Italy, Spain, and the territories across the sea. Charles was the fifth emperor of that name and the first as king of Spain, and it was said that the sun never set on his empire.

The empire that Charles V established was, by the end of the 15th century, already that *admirabile monstrum* ("admirable wonder") that it would seem to be to the theorists of succeeding centuries. Universal at least in name, the imperial Holy Roman monarchy consisted in reality of the kingdoms of Germany and Italy (the central northern portion of the peninsula), both of

Between Asia, the Atlantic, and the Mediterranean

To imagine ancient landscapes in our postindustrial age we must generalize, using surviving evidence. Swamplands were then more extensive, with immense stretches in northern Germany and Russia and behind the ocean dunes of the Landes in France. The Roman countryside, not yet romantic, was instead desolate, as were the Maremma and the Camargue at the mouth of the Rhone—the Slav name for the Hungarian plain, all grass and ponds, was *pustza*, which means "lonely." The broadleaf forests of Muscovy began to give room to fields of oats, just as agriculture and animal breeding were deforesting central Sweden. To the north were endless expanses of conifers and fur-bearing animals—sable, marten, beaver, squirrel, wolf, otter. In the countryside of woods, swamps, and moors to the east of the Elbe, German colonists had ended their advance, plowing the earth and founding cities, but south of Muscovy the agricultural conquest of the steppes had not yet begun. On the coasts of the North Sea, the struggle to wrest land from the ocean had met little success. In the Mediterranean world, from time immemorial, thickets with the odor of myrtle, lavender, and thyme had replaced the forests. Irrigation had already changed the environment of the Spanish plains and the Po valley, and from the plains to the highlands ran the tracks of sheep herds. From the former Byzantine empire, the mulberry tree had been introduced in Lombardy and the Rhone valley. In the immense Alpine region the conquest of the high valleys continued; there were already valley-dwelling families that owned, aside from a house, a hut in the summer pastures. Various places were already recognizable to a modern's eyes: the well-irrigated orchards of Spain, the rich and coveted land of Lombardy, the fertile land of Campania, the vineyards of the Medoc and Bordeaux, perhaps even all of France, "the most beautiful kingdom of the world after the heavenly kingdom" (Froissart), which was just returning to that state after the devastation of the Hundred Years War.

Green fields, villages hidden by the curve of hills, castles on rocky precipices, and the red glow of a sunset: another detail from the Resurrection, *by Hans Pleydenwurff. Halfway through the 16th century, Francisco de Hollanda, a Portuguese painter of Dutch origin, talking about Northern European painting, said that "one paints principally to reproduce deceivingly the external appearance of things." Painters "paint what people usually call a landscape, and they fill it with figures. Even though this may be pleasing to the eye, it is neither art nor reason." But it is precisely that "external appearance of things" from a past age that people search for and that fascinates.*

The empire was an institutional headache. One of its principal elements was Germany, which was subject to the emperor's authority only in theory. Maximilian became emperor in 1493, but he had already been a significant figure on the European scene for some time. In the German world he was hereditary sovereign of the dukedoms of Austria, Styria, Carinthia, and Carniola and the domain of the Tyrol. The rest of Germany was made up of a series of independent states, with about 30 principalities, 50 ecclesiastical territories, 100 domains, and about 60 cities. Below: On the title page of a register of the privileges of the merchants of Hansa (1484–1485), the emperor appears together with the seven "electors." The council of the elector-princes dated to the Golden Bull (1356) of the emperor Charles IV.

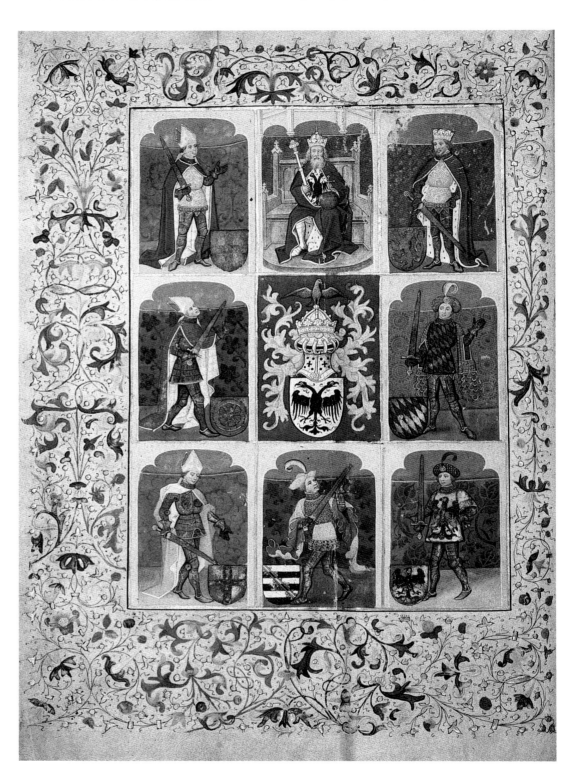

Top left: Maximilian, still as heir apparent, practices shooting with a crossbow; drawing from the Historia Federici et Maximiliani, by Joseph Grünspeck, ca. 1500. Above left: A tondo with a drawing by Jörg Breu the Elder, designed to be painted on glass, of the delivery of the city of Bruges to Maximilian in June 1485, sealing the dispute over Flanders.

promulgated a Golden Bull, a particularly formal document that fixed the number of electors at seven: four laymen (the king of Bohemia, the margrave of Brandenburg, the duke of Saxony–Wittenberg, and the count palatine of the Rhine) and three ecclesiastics (the prince-archbishops of Cologne, Mainz, and Trier). A family pact drawn up between Luxembourg–Bohemia and the Hapsburgs, and strengthened with the usual marriage ties, had ensured that the crown remained, between the 14th and 15th centuries, in the uncontested ownership of the two families. But the balance was unsta-

ble, nonetheless, constantly rocked by the turbulence of the electors (the true owners of a large part of Germany) and the failure of the politics of annexation through matrimony to add to the imperial framework. In fact, during the 15th century, Bohemia and Hungary, freed of the domination that the emperor Sigismund — son of Charles IV — had tried to impose on them, had set up national kingdoms, each burdened with its own weighty problems: the Hussite trouble in Bohemia, the nearness of the Turks for Hungary.

The empire did not benefit from the

exceedingly long reign of Frederick III, who was prepared — in the words of Pius II, who knew him well, having been part of his chancellery — "to conquer all of the world while remaining seated." Born in 1415, he was elected king of Germany in 1440 and crowned emperor at Rome in 1452. He witnessed the flight from his control of the two kingdoms of Bohemia and Hungary (Hungary's national king, Matthias Corvinus, had even conquered Vienna in 1485 and occupied Lower Austria, Styria, and Carinthia). Constant failures and frustrations beset even his nominal reign over 29

Above left: Frederick III crowns Enea Silvio Piccolomini with laurel as the "prince of poets." He was in Frederick's service in the imperial chancery and was to become Pope Pius II. The event is recorded in the frescoes by Pinturicchio in the Piccolomini Library at Siena, commissioned by Pius II's nephew, who became pope in his turn (Pius III). Above right: The last imperial coronation in Rome. Pope Nicholas V

crowns Frederick III on March 19, 1452; his consort, Eleanor of Portugal, is also present. The event is painted, taking elegant pleasure in its chronicle, on the front of a chest. Maximilian, Frederick's son, did not care to have himself crowned by the pope, as was customary since the time of Charlemagne.

France in the 15th century was on its way to becoming the first centralized state. Louis XI reigned from 1461 to 1483; due to a series of favorable circumstances, at his death the domain governed by the crown coincided almost exactly with the country's borders. Philippe de Comines, chronicler of the king's reign, remembers that the king "strongly desired that the people use one system of weights and measures." In this illustration he is depicted as the founder of the Order of Saint Michael. He was described as devout to the point of superstition, ugly, neglectful of his person, distrustful, and tormented, but he was acutely intelligent, astute, and energetic. He was more feared than loved: Philippe de Comines, for his part, says that "He was the natural friend of the middle class and the enemy of the powerful."

Germany, which was tormented by struggles among the princes and the cities and where the only groups able to govern with a modicum of stability were the economic leagues, such as the Swabian and the Hanseatic.

Even so, Frederick maintained his family's interests, which were centered on Austria. He managed to have his young and enterprising son, Maximilian — strengthened by acquisitions in the Low Countries obtained through marriage with Mary of Burgundy — elected in his turn leader of the Holy Roman Empire in 1486, thus assuring the Hapsburg succession to the empire. Maximilian entered Vienna in 1490, on the death of the Hungarian king Matthias Corvinus, and his rights were recognized over Tyrol and, thus, also over Bohemia and Hungary, both exhausted after their adventures in independence. On the death of Frederick III, Maximilian found himself master of an immense territory that extended from Trieste to Amsterdam.

This gain on the part of the Hapsburgs was not, at first, valued as much as it should have been, but on the political plane it closed the "Middle Ages" and opened the "Modern Age." The attention of a contemporary observer, however, would have been commanded by the lack of central authority in Germany and the success of limited but strong federal systems, such as the Hanseatic League or the Swiss confederation. After their victories over Charles the Bold at Grandson and Morat (1476), the Swiss were further united in a confederation that, from the three original cantons of Uri, Schwyz, and Unterwalden, had grown to thirteen by 1513. Thus they were able to thwart the efforts of Maximilian, who — both as heir of the Hapsburgs, their ancient masters, and as son-in-law of Charles of Burgundy — wanted to draw them back into the imperial fold, and the peace of Basil (1499) consecrated the independence of the "league of Confederates of Upper Germany."

30

Opposite: Charles VIII at a tournament as presented in an illustration of a chivalrous poem. He became king at the age of 13 and died before he was 30. He is sometimes described as being youthfully bold and heedless and as having imprudently read too much chivalrous literature. In fact, he proved himself energetic and wise, and his conquest of the Kingdom of Naples was prepared with diplomatic skill. As Machiavelli was to say, he could "take Italy with chalk" (a reference to the chalk with which military foragers marked the houses where soldiers had lodged). Much anger would soon be unleashed throughout the whole of Europe.

The resurrection of the imperial eagle by Charles V, therefore, took the Germans by surprise. For several generations, they had been joking about their sacred, papal, and impotent monarchy. The witty remark that Goethe put into the mouths of the jolly members of the Auerbachs Keller of Leipzig in *Faust* — "How on earth is that dear Holy Roman Empire still standing upright?" — could easily have come from the lips of a 15th-century German. But the eagle, according to the Bible and the medieval science of bestiaries, has the gift of being able to renew its youth — and this imperial revival, in dynastic garb, had a profound effect on the modern history of the west, from Bohemia to Mexico.

At the end of the 15th century, however, things were not so clear. Great disturbances in the continental balance were expected, instead, from France.

By 1453, the end of the Hundred Years War, which had been for generations a chronic affliction, the kingdom of the Valois had begun — first under the direction of the shady Charles VII and then under that of the cautious and enterprising Louis XI — the creation of a unity that would shortly become the first true example of an absolute, centralized state; that is, the first "modern" state. The age-old struggle between the crown and the aristocracy, which had begun in the 10th century and would end only with Richelieu and Louis XIV 700 years later, had by the second half of the 15th century taken a definitive turn. The nobles had launched a sharp offensive in 1465, which led to a civil war declared — irony of labels! — "for the public weal." They were backed by the duke of Burgundy and the king of England, but Louis XI wisely countered them with alternating military and diplomatic moves: while he provoked revolts in the duchy of Burgundy, he worked to magnify the contradictions within the alliance of nobles and to set the leaders against one another. England, herself in the midst of a civil war, was not able to give effective

Guillaume Juvénal des Ursins, chancellor of France in 1445, in a portrait by Jean Foquet. He was one of a series of royal functionaries who made France a modern state. Two of his brothers were at different times archibishop of Rheims and served the state just as their father, prevôt des marchands *of Paris, had served Charles VI.*

support to her French allies, and the ruin of Charles the Bold at the hands of the Swiss permitted a quick reduction of the large princes. While conducting a risky policy of territorial acquisitions in the Pyrenees (to the damage of Aragon), Louis liquidated the Angevin power: Anjou and Provence were returned to him in two renewals of hostilities, between 1475 and 1480, and were directly united to the crown in 1481. Only the duke of Brittany remained fiercely indomitable and capable of conducting his own independent policy when, in 1483, the prematurely aged king died.

His son Charles VIII, at that time 13 years old, was placed in the regency of his sister Anne and her husband, Pierre de Beaujeu. The nobles, now led by Louis of Orleans, emerged from hiding and began another civil war. But the new young sovereign revealed himself to be extraordinarily energetic and sage. He successfully subdued the new resistance and, in 1488, with the death of the duke Frances II of Brittany,

As the state gave way to administration, an invasion of official paper began: books of minutes, registers, account books, and also loose sheets. The evangelist Matthew was a publican — a tax collector — before Christ called him. Reynerswaele, painting his conversion, placed on a wall behind his counter strips of paper joined by a nail, a common sight in 15th-century offices. The growth of the modern state in France was facilitated by the passage to the crown of certain autonomous dynastic duchies, the last of which was Brittany. Assisted by her patron saints, Anne of Brittany appears here in prayer (from the Grandes Heures, illuminated by Jean Burdichon in the first years of the 16th century). The final union of Brittany and France took place by way to three marriages: Two involved Anne, heir to the duchy (the first in 1491, when she was only 14, to Charles VIII; the second in 1499 to the successor Louis XII, son of the poet Charles d'Orléans); the third involved the daughter of Anne and Louis XII, Claudia, married to Francis of Angoulême, who took the throne as Francis I. Neither Charles VIII nor Louis XII got from Anne, who was queen of France twice, male heirs who could unite, in legitimate succession, France and Brittany.

33

"We will unite the white rose and the red: Smile heaven upon this fair conjunction, That long have frown'd upon their enmity!" These words are spoken by Richmond in Shakespeare's Richard III. Having won the battle of Bosworth Field (1485), Richmond became Henry VII. Below: The king in an anonymous portrait by a Flemish artist. A cautious, parsimonious, and inscrutable man, he

was considered to be the initiator of "Tudor absolutism," an expression that has to be understood within the English context: "Had the king proposed changing any of the norms established by tradition," the Venetian ambassador to London said, "every Englishman would have given the impression of being deprived of his life."

Prison and knightly dreams

One of the most important English prose works of the 15th century was written during long years in prison: the *Morte d'Artur*, by Sir Thomas Malory. A gentleman from Warwickshire, Malory participated in the seige of Calais (1415-1416) and served in parliament (1445). He then became involved in rascally behavior, sacking convents and taking tributes from peaceful citizens. Arrested, he escaped (by swimming away) and again attacked an abbey. Caught again (1453), he passed the rest of his life in prison, entertaining himself with his pen. His long novel was published in 1485 by William Caxton. Caxton, too, is an important figure of the period. He began as an apprentice in the shop of a large silk merchant in London and was then sent to the Low Countries as governor of the Merchants Adventurers. A businessman, he also had literary interests: In 1471 he completed, after two years of work, *The Recuyell of the Historyes of Troye*, a translation of a French novel then very much in vogue, and offered the manuscript to Margaret, wife of Charles the Bold, and sister of the king of England, Edward IV. His friends requested copies, and Caxton, his eyes and hands exhausted by so much writing, had them printed at Bruges. This was the first book printed in English, and Caxton added to his occupations that of printer and editor.

The material for the *Morte d'Artur* is taken from "Breton cycle": King Arthur, the Round Table, Tristan, Lancelot, the search for the Holy Grail, tournaments, castles, enchanted forests, magnanimous wandering knights who risk all to save damsels in distress. Arthur, king of Britain (southwest England and central Wales), is of dubious historicity. He is mentioned in the *Historia Britonum*, by Nennius (perhaps from the 8th century). His acts are related more widely in the *History of the Kings of Britain*, by Geoffrey of Monmouth (12th century), and the entire cycle was, a short while later, literarily represented by the Frenchman Chrétien de Troyes. Malory recognized his debt to "a French book." His terse prose kept alive in England the image of the knightly world, all a dream.

reclaimed the protection of Frances's sister Anne. In vain, the duchess of the last large principality to still defy the unifying policies of the crown attempted a drastic resistance, offering herself in marriage to Maximilian of Austria and soliciting the aid of the Spanish. Charles VIII responded by breaking his engagement to Margaret of Austria and demanding—heedless of the double offense caused the Hapsburgs—the hand of Anne, to whom—in exchange for the union of France and Brittany—he offered the crown of the golden fleur-de-lis. The wedding took place on December 6, 1491. Finally freed from internal pressures, Charles began to listen with greater interest to the words of the Neapolitan barons exiled at his court following the failure of their conspiracy against Ferdinand I of Aragon in 1485. The exiles maintained that Aragon was a usurper and that the crown of Naples belonged to the good king René of Anjou, who had died in 1480 and of whom Charles was heir. For his part, Charles had not

forgotten that the French crown boasted dynastic rights to the duchy of Milan and that, as heir to René of Anjou, he was also due the nonexistent but prestigious throne of Jerusalem. He assembled an army, not very large but blessed with cavalry and good artillery, and at the same time dreamed of a Mediterranean adventure: a crusade to liberate Constantinople. He aimed at Naples, the coffer of the wealth of Italy and the port facing the Orient. To protect his rear—futilely, it turned out—he ceded to Spain Rousillon and Cerdana, which his father had illegitimately contested, and granted to the empire Artois and Franche-Comté, prestigious territories of the dissolved Burgundian empire. He then set off for Italy, completely unaware that he had made a potent contribution to creating the basis for the Austro-Spanish pincers that would threaten France from then on for nearly two centuries.

For its part, England was for the moment out of the game of political intrigue. With the victory of the Tudor Henry VII—related to both York and Lancaster and thus held to be capable of pacifying both the White Rose and the Red—over Richard III in 1485, the civil war had ended, but the country had to be put back together again. For the moment, France believed it had made the right choice in backing the Tudor camp, but time would prove this notion wrong, as the new king set England on the path of empire. Henry VII governed energetically and wisely, carefully managing the profits accruing to the crown from the large royal estates and the exportation of wool, relying on the recently elevated lesser nobles (the gentry) and the middle class, centralizing the government where possible on the French model, and giving support to naval activities. The modern age had begun in England. Who would have thought that in only a few decades that land of shepherds would become a major naval and colonial power?

34

Opposite: London at the end of the 15th century, in an illustration of the poems of Charles d'Orléans. The White Tower and London Bridge can be seen. Inside the White Tower, Charles d'Orléans, who was held prisoner in England for 25 years, is intent on his poetry. "There is no country in the world," the Venetian ambassador reported at the beginning of Henry VII's reign, "that contains so many thieves and robbers as

England. Very few venture out alone in the country except in broad daylight, and still fewer dare to go out at night, especially in London." To make income flow to the crown, Henry VII took advantage of both clergy from the middle classes and lawyers, who, according to Bacon, "could transform law and justice into one continuous theft, carried out with the system of gnawing woodworms."

Many Mediterraneans

The true meaning of the word *Europe*, the etymology of that famous name — beyond the myth of the girl abducted by Zeus — is still not known with certainty. The old theory that the word is related to the Akkadian *erepu* "sunset," corresponding to the derivation of *Asia* from the Assyrian *asu* "to rise" — and that thus the two continents got their names from their relative geographical positions, one to the west of the other — is by now dated, although certain scholars still defend it. For the Greeks, the name *Europe* indicated substantially all the lands north of the Aegean Sea and, in a wider sense, all the coastline that marked the north of the Mediterranean.

Throughout all of antiquity, Europe was seen as something coherent only in the south; its form and boundaries slowly vanished as one moved north. Awareness of the continent began to take shape—as can be seen in cartography — during the long period between the 10th and 16th centuries. Fifteenth-century Catalan and Danish mapmakers displayed a not too erroneous idea of the configuration of the north, and it was a widely held belief that Europe ended at the Tanais River (later the Don).

At the end of the Middle Ages, the Mediterranean was fundamentally a sea of active trading between continents. It was, in its turn, a "liquid continent," as Fernand Braudel has evocatively defined it: a sea that united, rather than divided, the shores that were reflected in it and the peoples who looked out over it. It had been that way for centuries, with periods of greater or lesser activity, of course. The *Mediterranean*, the "sea between lands," was a stretch of water limited by coasts, relatively well protected from inclement weather (and thus easy to navigate), as well as ploughed by the decks of islands. In fact, Europe is held between two "Mediterraneans": To the south is the true Mediterranean, with the smaller, adjoining Black Sea (which, in the irony of words, mariners called the "Great Sea" or the "Greater Sea"), to the north, the Baltic.

During the 15th century, the Mediterranean, Black, and Baltic seas were particularly well connected. Overland routes and

Europe — from Norway (ignoring the more northerly areas that were still sparsely inhabited) to Sicily — stretches almost one-third of the distance from the equator to the pole. This fact helps explain the variety of climates, landscapes, and living conditions found in Europe, factors that limited life far more in the 15th century than they do today. Deep-rooted historical factors, as well as the natural environment, distinguish

Mediterranean Europe, with its characteristic landscape. Above: The pleasant appearance of the Mediterranean environment, with olives and cypresses, in a contemporary photograph that nonetheless evokes the landscape of the past.

waterways cut across the mass of continental Europe, maintaining a series of relations that were strengthened by a system of sea trade along the coasts that had as its fulcrums the ports of Bruges (and, after it was silted up, Antwerp) and Lisbon, and that linked, by way of the North Sea, the Baltic and the Mediterranean. On the other side of the continent the ancient route "from the Varangians to the Greeks," made up in large part of Russian rivers, maintained heavy trading between the Baltic and the Black seas. Finally, Italian mercantile ships, for the most part Genoese, shuttled back and forth between the Black Sea and the Mediterranean, carrying various goods but mostly grain and slaves.

Federal empires began to form during the 15th century at the arrival points on this triangular system of Mediterranean trade, the first of which was Spain. The Iberian peninsula, which through the Reconquista of the Moorish kingdom of Granada had with difficulty gained by the 10th century onward its own identity, was formed of four kingdoms: Portugal, Castile, Aragon, and Navarre. The small and mountainous kingdom of Navarre can be dealt with quickly: During the middle of the 15th century, the Trastamare family, powerful nobles who had been struggling since the preceding century for the crown of Castile, asserted themselves there, but later events led to the kingdom being divided into Upper Navarre

This contemporary photograph shows the hard and rugged aspect of the Mediterranean environment: a section of calcareous land, fields dug out by clearing away stones, dry-stone walls, and terraces. Above all, one can see the fragility of an ecology dependent on irregular rains.

(an area south of the Pyrennes that was conquered by Ferdinand the Catholic in 1515) and Lower Navarre (united with France in 1589). Also of little importance at this time is Portugal, which by the end of the 14th century had successfully avoided, due to the help of the English, union with Castile. (This Anglo-Lusitania alliance is another of the characteristic features typical of modern Europe.) In Portugal, the new Aviz dynasty (descendants of John, bastard son of Peter I and the grand master of the military religious Order of Aviz) had asserted itself, following the waves of crusaders towards Africa and exploration of the islands in the ocean off the western coasts of the African continent.

We should pay greater attention instead to the nucleus of the Iberian peninsula: Castile and Aragon–Catalonia. Following a 14th century immensely troubled by bitter civil and dynastic disputes related to the Hundred Years War between France and England, these two great protagonists of the Reconquista were marching towards their own destiny: since this destiny could not be found in a natural union (their historical, ethnic-cultural, social, and economic differences were too great), they prepared for a difficult but unavoidable convergence.

Since the 12th century — when the royal crown had passed to the heads of the counts of Barcelona — the fate of tough and arid Aragon had been joined to that of wealthy and seafaring Catalonia. Stretched out into the sea but tied by a double knot to events in Barcelona, one of the greatest, richest, most powerful, and enterprising Mediterranean port cities, the kingdom assumed its astonishing role as a maritime empire. Between the end of the 13th and beginning of the 14th centuries, the Aragon rulers successfully installed themselves on the two largest Tyrrhenian islands, Sicily and Sardinia, and a group of adventurers, the so-called Catalonian Company, took possession by force of half of Greece. In 1442 the Aragon king Alfonso V the Magnanimous (son of Ferdinand of Trastamare, who in his turn had been installed on the Aragon throne because he was born of the marriage of a Castilian king with the daughter of the last heir of the old Aragon family), already king of Sicily, finally succeeded in installing himself at Naples as heir—after a tormented war of succession — to Joanna II of Anjou.

With the death of Alfonso V in 1458, the union of the kingdoms of Aragon and Naples again fell apart. Ferdinand I, natural son of the king, took the throne of Naples; the Aragon crown went to Alfonso's brother, John II, who was succeeded in 1472 by his son Ferdinand II. Mary, sister to Alfonso and John, married John II of Castile; from this marriage would be born Isabella. In 1474, Isabella, married for five years to her maternal cousin Ferdinand, took the throne of Castile; in 1479 her husband inherited, in his turn, the throne of Aragon, along with feudal rights to Sardinia and dynastic claims to Naples and Sicily.

The house of Trastamare, with its energy (which often expressed itself in cruelty) and its complex but coherent matrimonial policies, had maneuvered well to present itself as the "natural" unifier of the two contiguous kingdoms. However, differences remained. The maritime and mercantile economy of Catalonia suffered, penalized

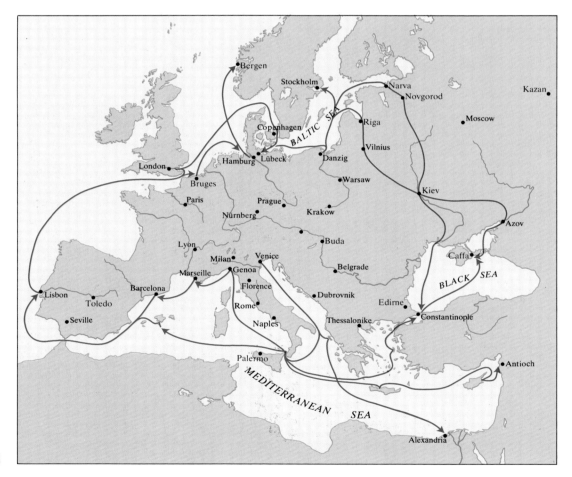

Europe, a slender Western appendix of the earth's major continental mass, has two "Mediterraneans," seas surrounded by land at a relatively close distance, reasonably protected, and not difficult to navigate; the Baltic and the Mediterranean. The Black Sea is almost a third "Mediterranean." In the 15th century, the three basins were connected by coastal navigation, roads, and waterways.

by the fiscal policy of the sovereigns, who were by then called the Catholic kings; they ruled jointly and kept strictly divided their respective kingdoms, which served them as reserves of financial earnings. They tended to favor the port of Seville, on the Atlantic, in which Spain did not intend to permit Portugal to develop hegemony.

The Catholic kings also decisively favored the mesta, the powerful corporative association of Castilian sheep owners, whose immense flocks annually flowed across a boundless territory — almost 400 miles long — in a wave of migration between the "lower" winter pastures and the "upper" summer pastures. The demands of the mesta created a well-known conflict — and one found not only in 15th-century Spanish society — between nomadic shepherds and settled farmers. The sheepherders needed free movement in the wide corridors they used for pasturing and migration; the farmers wanted enclosures as well as legislation to protect their crops of grain, grapes, and olives in response to a growing demand for these basic commodities of the Mediterranean diet. In the end, the sovereigns sided with the breeders, to whom, in 1501, they guaranteed the leasing of all the land that had been used for pasturing, regardless of the wishes of the current owners of that land. From then on, the rich wool of Spanish flocks made its way to ports for exportation. The predominance of shepherding had a powerful effect on the economy, culture, cuisine, and folklore of Spain; but it also highly compromised agricultural development and contributed to a sociocultural backwardness that weighed for a long time on later events.

The Catholic kings also laid the groundwork for a centralized government for their two kingdoms. They set up a royal council, organized a system of public officials in the royal service, and took back for the crown the powers taken from it by the cortes during the long civil war. They took pow-

erful control over the church by allotting all the military orders to the first grand master. The sovereigns then obtained from the pope, in 1482, the right to choose the kingdom's bishops: the archbishop of Toledo and confessor of the queen, Jiménez de Cisneros, watched over their morality. To guarantee the faithfulness of the newly converted — both the former Jews (*marranos*) and the former Moslems — the Inquisition was introduced in the two kingdoms between 1480 and 1484 and entrusted to the Dominican Tomás de Torquemada. To cement their work towards unification, Ferdinand and Isabella finally succeeded in capturing the last Moorish stronghold of Granada. After that, the poor but proud Spanish noblemen (*hidalgos*), who disdained any activity except that of arms, had no choice but to ask to take part in the new profes-

Ferdinand of Aragon and Isabella of Castile kneeling before the Madonna in an anonymous Virgen de los Reyes Catolicos. *The history of Spain as a united country, freed of the last vestiges of Islamic power, begins with these rulers. "Oh, great Ferdinand," exclaims a character in an allegorical play by Sannazaro given at the court of Naples on the occasion of the celebration of the capture of Granada in* 1492, *"you will give battle to the Turks and slaughter them!" But Ferdinand did not move against the Ottomans. In June 1493, the Spanish ambassador in Rome, distressed by the wars then going on in Italy between Christians, presents as an example his king, who "Continually endangered state and life for the salvation of the Christian faith and for his own greater honor, battling the infidels."*

Lorenzo de' Medici and the "felicity" of Italy

"Italy had never before known such prosperity or found itself in a state as desirable as the one it enjoyed in the year of one thousand four hundred and ninety and in those just before and after. It rested in peace and tranquillity, and the land was cultivated as much in the mountainous and more barren areas as on the plains and more fertile areas, nor was it under the control of any empire but its own, with abundant inhabitants, merchandise, and wealth; it was honored with the magnificence of many princes, by the splendor of many noble and beautiful cities, by the throne and majesty of religion, and flourished with excellent administrators of the public good and noble scholars in all the disciplines and in all the arts was illustrious and industrious; nor was it without, according to the customs of the time, military glory and was much adorned with gifts, so that its name and fame were deservedly known to all nations. This felicity, acquired as the result of various circumstances, was the result of several factors; but among others it was common to praise the industry and virtues of Lorenzo de' Medici, a citizen of Florence so far above the grade of private citizen that on his wisdom stood the republic, powerful because of its opportune location, because of the ingenuity of its citizens and the readiness of its money and the greatness of its rule. Having recently made new family connections, Lorenzo had forced Innocent VIII, the Roman pontiff, to give more than a little heed to his advice, and his name throughout all of Italy was grand, grand in the deliberations of all common authority. Knowing that it would be dangerous for both the Florentine republic and for himself were any of the major potentates to increase its power, he sought in all ways to maintain balance in Italy."

Tinged with bitter nostalgia, this is one of the first pages of the *History of Italy*, by the Florentine Francesco Guicciardini, written during the last years of his life (1537-1540), roughly 50 years—and important years—from the recorded "felicity."

sional army or leave for the New World in search of adventure. It was these uprooted and courageous nobles, along with the sober Castilian shepherds enrolled in the celebrated Spanish infantry, who later made up the victorious imperial troops of Charles V; and it was from these same social levels that came forth the conquistadors.

At the end of the 15th century, therefore, Christianity had overtaken Granada at the western end of the great sea ploughed by its ships; but, at the extreme opposite end, it had lost Constantinople. And both the Ottoman expansion by sea towards the Balkans and the aims and dynastic claims of the French and Spanish on Naples seemed to converge on the peninsula located at the center of the Mediterranean, the peninsula that had been reaping advantages from its position for four centuries.

The Italian peninsula, rich in populous cities and works of art, still the center of an important banking community and seat of the pope, was home to a new culture that had not yet conquered Europe but was already attracting with fascinated curiosity the gaze of all the learned men of the west.

Historians have tried to establish the 40-year period 1454-1494 as a model not only of peace and harmony in the peninsula but also of political wisdom and the desire for independence. Often repeated is the notion that thanks most of all to the wise diplomacy of Lorenzo de' Medici — "index of the scales" and "keeper of Italian liberty" — a politics of "balance" had been set up that had not only avoided conflict among the larger states but had kept foreigners from meddling in Italian affairs.

The truth is much more complex. First of all, because the 14th-century concept of "foreigner" was not at all what it later became, after the consolidation of national states and the extension of the concept — later considered "natural" — that every community that speaks more or less the same language is thus itself a "people," with the right to a state separate from that of its neighbors speaking a different language. Also, the "system of balance," presented as a guarantee against interference from across

The fear of spies. A page from the code to a form of cryptic writing used towards the end of the 15th century by the Sforza chancery in Milan to insure the secrecy of dispatches. "Aut" and "vel" stand, respectively, for the pope and the emperor, "plus" for the king of Aragon, "fac" for the Venetian state, and so on. The first four lines denote the alphabet.

The triumph of Alfonso of Aragon, an Italian illumination from a codex from the second half of the 15th century. Alfonso V, king of Aragon and Sicily, established himself in Naples in 1442 after a long war. Both he and René d'Anjou had, at different times, been designated heir to the queen of Naples, Joanna II. Alfonso made a great royal entrance into the city in a triumphal carriage, followed by allegorical carriages celebrating his virtues. Italy survived the second half of the 15th century in a precarious balance among five states (Milan, Venice, Florence, the Church lands, and the southern kingdom, which was detached from Aragon at Alfonso's death in 1458) and other minor powers.

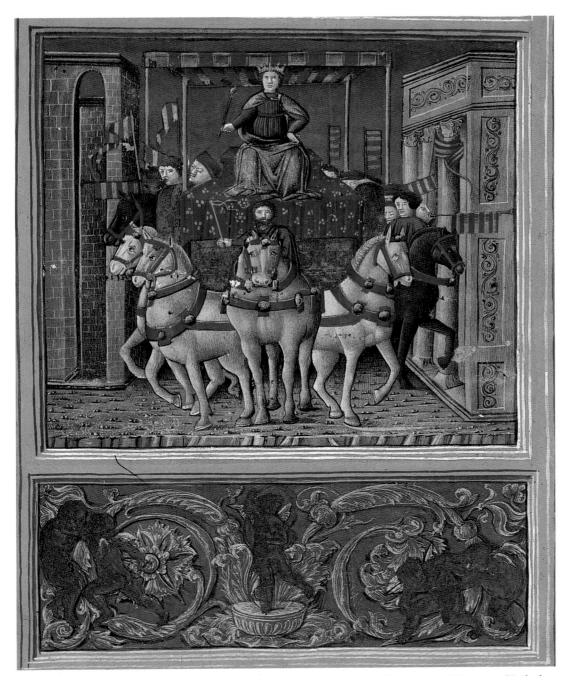

believe. Indeed, it was viewed first of all as a *respublica christianorum, corpus christianorum* ("Christian republic, body of Christianity") without any specific allusion to the Holy Roman crown; the principle was affirmed and spread that all sovereigns had substantially similar dignity.

Between the Middle Ages and the modern age, the winning system in international politics was that of the leagues and congresses, which also had a long life even in the contemporary world: The system was begun and came into common use because of practical and emergency necessities, such as the need to check the Turkish advance in the Aegean and the Balkans. The formal diplomatic conflicts that arose during every international assembly — essentially related to questions of precedence of this or that representative of this or that state and of their insignia and ambassadors — depended precisely on the idea that there was a hierarchy of importance and prestige among the Christian states (not always immediately connected to military power or wealth) but within a system of equal worth.

Thus, aside from a difficulty with language, a 15th-century Florentine did not consider a merchant from Ulm or Bruges to be much more of a "foreigner" than a Venetian or even someone from nearby Lucca; indeed, in a certain sense his relationship with the transalpine might be much

the Alps, was, in reality, entirely thought out and guaranteed by the presence of those very powers.

During the 15th century, as during all of the Middle Ages, European identity was the same as identity with the Christian world; as profound as was its crisis and as laughable as was its true political power, the "empire" remained a powerful moral and spiritual force in which people continued to

Lorenzo de' Medici in a detail from an illustration from the Vita, *by Niccolo Valori. The "needle of the Italian political balance," the head of the powerful Medici financial family (which had, however, deteriorated when he inherited it), was not as gifted in business as he was in politics. Machiavelli wrote that "as far as affairs were concerned, he was very unsuccessful."*

Negotiations. According to Philippe de Comines, God had organized Europe in such a way that every state had a traditional enemy next to it. Is this why war was apparently so inevitable? Negotiations could be both the source of war or its resolution. The rise of diplomacy created incidents that led to discussion; such discussions often led to war, which, in fact, was often their specific aim. Negotiations were often precarious

and were broken off when they came up against actual situations. However, the kings of the period seem to have trusted in these solemnly sworn agreements — or at least in the one that had been most recently sworn. In the illumination, from the Chronique d'Angleterre, *by Jean de Wavrin, the meeting for negotiations between John II of Navarre and Louis XI of France.*

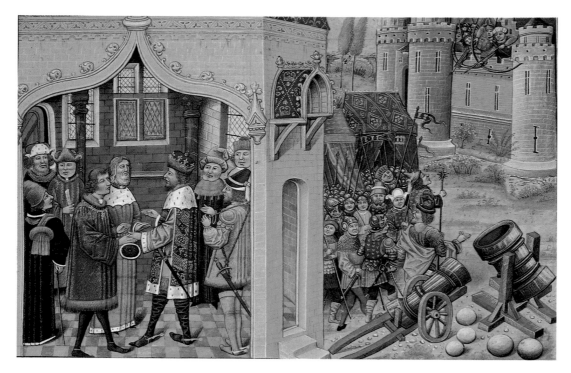

according to which the ten or so various communal states that had existed between the 12th and 14th centuries in the north-central area of the peninsula (to the south of the Abruzzi and Campania was a unified state, the Kingdom of Naples) had been reduced to a few units. The more prosperous, shrewd, and lucky cities had, by attraction or by force, progressively absorbed the other cities in a process of concentration to form nuclei essentially supported by the needs of the banking-mercantile class, and by their policy of acquiring territory and extending their areas of influence over an ever wider domain with a certain economic system and public order that favored their interests.

These territorial states were usually composed of a "dominant" city and a series of "subject" communities. The relationships between this city and each of the subject communities were anything but uniform

friendlier, since it would be less damaged by a tradition of enmity and vengeance left as a heritage of the period of the city states. People spoke of "Italy" frequently, and from Dante and Petrarch onward notions connected with its liberty had made headway; but the "Italy" that was thought of in such cases was always the "garden of the empire," tied to ancient Latin literature and the post–Carolingian idea of an independent *regnum Italiae* ("Italian kingdom").

For 15th-century men, the homeland was Christianity on one hand and a small "local homeland" on the other. The true problem of identity began when one tried to determine the size and borders of those "local homelands," or when it was necessary to decide the political-constitutional order to confer on them.

Fifteenth-century Italy witnessed the final development of a system of a few "regional states," more or less large and consolidated; this arrangement was the outcome of a process of selection by strength

Ambassadors. The arrival of an embassy at Siena in 1498, depicted on a "biccherna" (a painted tablet used as a cover for the account books of the magistrates who administered the collecting office, or biccherna). *Rulers kept their own agents in the courts and foreign capitals. In a Europe based on prestige and nobility, however, these agents were often of too modest a background to be able to conclude important agreements,*

although they could initiate them. They were then concluded by a special ambassador — a prince, a noble, or a high prelate. Intense diplomatic activity was often involved in arranging a marriage. The interweaving of the reigning families by marriage could cause visible changes in the political geography of Europe, as in fact did occur.

A kneeling courier delivers a dispatch for Charles VII of France (illumination from the Histoire romaine, *by Pierre Bersuire). Negotiations, embassies, and dispatches were the ordinary means by which the ever more complex network of international relations was managed. As the end of the 15th century approached, these relations became uncertain and tense. The protagonists were ready: France, undergoing* energetic economic revival under Charles VII *after the end of the Hundred Years War; Spain, united under Ferdinand and Isabella, who had brought the Reconquista to an end; England, reconciled after the Wars of the Roses; and warlike Maximilian at the head of the Holy Roman Empire.*

and easy and showed the effects of many historical memories — the outcomes of specific events, negotiations, settlements, solutions, problems, and well-founded traditions that changed from place to place. Far from being an anonymous identity equal to all the others in a mosaic of governing bodies, each of the subject communities — large or small, perhaps a center of importance or a dominion with feudal lay or religious character — had its own special relationship with the dominant city and performed its own unique role in the hierarchy of all the powers subject to that one leading power.

Less complex, perhaps, but more del-

43

The wheel of Fortune: detail from a 15th-century illumination attributed to the French Maître de Coëtivy. How far is this medieval symbol from Machiavelli? "Fortune is good in that it is chosen by man when he wants to achieve great things and he is of such spirit and of such virtue that he recognizes the opportunity she is offering him."

of Florence, and a true diplomatic-propagandistic duel took place between the chancelleries of the two states: The Florentines claimed that they were protectors of "liberty"; the Milanese replied by invoking the need for "peace." On the one hand were the values that stemmed from open debate and the confrontation between different ideas that are guarantees and preconditions for a free, communal life. On the other hand was the sense of high-class, princely experience and the idea of serene, superior arbitration; although suffocating debate among supporters of different interests, this created a superior moral and decisive level that guaranteed peace and kept confrontation from degenerating into civil struggle.

Both parties well understood the theoretical plan. "Liberty" in Florence was certainly not the same for everyone: the hierarchy of bankers, merchants, and tradesmen who governed the city and handled its relationship with the subject communities — more or less all of central Tuscany — held their own corporative and class interests

icate was the problem of constitutional order. According to contemporary sources, the question could be reduced to a dichotomy between those states that chose to govern themselves "in liberty" and those that instead were reduced to being "in tyranny." This meant — in the language of the time, which, following its cultural tendencies, absorbed much of the political terminology of Rome during the time of the republic — that in some states constitutional order was republican, while others had given themselves a boss or *signore* who — usually made official with some sort of imperial or papal backing that gave the ruler a suitable feudal title indicating his administrative privileges and his dynastic rights — had become a "prince."

At the end of the 14th century, a violent conflict had set the duke of Milan, Giangaleazzo Visconti, against the republic

44

Soldiers in a field of grain, detail from Rest During the Flight into Egypt, *by Joachim Patinir. Machiavelli maintained that good soldiers, not gold, were the sinews of war. But soldiers, both those good and those not so good, had to be paid and fed. During this period, the economic necessities of war were frequently underrated; armies sometimes disintegrated for lack of funds.*

foremost and acted accordingly. Florence's much vaunted "liberties" had nothing at all to do with the poor Florentines and did not extend, except in the form of an imposition, to the people of Prato, Pistoia, and Arezzo. And in Milan, Visconti was anything but a serene arbitrator. Spokesman for his illustrious family traditions and, without doubt, possessor of a certain personal charisma, he was nonetheless subject to influence from his supporters, who had their own interests. Thus the republic and the prince's dominion were both forms of a reality that — except for certain notable regional differences — was the same everywhere: At the top of each territorial state there was an elite of families and economic-financial powers that (alternating periods of relative peace with periods of great tension) led public affairs in the direction beneficial to their group.

Late 15th-century Italy was the result of this delicate, fragile, and not altogether coherent structure. The peace of Lodi had been signed in a rush in 1454 by Francesco Sforza — who wanted at all costs to be recognized as duke of Milan before the king of France could put forward his dynastic claims, which were based on family relationships between the Visconti and the Valois —and Venice, which, with the fall of Constantinople to the Turks in 1453, became concerned about the future of its colonial empire. This treaty had led to the creation of the Italian League, which included the peninsula's major states: the Sforza duchy of Milan; the oligarchic mixed-system republic of Venice (governed by a senate, though a supreme elected magistrate — the doge — held power for life, like a sovereign); the Florentine oligarchic republic (by then controlled by the Medici family, who, however, held back from any attempt to legally formalize their position); Rome and its crowd of city states and small feudal principalities among which the popes attempted to apply a connecting, guiding fabric; and the Aragon Kingdom of Naples (the only

state with a structure similar in some ways to the monarchies of France and Spain). This system of balance had gone through successive approximations and successive arrangements: It had been troubled by attempts at surprise attacks and by annexationist-expansionist moves by various signatories of the Lodi pact. Between 1478 and 1482, a conflict arose from Pope Sixtus IV's desire to drive the Medici out of Florence and replace them with his nephew Girolamo Riario. Between 1482 and 1484 there was a

war between Venice and the pope for control of Ferrara, and in 1485 there was a baronial conspiracy against Ferdinand of Naples that had the outside support of the pope and the king of France. On all of these occasions, the Italian states not involved in the conflict had been able to bring about a timely reestablishment of the pact. The climate remained one of constant tension, however, and only later could historical reconstruction make the period seem a time of open and faithful cooperation.

house of Este, the Malatestas of Rimini, the Bentivoglios of Bologna, the Montefeltros of Urbino, and many other aristocratic families of Genoa and Lucca.

But the image of the Italian *Prince* — the one formulated by Machiavelli, a mixture of fox and lion, protagonist of the state as work of art and master of his own destiny — is more the result of rhetorical amplification of small deeds of pride often only dubiously lionlike and ferocious and, not rarely, of vile treachery than a mirror of any true ability to acquire and keep power with energy or even pitiless shrewdness. Rather than lions, the princes of 15th-century Italy were more often hyenas; rather than sage foxes, they resembled martens in a chicken coop. But they had the good fortune — and, the merit — to have in their services the likes of Donatello, Piero della Francesca, Leon Battista Alberti, and Leonardo da Vinci — and to later have a failed politician but great political theorizer make of them a fascinating portrait. *The Prince* is a work splendidly normative, a eulogy written by a disenchanted republican for an impossible master. Machiavelli expressed his true ideas of Italian princes in *The Art of War*:

Before they tasted the blows of foreign wars, our Italian princes believed that a prince need only think up pointed replies in his study, write pretty letters, show in mottoes and words shrewdness and readiness, know how to weave plots, adorn himself with jewels and gold, sleep and eat with greater splendor than others, be lascivious, treat his subjects with greed and haughtiness, rot in idleness, distribute military ranks as favors, scorn anyone who tried to show him a praiseworthy path, wish that his words might be oracular responses; nor did these wretches realize that they were becoming prey to whomever attacked them. Thus were born the great fears of one thousand four hundred and ninety-four, the flights undergone and the miraculous losses.

Even so, the image that remains of Italy during the late 15th century — an image founded largely on the works of art created during the period — is one of a wealthy, peaceful, wise, and serene world. Aside from the splendor of the five great capitals of the leading states, this image comes in large part from the courts of the minor princes, all of whom were politically subordinate to their respective allied powers and all of whom frequently showed greater severity and cruelty in the use of power in their small states than did the great rulers. On the other hand, the minor princes knew how to organize their court life and how to use, sometimes wisely, their earnings from the exploitation of their subjects (and often their earnings from their professional activities as commanders of mercenary troops). They invested in public works, particularly urban development, and patronized the arts. All of this activity bestowed lasting fame upon the Gonzaga marquis of Mantua, the marquis and later dukes of the Ferrara

46

In northern Europe, other merchants and other knights tried to guide the lines of development in the other great "Mediterranean," the Baltic. Beginning in the second half of the 14th century, the great protagonist there was the Hanse, that is, the league of German mercantile cities guided by Lübeck, which, in 1397, had sponsored the creation of a confederation of Baltic kingdoms called the Kalmar Union, uniting Sweden, Norway, and Denmark under a single scepter. The union collapsed after 1434 following the rebellion of Swedish nobles; however, the Hanse still maintained its positions in the three kingdoms. What finally damaged the league was the growth in the west of competition from Dutch merchant fleets and the consolidation in the east of the Polish-Lithuanian kingdom and Muscovy, which made possible the use of trade routes different from those then controlled by the league.

In 1386, the Jagellon dynasty united under its crown the lands of Poland and Lithuania, which led to a conflict with the Teutonic Order, the other large Baltic power. With the Peace of Torun in 1466, the Teutonic Order lost western Prussia — including their own capital, the city-monastery of Marienburg — and eastern Prussia became a fief of the Polish crown.

The fateful year 1492 caught the Polish-Lithuanian kingdom at a moment of extraordinary expansion but also of difficult transition. In that year, Kasimir IV, who had governed since 1447 and who was the true author of "Great Poland," died. Between 1471 and 1490, his son Ladislaus had become king of Bohemia and Hungary, both valuable territories torn from the Hapsburgs in a weak and indecisive moment. Meanwhile, in 1485, the Danubian principality of Moldavia had become in its turn a fief of the Polish-Lithuanian crown. A great power, with a dynastic federal structure, was clearly emerging in the area from the Danube and the Black Sea to the Baltic.

But this concentration served only to increase the combined hostility of the Hapsburgs, Muscovy, and the Ottoman sultanate towards Poland. During that autumn of glory, the groundwork for Poland's age-old identity crisis, both as a nation and as a state, which has been part of European history to the present, was established.

The groundwork was also then being laid for the nucleus of another world power. Maneuvering among the Tartars of the so-called realm of the Golden Horde (which ruled southern Russia and to whom Russia was in theory a vassal), the Ottomans of Istanbul, and the Baltic powers, Great Prince Ivan III of Muscovy, aided by his nobles — the boyars — had profitted from the fall of "New Rome," Constantinople, to proclaim himself in turn *czar* (from *caesar* — that is, "emperor"). Moscow, his capital, thus became the "third Rome," cradle of orthodox Christianity and heir to the Byzantine imperial tradition. Beautified by Italian artists and celebrated for its hundreds of churches and monasteries, the city was from then on the true great capital of Euro-Asia, the crossroads of the Baltic world, eastern Europe, the Balkans, and endless Asia.

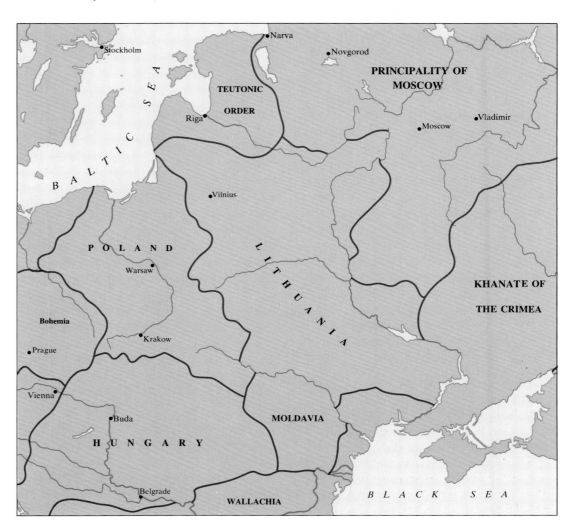

Popular opinion held that Europe ended at the Tanais, the great river of the Sarmatic plain that flows into the Black Sea. In eastern Europe, Vienna, and the Hanseatic cities of the Baltic, culture seems to have been more advanced than elsewhere. The Tartars, who still governed southern Russia, were in decline, but the principality of Moscow represented the first nucleus of a future world leader.

A small state
and a great power

How many divisions does the pope have?" This cynical question is attributed to Stalin, and whether or not he ever actually said it, the phrase displays no misunderstanding of history. Stalin was very much aware of the paradox presented by papal power and by the qualitatively different ways in which it has been used through the centuries.

The era of schisms opened in 1378, with the return of the pope from Avignon to Rome, and ended in 1449. For many prelates and men of the Church, it had presented the opportunity to discuss again the principle of the "monarchical" direction of the Church and to affirm, in its place, the different principle of a collegiate organization, the "prince" of which would have been the periodically convoked council. All the men who sat on the throne of Peter during the second half of the 15th century felt hostility — open or masked — towards the council, the sovereignty of which was one of the goals of many supporters of a moral — and in some ways also institutional — reform of the Church. Perhaps the best example of this is Enea Silvio Piccolomini, who had been a fervent defender of the council theories and had collaborated, between 1440 and 1442, with the antipope Felix V, whom the council supporters had put in opposition to Eugenius IV; but when he himself was elected pope, Pius II, Piccolomini became a stern zealot of the monarchist cause.

After 1449, the popes began to think with relative serenity about both their universal spiritual and legal power over the Latin Church and about their positions as sovereigns of a composite territorial state — composed of the regions known today as Romagna, Umbria, the Marches, and Latium — as well as of a dominant city. Rome was still medieval and in many ways poor and disorganized, with its shrines and its pilgrims' hostels, its unruly aristocracy and turbulent populace, its crumbling urban structures and general disorder. While the popes

were forced to adopt policies that bordered on true campaigns of "reconquest" of the subject territories, Rome was the visible center of their power and the goal of all the ambassadors and frequently even the great rulers who came to pay homage at the blessed papal seat. It had to become a splendid capital, and the incipient humanistic culture gave it a fascination beyond its relics and ancient glory.

If a 15th-century observer had lifted his

gaze from the humble and oftentimes sordid Rome of the hostels and inns towards the neighborhoods and palaces of the powerful, he might have perceived that the city was, in effect, an intricately woven fabric of courts, dominated by their relative "families" of bureaucrats, functionaries, courtesans, and parasites. At its center was the papal court, or Curia. The Curia's job was to administer not just the pontifical state or the style of life of the pontiff but, through the chancellery,

Pope Alexander VI in an illumination from the Missale ponteficis in Nativitate Domini *(1492–1503). Francesco Guicciardini says that he was "extraordinarily diligent and wise, had a marvelous ability to convince, and, in all serious matters, was incredibly prompt and skillful; but these virtues were far outweighed by his vices."*

the Church itself. The concentration of so many functionaries and their followers in one city — and, what's more, in a city with no solid administrative tradition, unlike those of other Italian states — created countless problems, which the popes sometimes sought to resolve with the time-honored recourse to bread and circuses: donations of money and food to the citizens and the pilgrims, processions, festivals, and tournaments. For the prelates and even for the second-rank dignitaries, great pomp in clothing and life-styles was both a status symbol and a kind of necessity dictated by the pressing need not just to retain public approval but also to recycle part of the accumulated riches in occasions of public generosity. The sumptuary regulations launched by Pope Sixtus IV in 1474, during a moment of austerity, served little purpose and had no evident effects for several decades.

The 15th-century pontifical court has been the subject of much scandalous literature. In reality, the papal court was no better or worse than any other court of that period, and the episodes of violence or corruption that occurred there were no greater than those that occurred elsewhere. The single — and certainly not insignificant — aggravating circumstance was that the people involved in these episodes were usually prelates or even the popes themselves. The fact remains, however, that the pope was not just the ruler of a state but a spiritual leader, and as such he was at the summit of a complex machine capable of administrating prebends and benefices, of granting exemptions of every kind (from the matrimonial to the fiscal), of pronouncing or lifting excommunications. The Church directed a complex legal, administrative, and fiscal organization. It affected all of western Christianity, including the governments of men, not just because many of these men belonged to the "minor orders" of clergy, but also because many sociopolitical situations that seem secular to us now at that time involved the Church. Nor should

that be surprising, when we remember that the kings, "the Lord's anointed," were consecrated with a sacramental act, and many bishops and abbots, as holders of government privileges, ruled peoples and presided over courts.

The flip side of the Church's involvement in secular affairs is that all those secular authorities were deeply involved in the internal workings of the Church. Not only did ambassadors, observers, and spies of all nations converge on Rome, but within the government of the Church each sovereign pulled strings in attempting to get special attention for his own ends. The papacy had been forced to pay a high price to diminish the support Europe's sovereigns gave to the idea of a council, which several of them had favored until 1449. Their preference stemmed not from the belief that a governing council would thus have left the Church closer to its original intent or less exposed to corruption — even the most devout of the princes took little interest in such matters — but because a council-led Church would have been easier

This xylograph of 1468 is an early example of the political use of an image. With a complex series of allusions, it comments on the relations at that time between the two great universal powers, the emperor and the pope (the former was at that time Frederick III, the latter Paul II, the Venetian Pietro Barbo, nephew of Eugenius IV). To the left appears Halley's comet, which had been seen in 1456.

to manipulate from within each country. To convince them to abandon their support for the council and the creation of "national" churches, the Holy See and its governing bodies — the pope and the Sacred College of Cardinals — were forced by events to become a sort of supreme international assize of the Christian nations.

While the pope was automatically due the chairmanship of any congress or any league of princes — which convened regularly when making preparations against the Turks — it is also true that each sovereign was due a certain number of places in the Sacred College — a certain number of cardinals' caps. During each pontificate, the cardinals—each one faithful to the king of France or the king of England, to Aragon or Castile, or to the emperor or some other Christian power—pursued his sovereign's interests and acted as unofficial ambassador of his country to the Holy See. During the periods of papal absence or during the conclaves to elect new popes, these cardinals wove alliances among themselves that in part responded to their personal designs and temperaments and in part to the needs and contingencies of the moment, but that also constituted each cardinal's fulfillment of the mandate given him by the power to whom he owed his purple cap and mantle. Moreover, many of these cardinals were important representatives of ruling families, noble houses, the Italian republics, or the elite of the government. In this way the pope embodied a dialogue among the Christian powers: The contest lay in gaining favors, getting the largest number of members in the Sacred College, and making the right alliances at the right moment.

The importance of "national interests" in appointment of cardinals and the mechanism by which the Sacred College functioned should not obscure another factor: Pressure groups and alliances of convenience — some of them with spiritual motivation — formed among the cardinals them-

49

selves, regardless of their places of origin. Like the empire, the papacy was an elective monarchy, but its college of electors was not hereditary. Thus there arose the need to find, for every pontificate, the most faithful court possible and to create the conditions under which the papal tiara could remain in the family or at least under which the family could continue to have influence. Since the power of the papacy extended to bishoprics and prebends, the reasons for this family interest are understandable. Nepotism — that is, the popular practice of having a considerable number of relatives, relations, and kin of the pontiff positioned in the grades of papal administration, in the ecclesiastical hierarchy, and even in the Sacred College — was necessary to insure a loyal following and to reward one's political supporters.

Beginning with the election of Alfonso Borgia, a Spaniard and great champion of his fellow countrymen, as Pope Calixtus III in 1455, the prominent dispute in the conclave concerned the Spanish and the French. But the Italians, who usually played an important role, were generally unfavorable to a non-Italian taking the pontifical throne and were usually prone to throw their weight into the international game.

One such struggle was caused by Guillaume d'Estouteville, a noble Frenchman and titular archbishop of Rouen and six other bishoprics. (The law at the time allowed prelates to enjoy in Rome earnings from their dioceses — one of the principal abuses challenged by the Reformation.) He was made a cardinal by Eugenius IV and heaped with benefices by Nicholas V. In 1458 he was on the point of obtaining the tiara but was overtaken by Enea Silvio Piccolomini — to the great pleasure and relief of the cardinals tied to Spain, Burgundy, the empire, and any other enemies of France. He was bypassed again in 1464 in a conclave that elected on the first round of voting (after only one "smoke") the Venetian Pietro Barbo, who took the name Paul II.

Along with the struggles carried on by heads of state through their cardinals, the

Rome: ancient ruins and venerated churches. The doctor and Nuremberg humanist Hartmann Schedel published a Liber chronicorum *in 1499, with engravings by Michael Wolgemut and Wilhelm Pleydenwurff; this is an engraving of Rome at the end of the century. The Porta del Popolo is in the bottom right-hand corner: immediately through the arch is the Via Santa Maria del Popolo, restored by Sixtus IV. We can also see the Pantheon and the Antonine Column. Beyond the Tiber is the Castel Sant'Angelo and the basilica of Saint Peter's (with the basilica founded under Constantine). Opposite, the* palatium pape *is the one on which work was begun under Nicholas V in 1450, using materials from other constructions. Farther away we can see the Belvedere, the small palace built by Pope Innocent VIII.*

50

... VI also called painters to the Vatican. ...io painted his apartments; Saint ... of Alexandria's Dispute with the ...ers before the Emperor *is part of that* ...n. The saint is wearing blue and red, the ...the Borgias, and is said to be a portrait ...Lucrezia Borgia, the pope's daughter, or ...rnese, his lover. In the background, the

...displays the bull, symbol of the Borgias, and is dedicated to the pacis cultori, *"the cultivator of peace." The Turkish knight to the right is Djem, brother of the Turkish sultan Bajazet and hostage of the Roman Curia. On the left, Pinturicchio has depicted himself.*

...ation that frequently decided the ... of conclaves was determined by ...ckeying on the part of the backers ...ersaries of the recently deceased ... first group eager to maintain with ...essor their commissions and pre- ...e second trying to insert themselves ... higher echelons of power.

...bists" and "Paulists" met in a bitter ...ation in 1471 at the end of a 13- ...n that began in 1458, during which ...popes, Pio and Paul, had alternat- ...e throne. The pope elected was the ...minister of the Franciscan order, ...o della Rovere. In 14 years of rule ...s IV, he revealed himself to be a champion of nepotism. He began by repaying magnificently the cardinals who had supported him and then raised six nephews to the purple, one of whom, Raffaelo Galeotto Riario, was barely 17. He distributed a high number of bishoprics, prebends, and benefices to other family members and, in 1478, while trying to create a principality for another relative, Girolamo Riario, he risked destroying completely the Italian system of balance.

When Sixtus IV died in 1484, the della Rovere family had become one of the most powerful families in Italy and constituted a real force within the Curia. In a single night of rampant bribery and promises (most of which he kept), Cardinal Giuliano dell Rovere, nephew of the dead pope (and late pope himself as Julius II), together wit Rodrigo Borgia, succeeded in literally buyin the pontificate for his chosen man, the Gen oese Giovanni Battista Cybo, elected o August 29. Eight years later, in Augus 1492, Rodrigo Borgia, then in conflict wit della Rovere, took the throne, no doubt du to the favor of the Catholic kings bu primarily because of the votes of the Sacre College, which he had paid well. He ha begun by promising his electors that if mad pope he would raise their incomes to fiftee thousand Venetian ducats — more than half quintal of refined gold.

The Good Things of Life — and Some Not So Good

Opposite: A trip along a canal to the music of a flute and lute in a 15th-century Flemish illumination from Les Heures de Notre-Dame. *Above: A couple talking, in an engraving by Israel van Meckenem; an image of a serene life, undoubtedly privileged. As often happens, the documents of the period regard only a small minority of the population, and historians cannot measure what was their happiness.*

Counting people, dividing spaces

For some time now, history has used "scientific" means, and one hears of "quantitative" history. The progress made in the technological fields has also influenced those disciplines that examine and try to reconstruct the past. Thanks to refinements and improvements in methods of philological and paleographic research, one can say things about written documents that, just a few generations ago, were beyond reach, except by way of hypothetical and deductive reasoning. Contemporary interdisciplinary methods and laboratory research — which put the newest results and discoveries in chemistry, biology, and mathematics at the disposal of the historian — allow us to reach conclusions about both the distant and recent past that were unthinkable before now and have forced us to drastically reexamine, sometimes even overturn, earlier theories.

However, one cannot expect a portrait accurate even in the smallest detail, not even from modern science. The precise or at least conceptual reconstruction of the past remains a Utopian objective, not just because much information has been lost or is

The canvas and the camera lens attempt to visualize how much Europe has changed. Above right: Woodland from a Flemish Virgin and Child, by the Maître aux feuilles brodés. Above left and top: The present-day landscape. The flock of sheep reminds us that sheep breeding had widespread importance, at least in England, Spain, and southern Italy.

irretrievable, but because the documentation produced in the past is often irremediably distorted by time and does not permit us to compare "numbers" or "facts," as is done in the exact sciences.

The quantitative method, so important to our way of thinking, was not so very important for the peoples of the preindustrial age. During the 15th century, most people knew the day and the month of their birth or baptism (such dates were necessary for calculating astrological configurations at birth and resultant horoscopes), for they were often given the name of the saint on whose feast day one of the two events had occurred. It was not rare, however, for people not to know with certainty the year in which they had been born and thus not to know their own age. During those days

of high infant mortality, it was not unusual for a woman, when asked by a parish priest or doctor how many failed pregnancies she had had or how many of her children had died at a tender age, to give an imprecise answer: "two or three," "three or four." That may seem unbelievable to us, in our age of intense certification, but any one of us who tries to rattle off, one after another and without consulting any documents, the ages and dates of birth of three or four close family members and soon encounters difficulties might judge our ancestors with more indulgence.

Demography is a recent science. Fifteenth-century governments were interested in knowing the number of their subjects only for fiscal reasons. When trying to work out statistics, historians make use of such documents as estimates and registers; pre-

There was plenty of space in the 15th century. Reclaiming land could be useful near towns, but the population had not yet fully recovered from the Black Death of the previous century, and as a result marginal agricultural land had been left free, and much land had still not been used for the first time. Above: The House on the Lake, *by Albrecht Dürer. Above right: A road winds towards a lake between houses, fields, and pruned mulberry trees in a detail from* Nativity, *by the Master of Flémalle (Robert Campin). Opposite: Detail from* Landscape with Saint Jerome *(ca. 1520), by Joachim Patinir. The desert to which Jerome withdrew to live an ascetic life at little more than 30 years of age was the Syrian desert, but the artist sets his pious portrayal of the saint in one of the most significant European landscapes of the era.*

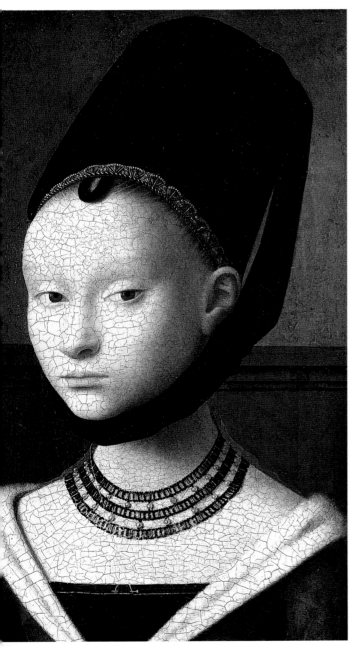

suspicion that the government was preparing for new kinds of taxes.

But the question remains: How many people lived in Europe during the 15th century? The problem is difficult to solve, because one would first have to establish precisely the boundaries of 15th century Europe (even today the definition of contemporary Europe varies). Then, while during recent years plenty of information has been gathered from demographic research for both long and short periods of time, this information has generally involved very limited areas. We can neither generalize nor extend the information that we have for certain territories to the larger areas about which we know very little. From these figures we can make estimates that may be not far wrong, but that is about all we can say.

pared chiefly for fiscal purposes, they furnish much precious demographic information. Such documents are not complete, not even the celebrated Florence population register of 1427, still well preserved in dozens and dozens of parchment volumes.

A similar problem exists in the case of determining national boundaries. No one in the 15th century thought of a boundary between states as a continuous, coherent line. Bridges, fords, and roads were marked with customs houses and guards, but the notion of a "territory" was similar to a spiderweb of inhabited areas joined by paths, rather than the idea familiar to us of a well-defined shaded area on a map. Fifteenth-century sovereigns and magistrates were not able to determine with precision the two calculations that seem fundamental to us today: the number of their subjects and the borders of their states. Furthermore, any investigation would have provoked immediate distrust among the people, since questions of that kind usually led to the

The painters must certainly have flattered them; but, of course, the members of the classes with the means to pay for a portrait in the 15th century did not want to see themselves unattractively. These have been chosen as representative of the many beautiful portraits known from the period. In the hands of a great master, each face holds personality. Above left: Young Woman *(1460–1473?), by the Fleming* Petrus Christus; *this may be a portrait of Maria Baroncelli Portinari, the wife of a Florentine in Bruges for business. Above center:* Portrait of Martin van Nieuvenhowe, *a young man of Flanders, by Hans Memling. Above right:* Portrait of a Woman *(ca. 1456), attributed to Paolo Uccello; this may be Elisabetta di Montefeltro, wife of Roberto Malatesta.*

Below: Portrait of a Young Florentine *(ca. 1469), first attributed to Andrea del Castagno but then to Sandro Botticelli. Below center:* Portrait of a Young Venetian, *an incomplete work that is one of Dürer's first works during his second trip to Venice. Below right:* Portrait of a Man *(1498?), by Luca Signorelli. This is probably a portrait of a lawyer, and the figures in the background give the work a humanistic nature.*

European continent; others have said 60. Around 9 million seem to have been gathered in Italy, 14 million in France, 10 in Germany, and 3 in England (the more the field of historical and demographic research is narrowed, the more credible the figures become). Thus about three-quarters of the European population was amassed between the Pyrenees, the Elbe, and the Danube.

The European continent was just recovering from a severe demographic bleeding. At the close of the 13th century, a period of good climate especially favorable to agriculture, which had lasted at least three centuries, came to an end. The population of Europe had doubled — growing gradually from about 40 million in 1000

It seems possible that around the middle of the 15th century, the world's population fluctuated near 300 million. Of these, from one-sixth to one-fifth were concentrated within the rough boundaries of what we now call Europe. Fernand Braudel estimates that there were 55 million in all of the

(according to some estimates, the population had already touched and then passed 50 million) to around 73 million (according to others, nearly 86 million) — when a long period of colder weather and greater humidity struck Eurasia, bringing with it a drastic reduction in available food resources, the consequent increasing frequency of poor agricultural years, and a relative lowering of natural biological defenses. The mortality rate — from hunger or respiratory diseases, 59

There are in Europe many old and even ancient cities. Buildings from the 15th century and even earlier are not unusual, but only rarely if ever are they set in a context that allows one to imagine the city as it was during this epoch. Paintings may bring us closer to the reality and certainly reveal what was in the eyes and mind of the painter and what, by extension, met with public approval. In landscapes, one must examine the details. Below left: View of gothic houses from the Très Riches Heures of the duke of Berry, the celebrated prayer book begun by the Limbourg brothers and completed by Jean Colombe. Below right: Detail from Shepherd Sermon (ca. 1480), by the Master of Santa Gudula. The view of the city is dominated by the large gothic cathedral with one tower left unfinished, a sight that was doubtless not unusual.

Novgorod, a distant city of merchants

From the gulf of Finland, by way of the Neva, Lake Ladoga, and the Volkhov River, German merchants of the Hanse and Scandinavians reached the great city of Novgorod, a sort of republic led by the *vece* (union of the people) and the access point for the rich commerce in furs. The city lay on both banks of the river, divided in five sections. To the left of the Volkhov was the "Santa Sofia side," with the cathedrals, the Kremlin, and the Nerevski (1) and Vasai (2) sections, in which there were smiths and silverworkers, and Castleback (3), with the courts of the boyars, the great landowners (there were three social classes of citizens: boyars, merchants, and the "black mass" of the common people). Beyond the bridge was the "commercial side," in which one found the market square (*torg*), the "German pier" for the rivergoing boats, the Jaroslav court—which, since the prince had been forced to abandon it, was used by the *vece*—and the two Slavno quarters (4) and the Carpenters (5). Near the market square was the "German court"—that is, the church of Saint Peter in the center of a porticoed enclosure used as a storehouse by the Hanseatic merchants. With the aid of the citizens of the rival city of Pskov, Ivan III, great duke of Muscovy, conquered Novgorod and later (1478) had the bronze bell with which the *vece* was convened brought to Moscow.

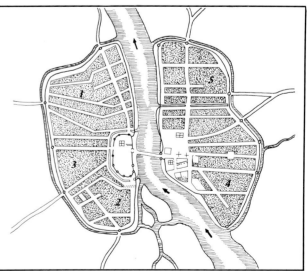

Top: A palace with a garden enclosed by a crenellated wall looking onto a city street: detail from the Nativity *(ca. 1453), by Rogier van der Weyden. Above: A glimpse of a city (perhaps the same city as in the detail above, judging from the castle to the left) and the surrounding countryside, seen next to and through the arches of the nativity stable, in a detail from the* Adoration of the Magi, *also by Rogier.*

Below left: Small doorways are situated along a path that follows the edge of a castle moat with swimming ducks. In the background, a woman wearing an apron approaches with a basket on her head. The setting is a Spanish town. A detail from the Samaritan Woman at the Well, *from the retable of the* Transfiguration *(ca. 1477), by Bernal Martorell. The Samaritan woman holds a terracotta jar tied to a rope: The anachronism*

reveals the world of the artist's time. Below right: Leaning on the balustrade of the loggia of a palace, a gentleman admires the elegant square in a detail from an illumination by Philippe de Mazerolles from the Histoire du bon roi Alexandre, *which belonged to Philip the Good, duke of Burgundy.*

Granada, the last city of the Moors

After the capitulation on January 2, 1492, part of the Islamic population—leather dealers, ironworkers, furniture makers, ceramics workers, silkworm breeders, merchants, mule drivers—remained. Also remaining were the wealthy of Albaicin, the class of nobles. The Darro River, before entering the Genil River, the largest tributary of the Guadalquivir, separates two hills. On one, the site of the Alhambra, the seat of the Moorish kings, the city had had its beginning as a military camp after the Arab invasion. On the other hill was the Albaicin (from the Arabic *al bayyazin,* "the quarter of the falconers"), the noble center, circled by walls. The city's planning shows its Moslem origin: a maze of narrow streets, blind alleys, asymmetric squares, and houses with patios and residences on upper floors. Although its population was halved after the capitulation, the former capital of the Islamic kingdom was Spain's second-largest city.

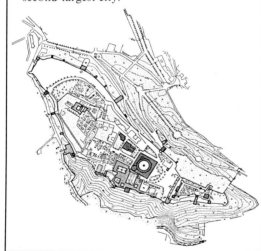

which most affected babies and the old — reached higher levels beginning in the second or third decade of the 14th century. The years between 1347 and 1350 saw the epidemic of the Black Death. Around the middle of the century, the contagion slackened; remaining in the form of an endemic, it came alive again several times until the next pandemic of 1630. During this time the

European population had been reduced to around 50 million: In four years (1347–1350) the plague had killed about 40% of the population, in some areas even more. The tragic chain of epidemics and famines continued to rage throughout the second half of the 14th century, accompanied by wars, which served to enflame both.

There were about 45 million Europeans at the beginning of the 15th century. Fifty years later, that number had risen to 55, and by the end of the century it had reached 70. (Some scholars, having reached very different conclusions, state that during the 15th century the continent's population rose to more than 80 million.) It is at least certain that the demographic curve had begun a constant rise during the early 15th century; but only during the course of the first half of the following century did the population again reach, and with certainty pass, the level of 80-odd million inhabitants it had

Other graphic documents give the flavor of daily life. Above left: A Spanish city (engraving from the History of the Emperor Vespasian, *Seville, 1499) encircled by tents; perhaps it is being besieged. Water is gathered with pitchers and containers made of animal skins and carried on mules. Above right: A miniature (Jean le Tavernier,* Chroniques de Charlemagne, *1460) shows the usual scene of the presentation of the book to the person to whom it is dedicated. To make the moment visible, the walls of a room in the palace have been removed (upper right); gentlemen chat in a courtyard, while others appear at balconies (which on the second floor are made of wood). Outside the city wall are the stands of traveling merchants; one of these is a simple round table.*

achieved earlier between the end of the 13th and the beginning of the 14th centuries.

It was not easy to count people who were only rarely surveyed (and then more for the value of their property and possessions), who were frequently nomadic, who lived in remote or isolated areas, who were unwilling to respond to questions, and who were governed by a ruling class insensible to the needs of the population. (The famines and epidemics had been made even more lethal because the policies to prevent and deal with emergencies furnished by the authorities were even more inadequate than the technological capabilities of the times would have made possible.)

People living in cities could be counted

Above: Shops protected by awnings, market stalls, and a cart that has brought vegetables from the country: the market square of a German city (pen drawing, ca. 1480–1490). Right: Nuremberg (1516); a recreation of the appearance of a transalpine city—compact within its walls and surrounded by dense forest.

Below left: An imaginary city. Since this is a detail from the Prayer in the Garden, *part of the decoration for the altar of San Zeno, by Andrea Mantegna, it should represent Jerusalem, but the artist has created it according to his own visual experience. The walls, towers, and castle are like those of a northern Italian town at that time, as are the modest houses and the road leading from one side of the town to the other. The houses even have Venetian-style chimneys. Below right: Typical architecture from beyond the Alps (steep-pitched roofs, the upper floors with their wood frames, floors marked by beams, and suspended toilets) appears in this detail from* Saint Anne with the Virgin and Child, *by Michael Wolgemut.*

more easily and more accurately, both because incentives for counting them were greater and they were confined in a smaller area. During the course of the 15th century, the major Italian cities — Genoa, Bologna, and Rome (which grew a great deal during the second half of the century) — each reached the level of about 50,000 inhabitants; Florence had more, but it must be remembered that this city, which during the time of Dante had contained 100,000 inhabitants, had suffered most from the pestilence of 1348. In France, the records of the hearth taxes (which took into consideration the "hearths," or family units, not individuals) give widely varied figures: Vienne, for example, in the quarter of a century between 1450 and 1475, is said to have gone from 406 hearths to 240 (in that region — Languedoc — each hearth accounted for three to four persons); on the other hand, by the middle of the century, Paris could count about 80,000 inhabitants. Ghent, the largest city in the densely populated and active Low Countries, had about 56,000 inhabitants around the middle of the 14th century, compared to, for example, the 35,000 of Bruges. During the course of the 15th and the first half of the 16th century, the population of Antwerp leaped, going from 18,000 inhabitants in 1374 to 50,000 in 1526. The most populous German city was Cologne, with barely 40,000 inhabitants, followed by such cities as Metz, Strasbourg, Nuremberg, Augsburg, Vienna, and Prague, which had just half that number. In England, only London had as many as 50,000 inhabitants, followed by York and Bristol, each of which swayed between 10,000 and 15,000. On the Iberian peninsula, only four cities achieved the considerable number of 40,000 persons: Barcelona, Cordoba, Seville, and Granada. With the exception of Cordoba, they were all located near the sea, and all of them, except Barcelona, had recent or very recent Muslim traditions.

Thus the major urban concentrations were in north-central Italy, along the Rhine, and in the Low Countries. Making a few rough calculations, we can deduce that the cities — for the most part the large capitals — accounted for 10%, more or less, of the population. But in Italy, as in the Flemish-Dutch region, there were many "minor" centers of a certain cultural, economic, and also demographic importance.

Comparing the general demographic growth to the growth of the cities yields additional information. Although 15th-century Europe was still an agricultural continent, if not a continent of marshes and forests, the population in the cities was growing faster than in the countryside. We can conclude that the growth in urban centers was a result of immigration from the surrounding area rather than a growth of the urban population. It is evident that the opportunities for work and for making a

The future awaits Antwerp

During the 15th century, the Venetians—who knew a lot about the subject—judged Antwerp to be the world's largest and most wealthy port. "Everywhere there," wrote an ambassador, "money flows with the sale of everything, and each man, no matter how low or lazy, becomes in his way rich." Although far from the sea, Antwerp was located on the large, easily navigable estuary of the Scheldt (below, a drawing by Dürer showing the port's wharves). Its fortunes exploded during the course of the 15th century because of three interconnected factors: When the English changed from being exporters of raw wool to being exporters of woollen cloth, they stopped dealing with Bruges, which was the major center of the Flemish woollen industry, and turned to Antwerp; at the same time, the silting up of the Swin made Bruges's contact with the sea increasingly difficult, ending that city's role as the world's largest marketplace; and when the sea route to the East Indies was opened, Antwerp became the distribution center for the spices imported by the Portuguese and distributed throughout central and northern Europe. By the middle of the 16th century, Antwerp had more than 100,000 inhabitants and was the center for more than a thousand foreign businesses.

67

The well-known Tavola Strozzi *is another splendid record of a 15th-century city: Naples, looking towards the port with the circle of surrounding hills, the capital and jewel of the Aragon dynasty. The Castel Nuovo at the water's edge and the charterhouse of Saint Martin on the hill of the Vomero are easily recognizable. Charles VIII of France entered Naples on February 21, 1495, as a conqueror but without* bloodshed and was "received with such approbation and happiness by everyone that it would be vain to try to express it; people of both sexes, of all ages, conditions, levels, and factions concurred with incredible exultation, as if he had been the father and first founder of that city" *(Guicciardini,* The History of Italy*).*

living were greater within the walls of a city. Even so, in certain areas of the continent — most of all in the east — urbanization encountered ideological and even legal obstacles: Many nobles were hostile to city life, which they considered plebeian; and in many areas feudal obligations made it impossible for the peasant or serf to leave the land for life in the city, where, according to a well-known German proverb, the air "made one free."

In Italy, the nobility and ruling class

68

The construction of buildings as shown in two German xylographs. Top: Detail from a woodcut illustrating the city of Cologne (Adam Woensa, 1531); the gothic cathedral is under construction. Above: The work on site: the crane for lifting materials, the stonecutter, laborers transporting stone, and the architect with a square in his hand.

Piero di Cosimo, Construction of a Palace. *Owning a palace became the ambition of anyone who had accumulated wealth. It is easy to imagine the reasons for this, but perhaps we should heed what a Florentine architect, Antonio Averlino Filarete, had to say: "Building is nothing less than a voluptuous pleasure, like when a man is in love."*

remained strongly attached to the cities but increasingly preferred a life that included visits in the country for at least certain periods of the year. The country was more healthy as it was less exposed to the dangers of riotous city dwellers and to contagion during times of epidemics, and it also conferred a certain status that was much appreciated in that period. The denizens of the city, on the other hand, included the members of a well-to-do middle class and also poor or impoverished peasants who hoped to make their way into that urban "preproletariat" that lived by public charity and day-wage labor. The great building

activity, both public and private, in 15th-century Italian cities offered much poorly paid work for those willing to accept the fatigue and perils of construction labor.

However, even with this spurt of growth, only during the course of the 18th century did the town walls of the major European cities — most of which had been erected or enlarged between the 12th and the 13th centuries, a few before the 14th — begin to show themselves unable to contain the populations. The great leap forward by the urban centers and city economies that took place between the 12th and 13th centuries was followed by a stagnation. In the

case of Italy, for example, the great development in textile manufacture throughout the 14th and 15th centuries was greatly curtailed during the following two centuries.

While the air of the cities may have made people free, it certainly did not make them healthy. A glance at the legislation enacted by cities of the period reveals a great concern for matters of hygiene and ecology. There are frequent and strict ordinances designed to isolate — if not relocate beyond the city walls — pollution-causing activities, especially work in the dyeing, skins and leather, and glass industries. There are regulations for keeping the drains for

69

The illustration at right, part of a large perspective map from 1562, shows the center of the city of Bruges. A few decades earlier—that is, around the end of the 15th century—the urban landscape was essentially the same. The large square in the lower portion, just below the big building with the high tower, is the Markt or Grand Place. Immediately to the left of the Markt is the Burg, a square almost completely enclosed by buildings. It was there, along the banks of the Reye River (the river can be seen crossing the city; *Bruges* means "city of bridges"), that, around the end of the 9th century, the counts of Flanders built a castle around which, on a sandy plain broken by swamps, the city arose. The Burg was the site of the town hall (built 1376–1420) and seat of the citizen government, which had long before freed itself from feudal rule. In the same square is the Chapel of the Precious Blood, in which was kept a reliquary containing several drops of Christ's blood, donated to the count of Flanders by the patriarch of Jerusalem in 1149. Up until the 14th century, the blood liquefied every Friday. The city's most important church, however, was the 13th-century Notre Dame, visible at the right with its 122-meter-tall tower, begun at the end of the 13th century and completed only in 1549.

Bruges was a great mercantile city, the most important in Europe north of the Alps. A sign of the mercantile character of the city is the two squares visible behind the Burg. The one on the left is the grain market; that on the right is the market of furs. The city's vital center, however, was the Markt, site of the Market Hall (begun in 1248); it was dominated by its tower, the upper octagonal portion of which was built in 1482. On the left side of the square, over the Reye River and between the Markt and the Burg, is the 13th-century Waterhalle, in which goods were unloaded directly from riverboats. Since the Reye flows into an arm of the sea that penetrates deeply inland, the city had always been in contact with the sea, but a North Sea storm in 1134 dug a wide gulf, the Zwin, one mile from the city. An outer harbor, the Damme, was immediately built at the spot and joined by canal to the Reye and the city.

Venetian galleys first arrived at Bruges in 1277, the English furnished wool for its industry, and heavy trading went on with the German merchants of the Hanseatic League. During the second half of the 14th century, the Spanish and Portuguese began to arrive. The merchants met at the home of the van der Beurs family, a few steps from the Markt, and created the first stock exchange. The Zwin began to silt up, and around 1460 the port was no longer usable. The growth of Bruges ended, and the city's contemporary topography shows many signs of its ancient mercantile importance.

The drawing at left presents another view of 15th-century cities: These suburbs are depicted in a perspective map of Bologna. At that time, it was common to orient maps with south at the top (this is also the case in the map of Bruges); this is thus part of the northwestern section of the city, in the area of Via delle Lame and the gate of the same name. Except for the line of that road, everything else since then has greatly changed. What immediately strikes the eye is the walls that mark the edge of the city (these are the third ring, dating to the 14th century) and, within the walls, the abundance of green space, with an increasing number of cultivated fields as one moves from the center of the city (in this case, the walls are 500 meters from the city's geometric center).

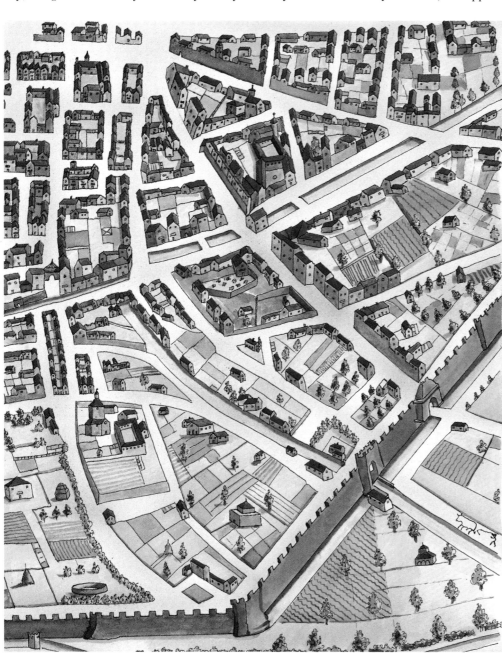

71

Below: The opening illumination from a Flemish codex (15th century) of Virgil's Georgics. *Because of the great nobility of the text it accompanies, it offers a complimentary and probably polished portrait of the agricultural world. It shows a sort of idealized farm that is rich and perfectly modernized, with the most recent technical developments. The plough used is heavy, with wheels and a container to pour the grain, and with a deep-cutting blade, as was needed in northern Europe. In the Mediterranean south, where the surface of the soil was softer, the ploughs used worked the earth to lesser depths. The enclosures are made of interwoven rushes, the stable is full (horses, sheep, and cows), and there are beehives (the farmer and his wife call the bees back by beating the copper basins).*

dead beneath the floors of churches and cloisters up to the end of the 18th century.

Providing water to cities always constituted a major problem, and the obvious fact that this was less critical in cities traversed by a large river reveals dramatic differences in hygienic and sanitary habits. Siena did not grow into a manufacturing center precisely because it lacked water, and Rome owed its relative hygienic security to its wealth of good water and to the abundant fountains with which Renaissance popes had decorated the city.

Stone and brick, the usual building materials in Italian cities, even for humble constructions, were certainly more secure and healthy than the wood, mud, and straw used in the cities beyond the Alps, materials that quickly filled with parasites, rotted in humidity, and easily caught fire. Fire was the great and constant enemy of the city, not only during the Middle Ages but even

"white" waters separate from those for "black" waters and instructions for the removal of garbage. However, as is often the case, the regulations indicate the existence of problems but do not guarantee that they were resolved, and we know that these laws were regularly broken.

Until the 15th century and even later, most cities were "demographic tombs," where it was easy to get sick and die and where life was good only in certain privileged neighborhoods — those containing the homes and palaces of the city's elite, which were regularly abandoned by their lucky inhabitants for long periods each year. Love for the countryside, an idyllic sensibility, and pastoral poetry became popular, in part because of this aversion to—in some cases this horror of — city life, with its miasmas, its sewage, and its turbulence. Only during the course of the 16th century were guidelines concerning burial and the keeping of animals regularly observed in cities; and people continued to bury the

A peasant in a German engraving, quite an unpleasant portrait. As "primary producers," peasants were at the basis of the entire system and certainly made up the vast majority of the population, but they were not well liked by their overseers. It is an "unbelievable thing how much wickedness there is in these ploughmen who have grown up on the land," writes Alberti, one of the bourgeoisie.

Some that arrived later . . .

Near the end of October 1492, Columbus reached Cuba and there discovered the potato and maize. As his son Ferdinand related in the *Histories*, he was offered "certain cook roots that tasted like chestnuts" and saw "a grain similar to millet that they called *mahiz* and that had a good flavor cooked, roasted, or ground into mush." The ship's log makes reference to tobacco ("Men and women holding firebrands of herbs to drink the smoke thereof"). The potato and maize were not the only edible plants that were still unknown to Europe at the end of the 15th century. Also unfamiliar, for example, were pineapples, avocados, bananas, kiwis, and other exotic fruits that have recently come into popular use. The banana is believed to have originated in the Far East; about 200 varieties grow in all the tropical zones, where some represent an important foodstuff. The variety that appears on our tables originated in Central America and came into common use only at the beginning of this century. Even the tomato was unknown in Europe. It comes from South America, probably Peru. It was brought to Europe in the 16th century and was not cultivated in Italy until the 17th. Tomato paste appeared at the beginning of the 19th century; pizza existed long before the tomato's arrival—it was simply made without it. Oranges—or at least the sweet variety we eat today—were also unknown in Europe. Of Chinese extraction, they were introduced to Europe by the Portuguese after they had reached Chinese ports. The Spanish and then the English brought the potato to Europe around 1580. Louis XVI put bunches of potato flowers in his buttonhole, while Augustin Parmentier (who lived between the 18th and 19th centuries) revealed that the tuber was a valuable food. Columbus himself brought maize to Spain; it was cultivated in the Po delta as early as 1544, but its cultivation in the rest of Europe did not begin until the 18th century. In English, French, Spanish, German, and Italian, its name is or once was "Turkish grain," a name that obviously has no true relationship to its provenance: During the 16th century "Turkish" was in a sense synonymous with the exotic.

The mercantile oligarchies had begun to invest in the land, seeking profit there as they did in other business enterprises. There was little harmony between masters and workers. Alberti's opinion of the workers: "Everything they aim to do is always designed to fool you; but they never allow themselves to be fooled for any reason. They never make a mistake unless it is to their benefit; and they always try every means possible to have and obtain what is yours." The peasant: "When he lives in perhaps more luxury than his master, then he will complain and say that he is poor; he always lacks something; he will never speak to you without causing you expense or woe." We do not know the peasant's opinion of their masters. Below: An illumination depicting work in the country.

with the introduction of electricity for lighting and heating.

All of these factors helped contribute to the development of urban gardens in 15th-century Italy. Following the 13th century, most of the arable land within a city's walls — including the gardens and patches of foliage near the walls and along the riverbanks — became construction sites and were filled with new buildings to make room for the growing number of inhabitants. Then the Black Death freed areas that would later fill again slowly. Fifteenth-century Italian architecture eased into these spaces, its forms inspired by Roman architecture, its solemn and restful rhythms, and its prevalence of horizontal over vertical lines. Gardens were planted alongside the beautiful aristocratic palaces and sometimes became parks circled by walls. They were healthful and paradisiacal, modeled on archetypes of Eden. Amid fields, fountains, and antique statues, privileged families lived in the middle of the city, just two steps away

from their thriving businesses, in comfort and peace identical to that of the countryside to which they frequently retired to lead their feudal existence and take care of their agricultural concerns. If one looks at such Italian regions as Tuscany, Lombardy, or the Veneto during the 14th century, one has the sensation that a happy and harmonious relationship had been established between the city and the country. One would see an agricultural territory dotted with sparsely populated areas loosely joined, much less marked by a human presence than even a city with abundant parks, cloisters, and gardens. This peaceful and pastoral landscape would belie, however, a terrible demographic crisis and a great socioeconomic impact on the environment.

To the ruling classes of the High Middle Ages, investing money in the land and in agriculture had been a kind of insurance against the reverses of commerce and banking. During the 15th century, however, the holders of capital among the new "bour-

geois" hierarchy — many of whose families had climbed to power and now lived a kind of aristocratic life, seeking and often obtaining titles and coats of arms — invested in agriculture for purely speculative ends.

The demographic pressure on Europe's territory was intense, which may seem strange since, as we have just seen, the entire population of Europe around the middle of the 15th century was more or less the same as Italy's total today. But if one takes into account that vast regions of the continent at that time were dominated by forests and marshes and that the technological means for deforestation, land reclamation, and fertilization remained rudimentary, then neither the scarcity of foodstuffs available, particularly for the less well to do, nor their high cost, nor the frequency of famine is surprising. The foods that formed the basis of the peasant's diet were cereals and vegetables (turnips were the symbol of the peasant's lot before the introduction from the New World of maize and the potato). Agri-

73

cultural yields were still low, even though
they were rising — a phenomenon that
usually accompanies phases of economic
contraction rather than expansion. During
the course of the 15th century, the yield of
wheat rose from 4.4 to 6.6 (that is, every
pound of wheat sown yielded an average of
4.4 pounds at the beginning of the century
and 6.6 at the end); the yield of rye zoomed
from 4 to 8.8, and oats from 2.5 to 4.4. Such
growth alone is not a sign of prosperity:
"yields" had been low during the 13th century because the growing population had
been obliged to cultivate marginal or less
accessible areas, such as high hills.

The gaps opened in the population by
the demographic collapse of the late 14th
century had made better lands available to
the survivors, and many poor areas had
been abandoned (giving rise to the phenomenon of the *villages désertes* and the
Wüstungen). By the 15th century, therefore,
only the better land was being cultivated,
which helps explain the higher yields. The
new landowners, former members of the
middle class or even peasants, were no less
exacting and greedy — to the contrary! —
than the former noble owners.

On a cultural level, the renewed interest
in the land and in the production and

*Beating grain; a xylograph from the 1495
Venetian edition of the widely known
agricultural manual by Pietro Crescentio from
Bologna. It was written at the beginning of the
14th century at the request of a Dominican
priest, with the title* Liber ruralium
commodorum *(The advantages of the country)
and made use of both the Latin classics and the
author's experience as a landowner.*

75

Pruning vines. This illustrates the month of March in the frescoes by Cossa and Roberti (second half of the 15th century) in the Hall of Months in the Schifanoia palace in Ferrara. In a French text, a traveling wine vendor advertises his product from the new harvest with these imaginative words: "Wine is again available, in large glasses and large barrels, good wine, pleasing, dense and generous, it runs like a *squirrel in the forest, without any sense of ill, nor of acid; it runs dry and lively, as clear as the tears of a fisherman: wine that is inseparable from the tongue . . . you can see it foam, shine, and sparkle; try a little on your tongue, and you'll feel its taste pass to your heart."*

The forest was much more widely spread than it is now. This was more true the more one descended from northern Europe towards the Mediterranean. Wood was used to construct houses, ships, bridges, furniture, barrels, and any number of utensils, and wood fires were the major source of heat. The forests were populated by coalmen, preparers of resin, and woodcutters. They were also a refuge for outlaws.

earnings that could be drawn from it led to a flurry of tracts on agricultural techniques (and especially the aspects of it related to increasing family incomes: even Leon Battista Alberti dedicated several writings to the subject). In 1305 the Bolognese Pietro Crescentio wrote a tract in Latin that was soon translated into vernacular Tuscan, and other texts written for townsmen who had acquired villas followed in the course of the 15th century. With the introduction of printing, many of these were widely distributed. The popularity of such texts must be considered parallel to the "return to the land" movement and the ethical-cultural reevaluation of country life, which also explains the renewed success of Georgic and bucolic poetry and the Arcadian movement. Both trends, however, should be seen against a background of experience and a concrete desire for investment and enrichment; agriculture was looked at from the point of view of the entrepreneur and — to use a term for the moment inadequate — the "capitalist," who was intent on profit and well aware that a rationalization of

efforts and technology used on the land would lead to such profit.

This entrepreneurial outlook also led to a substantial change in attitudes towards peasants. If the city dweller's "satire of the peasant" was a traditional literary genre — the peasant was greedy, dishonest, immoral,

dirty, violent, and intemperate — it was now loaded with suggestions to justify the obsessive fear, on the part of landowners, of being cheated out of part of their wealth and their land by those who worked it. Late 15th-century literature displays a kind of schizophrenia in this regard: Peasants and

shepherds sometimes appear according to the stereotypical models of bucolic poetry as innocent creatures, docile and close to the land; sometimes, on the other hand, they appear as brutes, much like Caliban in Shakespeare's *Tempest* or as the "wild men" of folklore.

Above left: A "literary" forest in a xylograph from the Hypnerotomachia Poliphili, *by Francesco Colonna, printed in Venice in 1499 by Aldo Manuzio. The story begins with young Prolifilo entering an allegorical wood that he will come out of with the guidance of Reason and Will. Above right: A swineherd takes his pigs to eat acorns in the woods: an illumination illustrating the month of October from the* Très

Riches Heures *of the duke of Berry. The decoration of this book was entrusted to three well-known artists, brothers from Limbourg. By 1416 they had finished 39 large illuminations, 24 smaller ones, and 86 initials. A subsequent owner of the manuscript, Charles of Savoy, had it completed by Jean Colombe in 1485. The month of October is one of Colombe's 23 large illuminations.*

77

In the garden

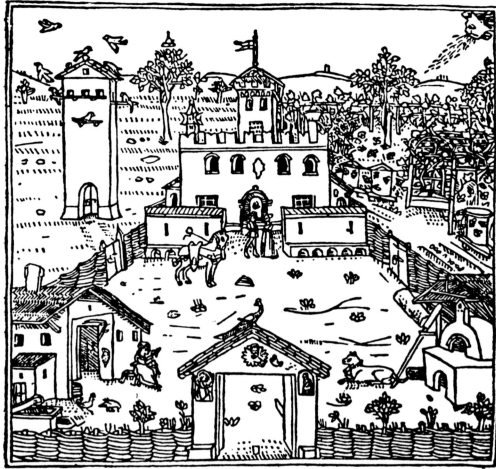

1

2

3

4

E tymology reveals the connection between the French *jardin*, the ancient French *jart*, and a word brought by the Franks, the Germanic peoples who entered Gaul, eventually changing its name to France. This word is *gard* (its relationship to the German *Garten* and English *garden* is clear). The word's original meaning is "vegetable garden." The etymon, or root, of this word—the Latin hortus—leads back to an Indo-European source: *ghorto*. In its original form the word could also mean an enclosure.

Passing from the word to the thing itself, the distinction between a vegetable garden and a flower garden— the first within the sphere of material utility, the second, it can be argued, superfluous— came about slowly. By the end of the 15th century, this distinction was not yet clear, even though separate vegetable and flower gardens already existed, differing, perhaps, more by the use made of them than by their form. Maps and views of 15th-century cities reveal an urban configuration in which houses built along streets have parcels of cultivated land—whether vegetable or flower gardens or both—behind them. The same can be seen in castles, monasteries (the Cistercians had a vegetable-flower garden for each cell), and the country houses that the merchant class began to build or create by adapting older structures. The enclosure fenced in by interwoven rushes in front of the villa shown in illustration 1 is something halfway between a field and a courtyard, but to the right of the house is another enclosure with plants, hives, and a pergola.

The growing of medicinal herbs was also widespread. Herbalists cultivated such plants professionally, but an implement for distilling herbs can often be spotted in the corner of a garden owned by "simple" folk in engravings of the period. These gardens became the first "botanical" gardens, and the herbs used in medicine led to the study of the science of botany.

In medieval culture, the idea of the garden is associated with a celestial paradise, while the terrestrial paradise was known as the Garden of Eden. Adam was buried just outside the Garden of Eden, and the tree that grew above the spot, the so-called tree of life, was to provide the wood for the cross of the Redemption. The notion of the tree of life supplanted that of the tree of the Knowledge of Good and Evil in Eden. From these religious connotations, chivalric culture absorbed two principal ideas, that of the garden as a place of blissful paradise and that of the garden as an enclosed space, an area aristocratically set apart. The garden is almost always protected by a high wall, which is usually crenelated (this detail of military defensive architecture has a certain significance). The bliss is that enjoyed outdoors beneath the plants, the pleasure of the green grass, and the flowers: a sampling of orderly nature. "Fields and shrubs and sweet choruses / on which steps the lovely foot of the Madonna / yellow, vermilion, and pale violet / well-grown grass, fronds, and happy flowers . . ." Thus begins a sonnet by Domizio Brocardo, doctor of law, public functionary, and Petrarchan poet of the 15th century. Such verses are difficult to "visualize" anywhere but in a garden ("well-grown grass").

"Madonna," of course, stands for the poet's lover. The garden is a place suitable for loving gazes, merry parties, and intellectual diversions far from the cares of existence. Such is the atmosphere of the *Garden of Love*, a Nuremberg tapestry of 1460 (4). Tapestries are household furnishings, and thus the garden, at least imaginatively, enters the home. The late 15th-

78

5

cord. The owner of the garden could admire these formations, which frequently formed his noble coat of arms, from an upper floor of his house.

Meanwhile, the gardener handed down and perfected his art: weaving fences of rushes (5); espaliering vines to form decorative patterns (8); hoeing and carrying humus in a basket (3); planting trees (2); grafting (6); and caring for flowers. And the poet (in this case Politian) sang: "I found myself, young girls, one fine morning / in the middle of May in a green garden. / All around were violets and lilies / with green grass and sweet young flowers / blue yellow white and vermilion. . . . "

7

8

century print (7) shows that in the garden one can play music, converse, and eat outdoors. There is frequent mention of lively and large feasts in gardens, especially in Venice, rich in aristocratic gardens along the Giudecca, on Murano, and even on the city's islands; diarists sometimes mention the presence of courtesans.

As can frequently be seen in paintings and illuminations, the garden was divided into rectangular flowerbeds in an orderly arrangement. Nature (of which the garden is a microcosm) thus acquires the geometric order that later characterizes the so-called Italian gardens. At first, the flowerbeds were bordered by square structures set on the ground or even buried in it that separated the soil of the bed from that of the garden. Later, green borders came into style. These gradually made their way into the beds themselves in imaginative or regular designs. Documentation beginning in 1494 mentions the use in England of knot gardens—formal gardens with the beds arranged in intricate patterns resembling twists of a

Like the fleur-de-lis

In 1335, just before the start of the Hundred Years War, Philip of Vitry, secretary of King Philip VI of France, set himself to describing — with the optimism that the times still permitted, though not for much longer — that which, according to him, was the harmonious order of society: "To avoid the ills they saw themselves facing, the people divided into three groups: one to pray to God; another to trade and work the land; and finally, to see that these first two groups did not commit any outrages or villanies, knights were put on the earth." This pretty and providential arrangement reminded the good Philip of the heraldric emblem of the kings of France, the three petals of the golden fleur-de-lis.

There was nothing new about Philip of Vitry's socioanthropological thesis, and it would remain, at least officially, unchanged until the eve of the French Revolution. In fact, this order had been described beginning in the 10th century: Christian society was divided into *oratores*, those who prayed (the clergy); *bellatores*, those who made war (the feudal-knightly aristocracy); and *laboratores*, those who sweated for everyone else to draw from the land the common and necessary sustenance. Everyone had his role, everyone had his duty to perform before the eyes of God and those of his fellow men.

In the first half of the 15th century, Oswald von Wolkenstein, feudal vassal and

The three traditional classes: those who pray, those who do battle, and those who work the land. Above: Saint Bertin welcomes into the convent as brothers the knight Waldbert and his son, from the stories of the saint in the altarpiece of the abbey of Saint Bertin at Saint Omer (1454–1459), by the Frenchman Simon Marmion. Right: An English gentleman receives his peasants, a woodcut from the Book of St. Albans *(Westminster, 1496). Opposite: A nobleman hunting boar on his estate. Louis Malet, master of Graville and admiral of France, is shown here in a French miniature from the* Terrier de Marcoussis *(1491–1493) with a text that describes the life of a great lord at the end of the century.*

poet of Val Gardena, gave a more disenchanted opinion of the providential tripartition of the human race:

God divided humanity in three:
the priest, the noble, and the peasant.
The first, more cunning, as is well known,
prays for the others evening and morning.
The second fights and reaps laurels
for the first and the third, not for himself.
As for the third, it is just that he works
to give to eat to all three.

A response to this serene, hierarchial vision of the world and the stratification of society came at the end of the 14th century: the furious chant of English peasants in revolt ("When Adam dolve [dug with a spade] and Eve span, who was then the gentleman?"). But as early as the High Middle Ages, the theory of the "three orders" had begun to be considered inadequate to give a schematic idea of the com-

A castle on a hill; detail from a codex of the Gospels, illuminated by Ferrara artists for Federico da Montefeltro, duke of Urbino. In the new monarchical system many nobles were still bellatores, *or warriors, but they fought in the service and at the expense of the king. There were still war stories to be told during evenings spent in the castle.*

Noblemen hunting. One of the members of the retinue carries a crossbow, another a horn (detail from the Altar of the Cross *from the monastery of Polling in Germany, ca. 1444). At the beginning of the following century, in the* Théâtre d'agriculture, *Olivier de Serres was to write: "The aim of hunting, which is a pleasant pastime, is connected to many benefits: it favors health, due to the fact that one has to get up early in the morning and exercise, and sobriety. Moreover, hunting tempers the spirit, making man patient, discreet, modest, magnanimous, bold, and industrious. We should not forget that hunting supplies the table with precious meats. Finally, it also allows us to check the land and hasten the work."*

plexity of social relationships and the division of labor.

Around the middle of the 12th century, the English encyclopedist John of Salisbury had dusted off the celebrated apology of Menenio Agrippa to create an image of the "social body" in which the head was the clergy, the arms were the knights, and the body the peasants: To translate this morphology in physical-statistical terms, it would have been necessary to resort to a microcephalic being with short, skeletal arms mounted on a dropsical body. As this anthropomorphic social organism would indicate, the "body," the portion later defined as the "third estate," composed 95% of society.

The growth of cities and an economy increasingly tied to money, commerce, and the production of marketable goods upset the blissful sociology in which Philip of Vitry pretended to still believe. The class of

Living in a castle

Many castles—or ruins—can still be found throughout Europe. Nobles, particularly the lower nobility, identified themselves as being "landed," and the life they lived in their castles (all year or at least during a certain period if they had a house in the city) can be judged, depending on preferences, to be either fascinating or uncomfortable. There was a great coming and going of grooms, swineherds, peasants, servants, and men-at-arms. But there was also great isolation, broken by traveling merchants or performers, and every so often visits—perhaps to arrange a marriage — and one could have a secretary, adept at the best Latin, to carry on correspondence with the most learned minds of the period. Castles were rather gloomy abodes; and yet, here and there, they were on their way to becoming more pleasant country residences. They were drafty, and against the cold one had only coats, draperies, bed curtains sometimes a room dressed in *boiseries*, and straw spread on the floors. Hearths, of course, spread their warmth over a limited range and gradually were made with seats around them. The food was monotonous and eaten with spoons and knives—there were no forks. Sometimes extravagant banquets were held, with the lord of the castle seated in his special chair and everyone else on benches and stools in rooms flaunting the family's precious crockery. Baths were uncommon; water was drawn from wells and was only rarely warmed for personal washing. Parasites were everywhere, and branches of mulberry were put under beds to ward off fleas. Even so, life in castles was for the rich—although perhaps less rich than the middle-class city dwellers. But how can one really appreciate this life? What did it mean to live according to the quiet rhythms of daylight and shadow? To follow the passing of hours and seasons from out in the fields, from a high window, or from a seat in the slant of a wall? To take part in dawn riding parties, through woods or across moors, to hunt for "larger" game (deer, boar, wolf) or "lesser" game (ducks or hare), rights that the nobility carefully protected? What was it like to take the fresh air from a balcony? And what of the silence of the nights?

83

This seems to be a scene from a chivalrous story: A lady comes out of the castle on a white horse (detail from the Madonna Enthroned with Two Angels, *by Hans Memling). Machiavelli spoke scornfully of "those who live idly on the abundant income from their possessions, without paying any attention either to cultivation or any other effort necesssary to live."*

birth to an entire undergound folklore. On the seas were fishermen, sailors, and oarsmen. There were vagabonds of every kind: peasants in search of new land to work, real or fake pilgrims, real or fake clergymen, wandering ascetics, charlatans, and beggars. There were also wandering men-at-arms who by then accepted, without great lament, being called *soldiers*; a few generations earlier this appellation would have seemed offensive to any warrior — even mercenaries — since it expressed the hateful notion of risking one's life for a *soldo*, or coin, though it would undergo in the modern age a destiny of progressive nobilization, finally becoming a title desired even by kings.

The mechanism of the complex social stratification also cut horizontally across the clergy. Setting aside those people such as university students who enjoyed an ambiguous state in the sense that they belonged formally to the clergy (because they were granted "minor" canonical orders) while they lived in practice like laymen, the clergy themselves, whether secular (that is, bishops or priests) or regular (members of traditional

the producers had been socially and technically speaking, differentiated. Instead of only peasants intent on producing that which sufficed in an autarkic economy of direct consumption, there were bankers, merchants, professionals, artisans, and city laborers employed in shops and yards. Even the "peasants" were, in reality, stratified into classes of small landowners, tenant farmers working the land of others according to various sorts of agricultural contracts, sharecroppers, manual laborers, and day workers. There were also the workers in areas considered "wilder" than the fields, such as the forests, heaths, and marshes: the shepherds, herdsmen, woodsmen, coalmen (and, in the regions of central and eastern Europe, the hunters and the gatherers of honey and wax), and the miners, who, especially in Saxony and Transylvania, gave

monastic or so-called mendicant orders), had very differing ways of life. There were also the members of the many monasteries and women's convents as well as the people who, particularly in cities, conducted lives suspended between the clergy and the laity: tertiaries, oblates, lay brothers, and devoted women (known as Beghards and "pinzocheros") who lived in a common house and passed their time praying, working, and helping their neighbors.

Certainly, various features united this society so profoundly differentiated and stratified. Aside from those who, under differing titles, were truly marginal — vagabonds, beggars, ex-criminals, prostitutes, lepers, and Jews — differences of class or social level were usually underlined by rigid codifications (though they differed from place to place) in dress and behavior. Fifteenth-century Europe had, in a sense, a "young" population. People aged rather quickly and lived short lives, at least according to the standards of today's life-expectancy charts. Forty years was an enviable milestone reached in a battered state, usually with few remaining teeth. This does not mean that there were no aged or elderly persons — past 60 or 70 or even more venerable — but in such cases — and they are frequent — one can trust neither the declarations of those concerned nor their acquaintances (memory distorts easily, and there is an inclination to hyperbole), nor their appearance. However, more than a brief life span, high infant mortality lowered, in a statistical sense, the average age.

It seems that women were somewhat less numerous than men, a fact that may hide one of those "dark secrets" that are difficult to penetrate without sure documentation. A certain frequency (which can be found in China and many other civilizations) of female infanticide is probable. Girls were held to be inferior in the peasant's world because they were less adapted to work and were a cause of worry to the

85

Bourgeois from the 15th century, from the cover of a tax register from Siena painted by Benvenuto di Giovanni. We know that the rich were found among the bourgeoisie, but how many of them were there? We can obtain only partial answers to questions like these, about an era that has left us no statistics, in the tax record. It has been calculated that out of 3,000 Florentine families (Florence is the city for which most information survives), those who paid between one and ten florins in 1457 (in theory, these made up the middle class) represented less than 16% of the whole; 227 families paid more than 10 florins; 165 families paid between 10 and 20 florins; 51 families from 20 to 50; 8 from 50 to 100; and 3 families paid more than 100 florins.

Jacques Coeur, a wealthy man

He was the wealthiest man in France: a half million florins, homes and estates in 50 villages, 30 castles, mines of copper, lead, and silver. In Bourges, the city of his birth, he built a magnificent palace (a detail is shown above). According to a popular proverb, "Jacques Coeur does what he wants, the king what he can." Born into a rich family, he had used his business skills to multiply his worth. With true mercantile know-how he had established relationships with the Levant, skipping Italian intermediaries. He speculated in gold and silver in France and the Orient: He sent ships loaded with silver to the Levant to trade for gold— there, of lesser value—and then traded it back for silver in France. Since slaves were expensive, he made up the crews of his galleys from "sluggards, rogues, and other worthless ones" captured in the streets. King Charles VII gave him a role equivalent to that of minister of finance. Inevitably, Coeur fell into disgrace. It was whispered—absurdly—that he had poisoned Agnes Sorel, the king's favorite, who had died in childbirth. He was accused of minting false coins, embezzlement, high treason, fraud, and furnishing arms to the Turks. Arrested, tried, and tortured, he was condemned to death; he escaped and fled to Rome. Calixtus III made him commander of a fleet being sent to liberate the Greek islands from the Turks, and he died at Chios, either of wounds or disease, in 1459. On his deathbed he wrote a last letter to the king of France, pleading again his innocence and asking that his children be cared for. Louis XI restored his good name.

middle-class as well because they were difficult to marry off without dowries. In spite of this numerical inferiority, the 15th-century European world was full of widows who populated the houses of the Beghards in Flanders and the "pinzocheros" in Italy. This was less a result of the fact that the average life span for men was shorter than that for women (in certain circles, such as that of the warrior nobility, this must have been dramatically true) than of the considerable difference — as much as fifteen or twenty years — in the average ages of spouses. It was then common for already mature men to marry young girls to assure the prospect of having many children — and it was necessary to have many, given the high infant mortality rate, if one wanted to be sure of having descendants.

People lived according to a clearly marked social stratification that was reflected in differences in clothing, in behavior,

Mules loaded with sacks of grain, a detail from The Virgin and Pope Calixtus III, *by Sano di Pietro. Goods circulated in ships by sea, in mule trains by land, and by river, the primary means of transportation. Goods being shipped were, however, subject to frequent tolls and duties.*

and in food from class to class and from level to level. These differences were neither all nor always rigidly codified. However, alongside a moderate degree of social mobility, at least at the middle levels, these differences were strong; and they were very real in the sense that people had a fear of slipping down the social scale.

If the tripartition defined by Philip of Vitry provides an inadequate description of the complexity of what in the future would be called the "third estate," it does not give even a minimal idea of the other two. For

Anecdotes of merchant life. Top: Merchants negotiating. The vendor is seated on his sacks of goods; the purchaser has a bag of money in his hand. In fact, by this time large-scale commerce was carried out by the use of documents passed between banks, and there was less actual movement of cash. Above: Merchants evaluate the colors of their samples of material.

The port of Hamburg: illumination from the Hamburger Stadtrecht, 1497. Hamburg is situated on the estuary of the Elbe, which opens into the North Sea; Lübeck is on the Baltic. Transport by land or by canal between these two cities, which were not far apart, allowed the seafaring merchants traveling between the Baltic and North Sea to avoid circumnavigating the Danish peninsula. This system, which involved

unloading and reloading one extra time, was suitable for goods of a high value that were not too bulky (and it was profitable for the merchants of the two cities). The history of commerce is full of arrangements of this type, which opened the way for free enterprise and contributed to the prosperity of cities.

Artists: their origins, workshops, and formation

According to a romantic anecdote, Hans Memling was a bloody and dissolute soldier who, wounded at the battle of Nancy, was taken in and cared for by the nuns of the hospital of Saint John at Bruges, where he began to paint for them. In reality, having established himself at Bruges, Memling made a career of his activity as a painter, acquired land, and put aside a considerable fortune.

Many other artists raised themselves socially by using their art, to which must have been added a certain entrepreneurial skill. Art was a business. Many artists came from the poorer classes: Piero della Francesca was the son of a cobbler of Borgo San Sepolcro; Antonello da Messina was son of a mason, perhaps a stone dresser or marble worker, not a bricklayer; Piero di Cosimo was the son of a goldsmith. The father of Sandro Botticelli was a tanner; not surprisingly, that of Antonio and Piero del Pollaiuolo (their family name means "poulterer"), sold chickens. Giorgione, Vasari said, was "born of the humblest stock." Others began from a more solid social position: Leonardo was born out of wedlock, but his father did not neglect him and was a person of a certain importance, a notary for Florence's signory. Michelangelo's family was of distant nobility, and when he entered the workshop of Ghirlandaio it was taken as a sort of social decline. Leon Battista Alberti was from an important family, but notwithstanding the importance of his work in architecture during the 15th century, it is difficult to place him socially with the other artists: he planned, and others built for him. Many other greats of this fecund period were born into families of artists. The father of Giovanni and Gentile Bellini was a painter, as was that of Raphael. Even Hieronymous Bosch was a "child of art" (but his mother was the daughter of a tailor, and his brother inherited their father's workshop; he married a rich aristocrat who paid some of the highest taxes in the city). Dürer was the son of a Hungarian immigrant who had set himself up in Nuremberg as a goldsmith.

According to the cultural schemes of the time, painting, sculpture, and architecture—our three great "belles artes"—were neither among the seven "liberal arts" (which included music) nor among the "mechanical arts." A few decades later, the *Standebuch*, by Hans Sachs (1568), illustrated with xylographs by Jost Amman, presented, according to its frontispiece, an "exact description of all the classes in the world, high and low, spiritual and secular, of all the arts, trades, and businesses, from the largest to the smallest." Of its 114 images, which begin with a father and end with a madman, at least 15 are dedicated to activities that we would today consider artistic or the work of a craftsman.

The area of artistic production was still the workshop, which provided for a surprising range of activities. Painters, for example, made frescoes for churchs and rooms in palaces, painted altarpieces, made portraits, decorated chests, ornamented banners, and made designs for stained-glass works, inlays, and embroidery. Sculptors—and any painter might also be a sculptor—melted precious plates and other objects when not sculpting monumental tombs, bas reliefs, and statues. Both painters and sculptors prepared ephemeral decorations for public holidays, processions, ceremonies, triumphs, and "entrances."

The workshop rooted the artist in tradition, but its role was not entirely conservative. The workshop was a concentration of artistic intelligence, and taste flowed from the workshop to the buyer and from the buyer to the workshop. An overly conservative workshop that offered nothing new would soon lose trade. The workshop was above all a place for the development of the artist; together with the "craft," style was passed from master to student. Sometimes a student was a clever innovator and influenced the master; often the student studied different masters, gaining that interweaving of imitation, formal borrowings, and derivations that are the delight and torment of critics. Travel, too, served a formative function: Visits to Italy were important for many northern artists. Dürer went to Venice twice, Jean Fouquet visited Rome in his youth, and Rogier van der Weyden traveled there for the Holy Year in 1450.

example, it was unthinkable to group together in one "order" all the *oratores*, or priests. Besides the Roman Curia and the "princes" of the Church — those who were clothed in purple and united in the Sacred College — this composite group ranged from bishops and abbots, vastly rich and bursting with prebends and who usually did not reside in their dioceses or abbeys but enjoyed the proceeds from them while staying in the pontifical court; to the archpriests and the parish priests, more or less well provided for; to the poor parish clergy of the towns or country, who were penniless, ignorant, without dignity, and left to themselves. The pastoral visits carried out during the 15th century, of which descriptions have survived, frequently present a picture of desolation: crumbling churches, filthy surroundings and furnishings, neglected church services, and squalid stories of priests who round out their meager earnings by taking up the practice of magic or who appear involved in incidents of seduction or sexual violence.

Similar differences in station and character are found among the nobles. Although it is relatively difficult to define 15th-century "nobility," we can use certain characteristics to define the "gentleman," the *proudhomme*, the *gentiluomo*, the *Edelmann*, the *hidalgo*. First of all was the knowledge and practice of arms, even if only in tournaments or jousts rather than in actual warfare. This was often marked by the bearing of various ranks of knightly honor conferred by a sovereign, a great lay or ecclesiastic noble, the grand master of an ecclesiastic knightly order or "court," or the citizen magistrates of an Italian republic. Also required was the possession of land and houses or palaces in cities, manors or villas in the country. The leading of a kind of "noble" life was considered important, a life that consisted most of all in an alternation between activities such as war, tournaments, and hunting while caring for estates. Finally, the noble's life was marked by the display of the family's heraldric arms, along with a more or less famous genealogy (false ones could be assembled) and by a family history of political marriages with other illustrious families. But these were things one could, in whole or in part, feign, solicit with relatively little expense, or buy outright.

Among the nobles, the levels of stratification were numerous. The high nobility, capable of competing even with sovereigns, was strongest in France, Germany, certain areas of the Alps, and northern Italy. The great aristocrats held court and often conducted personal foreign politics, including military expeditions, that might differ from or even conflict with those of the sovereigns to whom they were formally dependent. A nebulous crowd, difficult to define, thronged around the courts of the kings and great aristocrats. In addition to the "body" of

89

The painter at work in front of his easel, with pen, palette, and a bar to support the position of the hand and make the stroke as precise as possible. Detail from a picture by the Master of the Augustinian Altars of Saint Luke Painting the Madonna *(1487). Luke the Evangelist, perhaps from Antioch, was a doctor. In the New Testament there is no record of his having been a painter, or of his having painted Mary; this is a tradition that appears only in the 8th century. Artists, as members of society, were in a state of transition in the second half of the 15th century, though by the following generation Raphael would be treated as a gentleman (he died leaving 16,000 ducats).*

Copper Mine, *by Hendrik Met de Bles, known as the Owl. Mining was developing quickly at the end of the 15th century, especially in Germany, and German experts were summoned to many countries. The Saxon Georg Bauer, teacher of Greek, doctor, and* bürgermeister *(first magistrate) of Chemnitz, wrote in 1530 in the* Bermannus sive de re metallica dialogus, *under the name of Agricola: "The miner must possess* vast experience in his art, so as to know with certainty which hill, valley, or plain can usefully be mined. . . . He must know the ways that minerals run through the ground, the way stones are split and broken . . . the many and various types of ground . . . the characteristics and forms of everything that must be done under the ground . . . the art of examining every kind of material."

government or chancellery functionaries, it included members of illustrious families in decline or impoverished, a variety of social climbers, "courtesans" with various and imprecise functions ranging from the young companions of pederasts at court to councillors and jesters.

Stripped of its tinsel, of its banquets, spectacles, and tournaments, of its display of jewels (often pawned) and colorful clothes (often borrowed), court life could be very hard. One ate the leftovers of the masters and slept as best as possible and haphazardly. Hygiene was lacking, and there were privations and humiliations to be faced. Early in the 17th century, the great iconographer Cesare Ripa defined a court as "a union of men of quality in the service of distinguished and princely people." Far less elegant but perhaps closer to the truth was the definition that the pioneering authority on the world's "professions," Tommaso Garzoni, had supplied a few years earlier, in 1587: "an assembly of malicious foxes, a school of corrupt manners and a refuge of dishonest roguery."

The high nobility held court. Beneath it, the members of the lower nobility usually refrained from visiting the sanctuaries and halls of power and lived decorously apart,

90

Opposite: Page from the Kuttenberger Gradual, *showing the entire productive process of the silver mines at Kutna Hora in Bohemia in the 15th century. The miners work with picks in the bowels of the earth. A pulley worked by horses raises the minerals, which are then split and selected, and finally the merchants examine samples and negotiate, seated around a table in the presence of a royal representative.*

They had various and different names: *artes*, *guilds (from the* geld *tax levied to pay common expenses)*, fraternitates, ministeria, fraglie, maestranze, *and* paratica *(from the custom of parading behind their own standard). By the 15th century, such trade organizations had for the most part lost the political power they had had in relation to the center of power. Instead, they concentrated on social assistance and religious and economic ends (the protective control of production). In some places there were not many of them, so each grouped together several trades, but in Paris in 1268 the* Livre des Métiers, *by Etienne Boileau, listed a hundred organized trades. Below: An urban magistrate observes the work of two artisans; a miniature from a Flemish codex from the end of the 15th century.*

The price of learning an art

So that he might learn painting, the Paduan painter Uguccione put his son Francesco in the shop of another of that city's painters, that of the master Francesco Squarcione in the San'Antonio district (Andrea Mantegna also worked with Squarcione). A contract was drawn up before a notary, with Latin in the premise and vernacular Paduan in the clauses. Dated October 30, 1467, it was witnessed by Federico di Vigonza and Sire Bartolomeo di Rinaldino. The course of study is outlined meticulously (concerning drawing and perspective). As far as the student is "capable to learn," Squarcione agrees to use his "knowledge and experience" to teach him to put a background in perspective and to "place figures on that background, one here, another there, in different places on that background, and to put there also furniture, that is, chairs, benches, and houses." Next comes the drawing of a head along with "the proportions of a nude body from front and behind with the placing of eyes, nose, mouth, and ears on the head of a man in the correct places." The master pledges the student that he will "give him progressive lessons in drawing with white lead on paper and to correct him" and point out his errors. The teaching, planned to last four months, was to cost the father of the student a half golden ducat each month, plus "the usual gifts": a goose "or pair of chickens" for the feast of All Saints' Day, *focaccia* (a flat bread) and wine for St. Martin's Day, two liras' worth of lemon juice or "enough pork sausage to stuff a pair of pigeons" for Christmas, and "a good quarter of a kid" for Easter. Squarcione adds that he does not want to be bound to teach on obligatory feast days and warns that the student will have to pay him for any drawings he damages.

This document is only one of many such agreements; reading it gives a sense of the breadth of humanity in the economic dealings and customs of the times. Since it is a legal document, it includes a provision for compensation in the cause of default: a fine of 25 liras.

looking after their knightly honors and meager earnings from the land. In fact, if such nobles had other sources of income (and they frequently did), they tried not to let it be known. During the 15th century, Florentine and Venetian merchants, with their new heraldric arms freshly painted and their knightly decorations newly gilded, were nevertheless of the opinion that only the land truly ennobles. This century saw cities, most of all Italian and Flemish, made illustrious by the presence of a patriciate of

*A unique mobile bread oven in a colored xylograph from the beginning of the 1400s. In a Nuremberg document that lists about 50 artisan groups in the city, the bakers are quoted as one of the largest, with 75 masters (third after the shoemakers and tailors). Local place names used in Venice indicate two different groups of artisans, one of which mixed the bread (*pistor*) and one that cooked it (*forner*).*

more or less recent establishment that had lost noble splendor but did not refrain from banking or mercantile trading, for the patriciate was usually formed from a political mixture of alliances among aristocratic and the upper-middle-class families.

In Germany, meanwhile, the *Ritters*, however penniless the knights might be, disdained living in the city and responded to their poverty by turning their castles into

centers of brigandage, which they took as a privilege of rank. Plundering the hated and scorned *Bürgers*, who made themselves rich with usury and the spice trade (the nobles called them *Pfeffersacke*, or "pepper sacks") was considered a knightly right and an act of justice. The peasants often shared the knights' opinion, and this ill feeling exploded dramatically in the wars of 1523-1525, at the beginning of the Reformation.

For their part, the merchants in cities grew strong from their wealth and often hired some of these knights to protect them. The *Ritters'* brothers called such mercenar-

ies "blood merchants" and felt themselves betrayed.

It was the cities, where people lived elbow to elbow, that provided the most dramatic evidence of the period's disproportions. There, amid the bankers and merchants, strutted, flourishing and haughty, a class of professionals who proudly displayed the symbols of the liberal arts that distinguished them: solemn headgear, long coats lined with fur. These notaries, lawyers, and doctors were professionals, surrounded by extraordinary social prestige as well as a reputation for greed and, often, incompetence. This accusation fell most heavily on the doctors, since 15th-century medicine was still in large part an activity of theoretical philosophy supported by the wisdom of Hippocrates, Aristotle, and Avicenna. Doctors delivered learned disquisitions on dis-

Above: A fishmonger's stall from the beginning of the 15th century; the illustration is taken from the Concilium ze Costenz, *a chronicle written by Ulrich von Richenthal. Above right: A xylograph showing the familiar work of carding and weaving wool, from the* Spiegel der Menschlichen Lebens, *the German translation of the* Speculum humana vitae, *by the bishop Roderigo de Zamora, written in 1477. The*

lanificum, *the most important of the manufacturing processes, was fragmented into a long series of operations that transformed the raw and semiworked material from various places of production both within and outside the city. The woolworker, owner of the raw material, strictly controlled the production process, even though this could involve the work of artisans who were more or less independent.*

The carpenter in his workshop (from a triptych by the Master of Flémalle). Among his tools are a hammer, pincers, chisel, saw, axe, and drill. Carpenters are frequently represented and are always depictions of Saint Joseph (whom the Gospels refer to generically as teknon, faber *in the Vulgate; the interpretation of this to mean carpenter appears in a Syriac version and is asserted only from the 2nd century onward).*

The tailor's workshop. Like the miniature on the opposite page, this illustration comes from the Behem Codex, *a collection of privileges and statutes from Krakow with the regulations of the city's guilds, compiled by the scribe and municipal notary Baltazar Behem and illustrated by a local painter (ca. 1505). The presence of a goat in the workshop, behind the client who is trying on the clothes, is an allusion to a popular*

tale: A tailor who subtracted some of the material he should have prepared for a client is sentenced to feed the victim's goat for twelve months. In a Nuremberg list of artisans, the clothing category includes tailors, boot makers, cobblers, furriers, cloak makers, hat makers, and makers of ribbons, gloves, and bags (not to mention leatherworkers, tanners, woolworkers, and dyers), comprising a total of 337 masters.

ease and on ways of maintaining or regaining health, but they usually did not stoop to the actual practice of therapeutic activity, which was left to apothecaries or, in the case of surgery, to barbers, To a host of obstetricians and gynecologists — whose practices often bordered on witchcraft, though they must have often been empirically effective — was entrusted the job of treating women for the problems and afflictions of their sex.

The organization and regulation of production, costs of products and salaries, work hours, the recruitment and training of professionals, merchants, and specialized artisans, and negotiations with common laborers were all matters not thought to properly concern the state. Governments limited themselves to inflicting on the wealth, real estate, and property accumulated by their subjects a host of direct and — most often — indirect taxes. As had happened during the entire period of the Middle Ages and would continue until the French Revolution, such regulation and organization was entirely the duty, city by city, of professional associations of bankers,

merchants, or artisans — those who could call themselves *universitates, communitates, artes, officia, scholae,* commonly called guilds.

Each guild had its functionaries, courts, archives, and sometimes even its own body of men-at-arms. Membership in the guild required a rigorous apprenticeship and then the necessary economic and professional qualifications. The guild resolved questions of disputes pertaining to work and severely repressed any sign of uncontrolled economic competition among its members. It oversaw the quality and quantity of finished product and made laws concerning costs and means of production. The guilds also regulated and repressed the pretensions of its members. Partnerships among the subordinates were usually forbidden, even such brotherhoods organized for the simple pur-

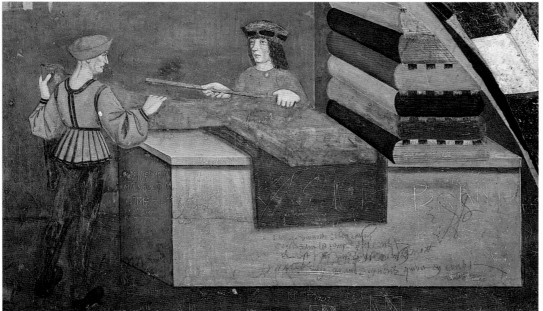

A wooden counter, bolts of merchandise, and a vendor with a ruler in the clothseller's workshop (from 15th-century frescoes). Commerce enriched many families. In the following century, many people hid the fact that their wealth originated from trade. It was often necessary to do so: In 1546 the families of those who had been in contact with the "mechanical arts" were excluded from the citizen council of Brescia. Shortly

afterwards a trial was begun for "accusations of mechanics," in which an inquiry was made into the life of the father of a councillor, a certain Francesco Tarello, who had died at the end of the 15th century. A witness claimed to have sometimes seen him "measuring, cutting, and selling clothes" and that he had heard him say "He has power whose patrons get their hands on his things." His son lost the case.

The blade-maker's workshop (from the Behem
Codex*): He produces knives, razors, swords, and
scimitars. There are two interesting details: A
figure on the left (a client?) is wearing Oriental
clothes — south of the Carpathian mountains the
steppes were still in the hands of the Tartars.
There is a wash basin in a recess in the wall, with
a hanging metallic basin and a pouring spout.
Next to it hangs a long white towel.*

pose of prayer. Guilds were organs of "masters" — that is, of entrepreneurs, great professionals, and owners of banking and mercantile companies. Salaried workers had no rights, and it was not rare that their salaries were beneath the minimal level for sustenance, forcing them to round out their earnings by begging or relying on public charity. The city hospices and fraternities dedicated to assistance in the form of material goods and the distribution of frugal meals intervened, furnishing a kind of supplement to the salaries of the classes less well off and thus serving the social balance and maintaining order.

Many riots, both by citizens and peasants, took place in Europe between the end of the 14th century and the early 15th century, often with religious motivations (the Lollards in England, the Fraticelli in Italy, the Hussites in Bohemia); but the second half of the 15th century was a period of apparent social peace in Europe. The flames, however, smoldered beneath the ashes, to catch fire between the second and third decades of the next century, the years of the Protestant Reformation.

The fuel of the city economy was money, and although the basic instruments and practices of credit that even today support banking activities were already in place, money meant "hard currency." During the 15th century, the monetary system of the Euro-Mediterranean area was based on a bimetallic standard, with gold coins used for large, international transactions and silver coins (often of poor quality or nominal value) or even base-metal coins or coins of relatively poor alloys used for small expenses or to pay salaries. Establishing the exchange rate between gold and silver gave entrepreneurs and employers a further premium: They easily speculated, paying for work in poor coins and selling products in exchange for gold.

The Florentine florin and Venetian ducat (both nominally of pure gold, the first

weighing 3.536 grams, the second 3.559) dominated the monetary scene of the 15th century and were honored even in the ports of the Levant, although the Muslim powers had their own gold coins made to resemble the old denarius or hyperperon of imperial Byzantium. Traded alongside the Florentine and Venetian coins were the papal florin,

the genovino of Genoa, the ducats of Hungary and Bohemia, the Portuguese cruzado, the "half noble" of England, the cavalier of Burgundy, and finally the excellente of the Catholic kings of Spain, who began minting it in 1497. Each of these coins weighed around 3.5 grams and was nominally pure. Within the Holy Roman Empire, the best

The mechanical arts

Ugo di San Vittore was a 12th-century theologian. A Saxon, probably the son of a count, he became an Augustinian and taught in the abbey of Saint Victor at Paris, from which comes the name by which he is known.

In the first chapters of

one of his books, the *Didascalion*, he discusses the liberal and mechanical arts. These xylographs illustrating the mechanical arts are from an Augsburg edition of 1475; there is thus a wide gap in time between the formulation of the classification and its iconography, which is clearly more modern.

The scheme represented is traditional: The mechanical arts, younger humble sisters of the liberal arts, are divided into seven, as are the liberal arts and the virtues of the religious canon (theological virtues and cardinal virtues). Their characteristics as listed may seem bizarre to us. Armor, or the making of weapons; Medicine; the Venatorial arts, or hunting; Lanificium, or the manufacture of woolen cloth; Navigatio; Agricultura; and Theatrica, or scenic arts.

The images are sketches from the period. The manufacture of wool shows a carder, a wool winder, and a

horizontal loom with pedals. In the shop of the armorers is part of a suit of 15th-century armor. The ship's rudder is hinged to the sternpost, which is not accurate for the time of Ugo di San Vittore (the passengers jammed onto the open deck of the ship do give a sense of the discomfort faced by pilgrims to the Holy Land when traveling by sea), nor was there then the heavy wheeled plough shown in the farming scene. The nobility is shown using dogs to hunt deer. A doctor examines urine while another heals a fracture with the patient's leg supported on a three-legged stool. The theatrical arts are represented in action, with nearly nude wrestlers and

duelers with swords.

More celebrated than this modest German work of xylography is the representation of the same subjects in the 14th-century panels of Giotto's belltower at Florence. The same mechanical arts are depicted

with two significant additions that give a singularly "modern" touch, as might have been expected from the great Tuscan community: architecture and painting. Ugo di San Vittore's formulation is doctrinal. The reality of material culture was much richer; there were dozens of specialized "trades," each regulated and protected by a guild.

96

gold coin was the gulden of the Rhine. In France in 1475 the old scudo *à la couronne* ("crown coin") was replaced by the new scudo *au soleil* ("coin of the sun"), more in keeping with the European standard. The moneychanger's task was further complicated by the good silver coins, which were usually called, according to the time and place, "thick" or "white."

Despite a tendency towards standardization in coinage, the 15th-century economy

Above and opposite left: Monks and nuns working. These are Humiliati taken from the Historia ordinis humiliatorum. *They belonged to a medieval movement that began in Milan, and they organized themselves into communities to live Christianity "in the same way as the original church," supporting themselves by working. Unlike the Waldenses, members of a movement that began at more or less the same time and*

Commune employees being paid, from a Sienese tablet of the 15th century. The imperfect two-metal system — whereby gold coins were used for large commercial deals while silver or cheap metal coins were used for smaller sums and for paying salaries — allowed those with capital to effectively reduce salaries. Salaries were, however, fixed towards the end of the 15th century.

was far from coherent. Usury was constantly condemned, but loopholes of all kinds kept it legal, at least in certain forms. Gold and precious stones, which seemed an excellent investment, and the immense treasures of sovereigns and cathedrals were regularly used as pledges for loans, but those objects were also desired for their own sake — for the prestige and, one can say, the "magic" force that emanated from them.

Guilds united professions and trades

with the same intent, the Humiliati did not overstep the limits of heresy. In the beginning, most of the Humiliati came from the working classes, in particular weavers and woolworkers, and they played an important role in the spread of textile manufacture in northern Italy. In the 15th century the order attracted not only pious souls but also those in search of comfort. The movement was suppressed in 1571.

that to us seem heterogeneous. There were products that, to be perfected in every detail, had to pass through the hands of shops belonging to two or three different guilds. In Florence, meanwhile, painters were usually enrolled in a school of medical and chemical arts (the same substances were used to make medicines and pigments).

The 15th century, heir to the Middle Ages, was neither irrational nor prelogical; it simply reasoned in a different way. And, most of all, it recognized neither the supre-

macy of the economy nor that of production. Similarly, it did not know political consistency. The king of France or England may have been a broadminded politician, but this did not keep him from being anointed with blessed waters on the day of his coronation or from attempting to heal scrofula with a touch of his hands. A king's hands were sanctified, by both definition and consecration, even when — as often happened — they were the hands of an assassin.

97

The cardinal's nine courses, the peasant's turnip

English sumptuary laws of the 15th century specified precisely the number of courses required during official banquets for the various dignitaries of the Church and the realm. If a cardinal were present, nine courses were served; bishops, archbishops, counts, and dukes had a right to seven; peers of the realm and knights of the Order of the Garter had to content themselves with six. In 1460, the Venetian senate banned banquets, which had come to cost more than a half ducat a head, and, except for carnivals and other festivals, prohibited certain luxury foods, such as partridge, pheasant, and peacock. Other sumptuary laws, which were found just about everywhere in Europe, included rules against costly habits and overly luxurious clothing, conceding with extreme parsimony the right to certain kinds of necklines, trains, ornaments, belts, and jewels. Domestic inventories and paintings of the time fairly accurately inform us how well and to what extent these prohibitions were respected. What's more, they were fundamentally ethical, symbolic, and social, rather than economic.

Sumptuary legislation, together with the sermons of the Franciscan and Dominican friars who dominated the city squares of the time, reveal a great deal about the unequal struggle waged by 15th-century Europeans against their taste for pomp, luxury, color, splendor, and feasting. We are given the impression of a society decked out in finery — at least that is the way they saw themselves. And the "popular" classes figure in that image no less than the aristocracy. The exception might be made for what we might call the "middle class," the austerity of which both aristocrats and the downtrodden saw as the stinginess and avarice to be expected from a class of usurers.

Much of 15th-century life took place in city squares, in the streets, or — in the north, where the climate did not permit

This was a society that loved ostentation and had a bent for consuming in excess, perhaps because of the background of general scarcity. Above: Gold plate is used at a country feast. This detail is from a painting illustrating the celebrations of the third marriage (to Isabella of Portugal, in 1430) of the duke of Burgundy, Philip the Good. In 1484, writing to his brother Lodovico il Moro, Cardinal Ascanio Sforza described the apartments of Cardinal Rodrigo Borgia (later Pope Alexander VI): "He had a chest full of finely worked silver and gold plate along with numerous other plates, bowls, and chinaware that were indeed a beauty to behold." Opposite: Sumptuousness, merrymaking, and other pleasures at a different social level—archers feasting in a garden, by a master of Malines or Antwerp (1493).

The delight taken in dressing sumptuously is revealed in an infinite number of details. Below: Dark-skinned figures with Oriental features mingle with various characters decked out in plumes and feathers mounted on caparisoned horses; these are members of the train of the Three Kings, from Dürer's Adoration of the Magi. The Turkish borrowings are a reminder that a similar atmosphere pervaded in the feared Eastern, Muslim empire. Sebastian Brant, in the Ship of Fools, reflects a more moralistic, traditional approach. The comments on the prints relate certain themes: Countryfolk exceed townspeople in vice, vanity, outlandish dress, and fancy appearance; the example of foolhardiness given here (below right) is the "countrywoman remade."

Above: Another example taken from the Ship of Fools disapproves of the lack of austerity. Shaven faces, depilated bodies, elaborate hairstyles, gems, jewels, and gaily colored clothes all exude corruption. Others made more specific recriminations, including the complaint that "extravagant modes of dress have ruined the German nobility in their attempts to keep abreast of the rich city merchants."

Finery of a rather fantastic nature. A hunting scene from a miniature for the month of August from the "calendar" of 24 pictures illustrating country activities of the nobility in the various periods of the year, from the Grimani Breviary, *illustrated by the masters of the school of Bruges and Ghent at the end of the 15th or the beginning of the 16th century. Although clothes were costly, one did not consume many in a lifetime.*

Minstrels and troubadours

Professional performers usually traveled either alone or in small troupes, visiting castles and inns, the banquets of the middle class, and peasant celebrations of weddings or baptisms. For many centuries, the Church had declared them *infames, instrumenti damnationis*; they were vagabonds, not so much on the margins of society as completely outside society's framework (even so, Ugo di San Vittore, in the 12th century, included the theater among the "mechanical arts," considering it useful for regaining the *laetitia*, or "happiness," lost with original sin). They delighted their public with broad gesticulations and streams of nonsense rhymes. During the 14th century, a bishop of Salisbury claimed there were three types of performer: those who contorted their bodies with base gestures and horrendous masks; those who gained favor at courts by slandering those who were absent; and those who sang stories of princes and saints. By the end of the 15th century, the "mystery," or "sacred play," had reached the height of its popularity. In court, and with inspiration from humanism, the revival of classical theater began, but the minstrels and troubadours long remained a vibrant form of theater and "popular theatricality."

outdoor activity — in the great churches and guild halls. It can be said that 15th-century aristocrats and plebeians lived with a kind of "elbow contact" that led to — rather than hostility or cooperation — a sort of parallel life. The privileged classes sought their illuminated manuscripts and later printed books; the downtrodden relied on the paintings and sculptures in churches as well as ballad singers in the squares. When they fell ill, the privileged followed costly regimens that included medications made of rare spices or even pearls and gems

dissolved in astonishing — even if disquieting — mixtures to form pasty electuaries; the lower classes depended on their trusty poor-man's remedies made of herbs and roots, which were more effective notwithstanding their much lower cost. The privileged enjoyed their feasts at court; the poor held theirs in the squares, although religious feasts were a time of confusion in which the strict social orders broke down and everyone took part.

In preindustrial European cities, most feasts were celebrated on Sunday, contrary

Tournaments initially arose from the need to train combatants in the use of arms and to foster individual ability and valor in a period when the outcome of battles was determined by a succession of individual duels. Later on, aristocratic pride took over, combined with a sense of dashing honor, further embellished by the fantastic transfiguration of erotic symbols. Thus a tournament was both sport and entertainment; for those not in the noble class, its delirious aspects were clearer. Perhaps better than the unheeded strictures of the church, the critical comment of a Paris burgher captures the wild spirit of the event: "I do not know for what insane reason they took to the field of battle." Here, in an English miniature from about 1485, knights are engaged in combat.

The knight, the lady, and death

This unusual, extremely elegant tournament shield, made of gilded wood, painted with tempera, is a work of 15th-century Flemish art. The notch on the top edge is a lance rest. Since the faces of the people seem to be portraits, this shield is believed to have been made for some special occasion, one of those elaborate *pas d'armes*, full of erotic, heroic, or chivalric symbolism, with which the nobility of the age expressed its favorite views of itself. The knight has laid his helmet and lance at the feet of the lady. Death is lurking behind him. Written in the scroll is "*Vous ou la mort*"—a weighty choice. The age, however, found room even for irony concerning its languorous, emotional literature. In one poem, a knight leaving for war makes this resolution: He will either win the promise of love from his lady before leaving, or he will take, on his return, the first woman who accepts him—on condition she has twenty thousand scudos.

to Church regulations, and the day of rest was frequently broken, most often by artisans. In response, the Church inaugurated a new cult of the "Sunday Christ." The vivid iconography centered on a bleeding and wounded Christ, reminiscent of the Passion, whose wounds were inflicted by work tools — hammers, tongs, shears, gouges, chisels, burins — painted all around His image. Whoever broke the sabbath tortured Christ anew — motivated by a thirst for money, the sole excuse for an artisan's working on Sunday. (Agricultural work, which demanded during certain periods indispens-able daily chores, was permitted.) However, the portrait of the population suggested by

102

Exhibiting the contestants' colors at a tournament; a miniature from the Traité de la forme et devis d'un tournois, *by René d'Anjou (according to tradition, the prince himself was the miniaturist). Duke of Anjou and count of Provence, "good king René," as he was remembered by the people of Provence, vainly contested the Aragons in their claim to the kingdom of southern Italy.*

the inauguration of these Church prohibitions is refined by looking more closely at the occasions of feasts in any city of the time.

There were, first of all, the great Christian feasts, to which were added various local celebrations — carnival, Mid-Lent, or May Calends, to name a few, as well as the feasts of the patron saints of cities and professional guilds. Festive occasions were also prompted in the city by the arrival of an illustrious person or by any great news

(the election of a pope or the crowning of a sovereign, the arrival of firstborn children, or victory over an enemy, primarily the Turks). It has been estimated that the total number of workdays for the city dweller — that is, for artisans, manufacturers, and laborers — was not more than about two hundred annually.

At the heart of the feast was the spectacle. The solemn Church liturgies for feasts and processions were certainly impressive. Jousts and tournaments, in which the local

aristocracy offered itself to the admiration of the populace, were staged. These confrontations were taken so seriously that — as happened in Germany, where they were regulated and registered in special *Turnierbücher* ("tournament books") — they sometimes became the means by which knights maintained and extended their authority. Commoners pursued their own pseudomilitary activity: They participated in farcical tournaments with "ignoble" weapons (mostly clubs), or they took part in

103

The dance

1

2

3

Two women and a gentleman dance contritely to the strains of a harp (3) in an illumination from *De arte tripudii*, by Guglielmo Ebreo, depicting a scene from court. At the courts of the 15th century, the prince was surrounded by spectacle, and during celebrations, his followers made a spectacle of themselves (and had a good time doing so). From what we know of these celebrations, they were mixtures of various entertainments (banquets, dances, interludes of dances following a narrative line, even theater with classical texts or texts for the occasion). They took place following solemn occasions—marriages, births, important visits, or "entries"—and often lasted several days. Sometimes everyone danced, each doing his or her best; while at other times only a few experts performed during the interludes. It was from these celebrations that the "dance master" appeared. The first such master known in Italy was a certain Domenico da Piacenza, a "worthy and noble knight," as is written in a work bearing his name that is either a collection of notes used in teaching or the rough outline of a work never fully polished. Domenico gave the first classification to dance steps, dividing them into the "natural" (simple, double, restrained, reverent, half turn, movement, and jump are the steps derived from spontaneous movements) and the "accidental," which is to say artificial (interpositions, quick movements, changes). This technical language of dance was later expressed in French: *pas simple, demitour, pile* (the restrained step), *pas couru* (the quick step). Also important is Domenico's catalog of the dances of his age: There are four, "according to

104

("quaternary"), is a bit faster, and even quicker is the festive *saltarello*, a style involving leaps; fastest of all was the *piva* ("hornpipe"). Both the *piva* and the *saltarello* were later replaced by the *gagliarda* ("galliard").

A worldly entertainment, courtly dances often became costume balls, for which the participants had to dress accordingly. During the 15th century, "theme" dances took their inspiration, instead, from the ways of love. The engraving, the *Dance of the Golden Ring* (2), by Israel van Meckenem, is an example of this. To the rhythm of a single instrument, four dancers compete for possession of the ring shyly offered by a young girl. The dance has a story to tell and is witnessed through the window by the passing public. Thus, in the world of the courts, dance was moving towards ballet.

Some of the dances that Domenico choreographed already displayed narrative aspects—situations interpreted through various steps and specific dances, performed by an established number of dancers. Indeed, it was one of the students of Domenico, Antonio Cornazano (born at Piacenza, he died at Ferrara in 1484), who coined the word *balletto* ("ballet").

Outside the world of the courts, the customs of which also included those of the mercantile oligarchies, popular dance existed. Lively and impetuous, it is well recorded in the engraving by Albrecht Dürer, *The Peasants' Dance* (5). Between courtly dance and popular dance there was an ongoing exchange; the latter was a source of inspiration for the former, and courtly dance, for its part, influenced the styles of popular dance.

the tempo," each a sixth more lively or faster than the last. The slowest is the *bassadanza*, performed "in as many lines as desired"; this is a dance in which everyone could participate. It is probably a *bassadanza* being performed in the engraving *Herod's Banquet*, by Israel van Meckenem (1). The rather haughty marriage dance in the xylograph (4) by Hans Leonard Schafelein (1490) is certainly a *bassadanza*. In effect, the *bassadanza* was a style that allowed for the encumbering clothing of the period. It lasted until the beginning of the 17th century, when the even more severe and majestic pavan came into style.

The second dance listed by Domenico, the *quaternaria*

4

5

subsistence, might seem wasteful in these extravagant displays. However, these excesses fueled much economic activity: Festivals were the occasion for a large consumption of food or the sale of artisans' crafts. While festivals and holidays were periods of dangerous instability during which fights and riots might occur (and in fact frequently did), they played an important role in pacifying the populace and providing cultural integration.

Leaving the courts, the squares, and the streets of the cities behind, is it possible to recreate the private life of the 15th-century family? It is difficult to gather information or make generalizations about an existence that differed markedly — from Stockholm to Palermo, from Lisbon to Prague — and for social conditions that varied so much from place to place. Even so, similarities to modern family life can be found in the 15th century, along with behaviors and attitudes that, to a certain extent, we recognize our-

bloody confrontations with fists and stones during which various districts of a city might challenge one another.

City squares could also be used for visual spectacles, often depicting religious subjects. The miracle or mystery play or the *sacre rappresentazioni* narrated the story of a martyr, or "theme tournaments" might include a military display, with scenery and costumes, related to a biblical story. The plots often followed those of chivalric tales: a castle must be defended or conquered, a bridge could be crossed only after meeting a challenge, or a damsel held prisoner must be rescued from her abductors.

The solemn entries were, in this sense, the most refined and complete festive occasions because such opportunities made possible the wedding of various forms of spectacle: from the religious procession with its "tableau vivant" (the "mystery"); to the

"triumph," with its cart in the antique style (in a celebrated poetic work, Petrarch had provided the first model); to the historical-allegorical reevocation of biblical and mythological events; to the chivalric tournament and the clash of popular factions; to the race for prizes (the "palio"); to battles between ferocious animals of the same or varying species.

Special companies (the Venetian della Calza troupe was particularly famous) modeled on the devotional fraternities or knightly "court" orders (the latter a 15th-century passion, exemplified by Burgundy's Order of the Golden Fleece or the Angevin Crescent) took it upon themselves to organize special festivals and to finance them in whole or in part. If modern European society can be defined as a "consumer" society, that of the 15th century, which was supported by an economy that was just above

Street games. In this tondo by an unknown 14th-century Florentine artist, three youths are playing at civettino *amid the distracted curiosity of passersby and the indifference of a group of children playing with a dog.* Civettino *was a time-honored, rowdy game in which each player in turn was hit, punched, or slapped from behind and had to guess who had administered the blow.*

Street theater. The most popular form of entertainment (also meant to edify) was the "mystery," or "miracle" play. In this French miniature in two parts (below left), one can see an actor who, assisted by a prelate, is dressing up as a devil—the role he will perform on the other side of the picture. In the miniature below right (from a book of hours of Etienne Chevalier, by Jean Fouquet), the martyrdom of Saint

Apollonia is recreated with brutal realism. The stands at the edges are seating for the guests of honor. The general public is packed in below. Holding book and baton (center right) is the theater director. These spectacles often lasted many days (in one case, 25).

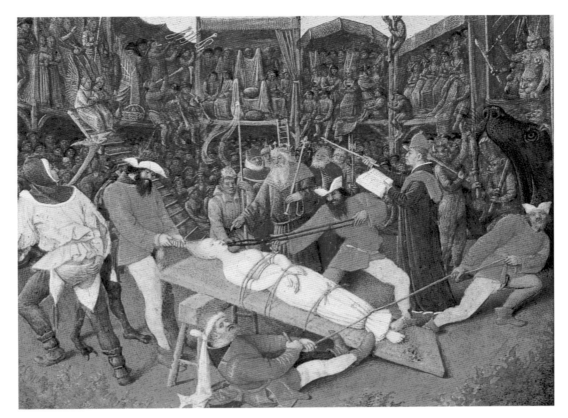

selves. We may react very differently to the problems of relationships between the sexes and age groups today than did our ancestors of five hundred years ago, but we can still recognize the important role they play in our lives.

In a 15th-century home — modest but not too humble, perhaps a well-to-do household in the city — we might, in a general way, feel ourselves at home, but we would find privacy and comfort strikingly absent — concepts that are, of course, modern. There would be no glass in the windows ("white" glass became widespread only at the end of the 15th-century; while leaded glass was used mostly in churches), which would be closed with wooden shutters or covered by frames of mounted cloth treated with turpentine, grease-proof paper, or some other waterproof material (oil in the south and wax in the north were the common and

least costly materials for waterproofing). The few pieces of furniture might include folding chairs, tables made of wooden boards set on sawhorses, and perhaps a few chests that served at the same time as cupboards, closets, and seats. In the most well-to-do homes one might find additional pieces of furniture that were more refined and costly, ceramic or even glass crockery, and brass or pewter containers. Shiny copper and smooth brass were found most often in the Mediterranean area, near the fine copper mines of Cyprus, while tin-, lead-, and silver-cast materials were more widespread and less expensive in the north. In the Mediterranean, glazed majolica was becoming popular, with its brilliant colors and iridescent reflection. Mirrors were rare and highly valued, the objects of fascination and superstition (they were used in certain magical rituals). (In Jan van Eyck's portrait

of the wealthy Arnolifini couple [1434], now in London's National Gallery, a splendid mirror hangs from the wall and a magnificently ornate chandelier is suspended from the ceiling. The artist's own reflection appears in the mirror.)

The beauty of the homes of the well to do owed more to decorative fixtures than furniture: colored ceilings and walls, tiled floors, fireplaces, washstands, and — in the north — stoves of carved stone. The Spanish easily grew accustomed to the luxury and cleanliness of the Arab homes that they occupied, and they learned to imitate them.

After the great dynasties, the type of 15th-century family about which we know most is that of the well-off city dwellers, based on information found in registry books, wills, and memoirs. Little record remains of the poor; they had nothing to register, had no reason to make out wills, 107

Flemish interior from the second half of the 15th century (detail from a Madonna and Child *attributed to Petrus Christus). Only the upper portion of the window is glassed (with lozenge- and diamond-shaped pieces joined by lead). The vertical bar of the frame below serves as a stop for the wooden shutters, which are folded into the jamb and divided horizontally into three parts.*

The candle and the chandelier

The darkness of night was not truly driven from homes until the use of gaslight in the 19th century. Until then, candles and oil lamps were used. The object shown above, in a detail from a 15th-century painting, is still familiar—as is the painfully small circle of light it creates. The candle—a wick surrounded by a combustible substance that feeds the flame by melting—seems to have appeared at the beginning of the modern era. Apuleius (ca. A.D. 150) speaks of wax candles (beeswax) and tallow candles. The latter seem to have come into common use during the 15th century and were prepared by dipping rows of wicks hung along rods into containers of liquid tallow (the fat of ox or sheep). They gave off both a bad odor and a sooty flame and burned more quickly than beeswax candles, but they were less expensive. The chandelier was born of the need to multiply light sources. German versions made of deer antlers appeared during the 16th century, followed by those of Bohemian crystal and Murano glass. The branched chandelier with candles (below) is from *Madonna and Child*, by Petrus Christus (who died around 1472). On the wall is another common lighting apparatus: a candlestick mounted in front of a reflecting plate.

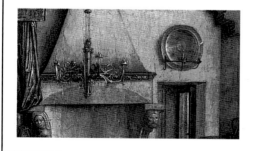

and only rarely wrote memoirs (usually because they did not know how to write). Moralists and sermonizers also had a great deal to say about the family. Although the ties between spouses and among relatives were strong, our concept of the "patriarchial" family does not apply to the 15th century, where we find broad families in which inlaws were welcome. Leon Battista Alberti, who left detailed information about the Florentine family, describes the custom, slightly out of fashion, of brothers, their wives, and children, all living together under the same roof. The "average" 15th-century family was not much different from our own. Sources for Tuscany, Lombardy, the Veneto, and France record families of four or five members. However, the custom of related families living near one another led to a larger cooperative social group with a spirit of community and interdependence.

The woman who married into a home of this kind was usually subject to the vexations of her husband's relatives, unless

In the kitchen. This 16th-century German print presents a very busy cook: While stirring one pot she is adding ingredients to another. The cooking pots used on this wood-burning stove are made of earthenware (probably German grès*). Those hanging above are of metal. The dishwasher labors over a tub, while a spitted bird roasts over a fire.*

she belonged to a higher social rank. In addition, according to the habits and needs of the time, men were often forced to spend long periods away from home, often for business. They considered it desirable that their wives be pregnant every year — to ensure marital fidelity and, considering the high infant mortality rate, heirs. Wives were usually ten, fifteen, and even twenty years younger than their husbands. Jealousy, which did not exist in polite society and was considered a grave and ridiculous fault, was a middle-class sentiment.

The wife who was widowed faced a sad future since remarriage was more or less frowned upon. She could either accept the hospitality of her husband's family, where she would be treated as something of an intruder, or return to her family's home, where she might be unwelcome and considered useless. Many widows decided to avoid dependence and gossip by living in communal homes under the protection of the Church, thus achieving a kind of liberty otherwise denied them.

Eating meat. There are knives and glasses, but no forks in this detail from the Triptych of Lazarus *(1461), by Nicolas Froment. Above right: Setting the table, from a manuscript of* Bella Melusina *(1468), by Thuring von Ringoltingen. The rich and the poor did not eat alike, of course. Although polemical and openly sarcastic, the humanist Bartolomeo Sacchi, known as Platina, may not have been far wrong in his* De honesta

Reconstructing the institutions and forms of family life of the 15th century is one thing; investigating the sentiments of groups or individuals is another. It has been proposed, for example, that affection for children is a modern development and that in medieval society they were treated like small adults, with their specific needs gener-

voluptate et valetudine *("Of true pleasures and health"), the first classic of gastronomic literature, in which he compared* cepam et allium *("garlic and onions," the food of the poor) to the* pavones et aves esculentas *("peacocks and succulent birds"), with which all the best dishes were prepared, suited for royal and princely tables (and that the plebeians and common people should not dare to even taste).*

ally ignored. It has also been argued that the elderly were granted authority and prestige. Both ideas are generalizations. The many paintings of the Virgin and Child, the charitable institutions for abandoned children, the memoirs that speak with tender affection or that recall with agonizing sorrow the premature deaths of babies or children, and

109

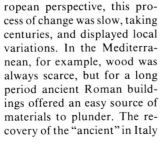

In a well-known phrase, Leon Battista Alberti contrasts the cities "made all of boards" of his youth with the marble cities of his later life. Thus is expressed the change, over a long period of time, from the use of mere wood to that of the richer materials of stone and brick. From the European perspective, this process of change was slow, taking centuries, and displayed local variations. In the Mediterranean, for example, wood was always scarce, but for a long period ancient Roman buildings offered an easy source of materials to plunder. The recovery of the "ancient" in Italy was preceded and accompanied by this plundering, which could be considered a means of becoming familiar with the past. London's Great Fire of 1666, which destroyed more than 12,000 houses—three-quarters of the city—provides a good measure of the widespread use of wood.

7

8

9

10

11

12

13

The illustrations on these pages compare a 15th-century Italian villa built in stone (1) with a transalpine building with wooden framework (7). These two homes display typical forms in widespread use in the areas south and north of the Alps.

The principal characteristics of the Italian villa—the courtyard encircled by open galleries, the flat ceilings, the symmetrical tendencies of the facades, with framed windows and cornices, the square shape made to occupy a city block—are as distinguishing as are those found in the example inspired by a German farm, with a stone basement and ground floor, wooden reinforcements with uprights, cross beams, tie beams, and diagonal struts, into which are built the windows, other areas filled in with light masonry. The two different structures give way to different interiors: even today—although there are many exceptions—a traveler from the south of Europe notes the

smaller living spaces in homes in the north, while the traveler from the north is struck by the sense of grandiosity in homes in the south

Less furniture was used inside homes during the 15th century than is common today, and there were fewer kinds of pieces (many new forms coming into use during the three centuries following the 15th). The two interiors (2,3) from xylographs from the *Hypnerotomachia Poliphili* (Venice, 1499) are examples of tidy elegance. Along the wall in the bedroom are chests (this period's universal storage unit), the bed is placed between two arched windows, the columns and head of the bed are carved (the carved lion's-paw feet have a long history), there is a canopy, and other chests are placed along the sides of the bed; chests are visible along the walls in the other room, the desk is topped by an inclined writing surface (both writing and reading were performed on inclined surfaces, a

form sometimes still encountered in schoolrooms), the box with its ornamental cover serves as a chair, and a religious subject hangs on the wall (the painting of sacred works for private use had just begun).

The examples of furniture shown on these pages include just about all the types then in use: the bed with hangings made to be placed in a corner is English (4); the bed surrounded by chests is from Tuscany (6); the gothic-style standing closet (an article of furniture still rare at the time) is German (5); the table (13) is based on one in a Dürer painting; among the chairs is an unusual medieval example with a metal framework and seat of strips of cloth and leather (8), one from northern Italy (9), a small armchair with semicircular seat and arms from the Rhine area (10), a three-legged Tuscan chair (11), and an Italian "pincer" chair (12), a piece of furniture in which elegance competes with ingenuity.

111

the frequent and widespread appearance of toys all tell a different story. As for the elderly, there are many accounts of estrangement or abandonment, of ingratitude of children towards their parents, and acts of fraud and violence committed against the aged. Historians have only recently begun to explore the complex web of those relationships.

Abortion, the use of contraception, even instances of infanticide masked as accidents and the deaths of abandoned babies not promptly found by charitable persons or institutions were not unusual,

This painting (above left), with its own mysterious fascination, is found on the back of a portrait of a German nobleman and is attributed, with some doubt, to Jacopo de Barbari, born around the middle of the century, probably at Venice, and active in Germany. The object the woman is looking at may be a crystal or a mirror and has been interpreted as a love spell. Above right: Young maids hard at work from an

allegory of the month of March from the frescoes in the Schifanoia palace, Ferrara. The period required brides-to-be to be hardworking, honest, and furnished with an ample dowry. It seems that at the time the size of dowries increased, since limits were set by laws in various places, only to be subsequently increased. In 1469 in Rome, dowries were set at 800 florins, but this sum had doubled by the end of the century.

and violence against children was not un-heard of. (Though some abandoned babies were furnished with "signs" — pieces of coral, small necklaces, or coins — to aid their eventual identification.) Illegitimate births were common. Fortunately, theology came to the aid of the mother who would not or could not name her child's father: Saint Thomas maintained that demons in the form of succubi could take sperm from a man and then inject it into the "natural vessel" of a woman. It was impossible to identify a father, and all that remained of this encounter was a troubled dream. Happily, children conceived in this manner would be normal, not diabolic.

But the promiscuity of the times and — for men — the frequent opportunity for sexual encounters produced many more illegitimate children than the reproductive acrobatics of demons could account for. Domestic servants and slaves — usually from the Balkans or the Caucasus, including

113

A Venetian woman and a woman from Nuremberg in a drawing by Dürer (ca. 1495). In the first part of the 15th century, Alberti said, "Defend your woman, lock her up at home with your belongings." Ninety years later, Castiglione held that women should "know some literature, music, and painting, and know how to dance and make merry." One is speaking of a middle-class wife, the other of a woman of court.

Lovers in a country scene, part of an Allegory of Life and Death, from an engraved relief by a master of the upper Rhineland, ca. 1480. Astrological calendars often showed scenes of lovers in natural settings. François Villon: "S'ils se vantent coucher sous le rosier. / Lequel vaut mieu? Lit côtoyé de chaise? / Ou'en dites vous? Faut il a ce muser? / Il n'est tresor que de vivre a son aise" ("They boast of lying beneath a rosebush, what could be better? A bed with a chair beside it? What do you say? But need one say more? There is no treasure like living at one's ease").

A married couple: Iñigo Lopes de Mendoza, marquis of Santillana, and his wife, painted by Jorge Inglés. In this case the donators of the work, commissioned in 1455 for a hospital chapel, occupy the two main panels. The marquis of Santillana was a person of some standing, a man of war and letters and author of a collection of proverbs meant to instruct the heir to the throne.

Sveva and Giannantonio: marriage and death

Giannantonio was the son of Antonello Petrucci, secretary of state to Ferdinand I of Aragon, king of Naples. He married Sveva Sanverino, member of a great baronial family that had been in frequent rebellion against the monarchy for five centuries. The two families became involved in the baronial conspiracy (1485) undertaken during a war against Pope Innocent VIII. The conspiracy failed; the pope himself negotiated with the king of Naples for the pardon of the rebels, but using a deception Ferdinand succeeded in capturing the most important of the conspirators and bringing them to justice. Giannantonio had had only a marginal role in the plot, but in August 1486 he was arrested, and on December 11 he was beheaded. During his months of imprisonment he revealed himself a poet: "Although fortune has left me in an arid region, shattered by the storm." While in prison he wrote eighty-odd bitter sonnets, rediscovered and published only at the end of the last century: "Dear wife whom I love so tenderly/the twenty-two days that we passed together/I don't know if my heart moves you/only that fortune has turned against me./I don't believe you have changed at all/and I think you curse this cruel fate/I think that day and night you moan for me/and in your face you have been transformed."

The loving worries of a mother

Alessandra Macinghi, widow of Matteo Strozzi, wrote from Florence to her son Lorenzo at Bruges. Strozzi had belonged to the party that had exiled Cosimo de' Medici. With the return of the Medici, he was banished from the city. Alessandra's three sons were still in exile; 20-year-old Lorenzo worried her because of his passion for gambling. The year was 1452:

" . . . you have reached the age to behave differently than you do, and more than ever you must correct yourself and direct yourself towards living better; up to now you were considered a child, but such is no longer the case, and you should change, for your errors can no longer be attributed to ignorance or because you don't understand what you're doing or because you don't know right from wrong—particularly since you have your elders to show you the way. I'm afraid that one day or another you're going to come to ruin, for he who does not do as he should in the end receives what he is due. Along with the other worries I have, you are the greatest. I thought that to end all these worries and to help you right yourself, I would sell the land at Antella and, having paid my debts, I would have left eight hundred florins, and Filippo has three hundred: and I figured that you and Filippo could then go into business and begin to put aside something every year. But from what I hear, you're better at throwing money away than at saving even one coin, and that is precisely the opposite of how you should be. In my eyes, you bring harm and shame on yourself and on us. Admonishing you serves no purpose, for you respond poorly and make me take back every good thought I have of you. I can't understand why you do as you do since you know, first of all, that you displease our Lord, who watches over all of us, and then you displease me, because I am greatly pained when I hear of your failures, and I'll leave it to you to ponder the harm and the shame that follow on your acts. If you began to correct yourself now, there might be hope for you, but by now years and years have gone by during which you have done no good, and I have put up with you only because of my love for you."

Slavs, Tartars, and Circassians, but also dark-skinned women, the fruit of Portuguese exploration of the African coast — commonly served as sexual vassals for the young of men of their master's family or as the concubines of the familial head.

For young men who lived in an environment where women and girls were carefully watched and in which an act of seduction could led to a dramatic series of family vendettas — and for men whose perpetually pregnant wives became prematurely disfig-

In the Très Riches Heures *of Turin, John the Baptist is born into an exemplary 14th-century Flemish interior. The bed with hangings, the pitchers and other objects on the shelf above the door, the chest, spinning tools, triangular chair, and wooden tiles are only some of the significant details of this delicate, well presented scene of private life. Concerning the relationship between fathers and sons, a chronicle from Modena includes the following: "If between seven and fifteen years he frolics, use the stick. . . . If he should slacken between the age of fifteen and twenty," the only solution is prison; at thirty punishments are no longer effective, and the son should be sent on his way. The text adds, however, "do the best you can." Girls passed from the authority of their fathers to that of their husbands.*

115

As the great papal librarian and historian Platina maintained in his treatise *De honesta voluptate et valetudine* ("Of true pleasures and health"), a milestone in humanistic gastronomy, culinary arts were closely allied with medicine: The same spices were used by the apothecary and the cook. But while gastronomy triumphed at the courts, it had

ured — casual opportunities for sexual encounters were less certain. For them there were the public baths, which were frequented by prostitutes, and taverns, where, in addition, one could gamble at dice and cards. Tarot cards began to come into use around the first half of the 15th century, and by the end of the 1400s their production had become common, while beautiful illuminated decks were used in the games at court. There were laws prohibiting gambling as the cause of arguments and source of corruption, as well as association with the devil — it was not by accident that dice and cards were used as instruments of divination — but such prohibitions were often ignored.

A well-dressed child shows his face at the door in the Annunciation with Saint Emidio *(1486), by Carlo Crivelli. Opposite top: Infants in swaddling clothes, a detail from* The Madonna Protecting the Innocents, *attributed to a follower of Francesco Granacci. The use of swaddling clothes for newborns continued up until fairly recently; the expression "in swaddling clothes" is still common.*

little effect in daily life. Throughout Europe, the 15th-century table was simple. The mainstay was pork, both fresh and preserved, and the meat of sheep and goats; fish, both from fresh water and the sea, was also important, especially during the frequent periods of abstinence enforced by the Church. Customs and tastes, of course, changed with climate and latitude. Heavy, resinated wines were common in the south, giving way to the clear, light wines of central Europe — which were, however, strengthened by cooking or by the addition of spices, honey, and even, among the most well to do, sugar, which was a rarity that saw more use as a medicine than as a food. Popular also were beer, cider, and mead.

In the Mediterranean area, the preservation of foods depended on the use of salt,

117

Saint Zanobi Revives a Dead Child *(ca. 1461), by Benozzo Gozzoli. How many children? Research on the nobility (the class most likely to have conserved records of family members) gives us partial information: It seems, for example, that at the end of the Middle Ages the Polish nobility had an average of eight births per family. The number of children in French noble families, which had been between four and seven from the* 10th to the middle of the 12th centuries, decreased to fewer than four in the first half of the 15th century. Alberti, in asserting that the state should honor "those who have the greatest number of children," seems to voice fears of demographic regression. There is no doubt about the high rate of infant mortality; "miracles" like the one depicted here reveal a consciousness of this dramatic phenomenon.

Below left: Imaginary eroticism from a miniature in a 14th-century codex of De Sphaera *from the Este library. An astronomical treatise,* De Sphaera *enjoyed great popularity throughout Europe for over four centuries. A collection of elementary notions derived from Ptolemy and the Arabs Alfragano and Albategnio, it was the work of a 13th-century English astronomer known as John of Holywood.*

while smoking was used in the north, where salt was less common and wood more abundant. Various methods were employed to preserve milk products, eggs, and vegetables (ash, vinegar, animal or vegetable fats, and lime were all used). The fat of pigs and in certain areas that of mutton was used instead of butter. Olive oil, although abundantly produced, was put to innumerable medicinal and manufacturing purposes but was used relatively little in cooking. In part, this was due to the fact that the practice of cooking with oil was typical of the Jews, who were looked upon with suspicion. In turn, the Jews were horrified by the consumption of pork fat, and, even worse, pig's blood, which was used in blood sausages (seasoned with pine nuts, raisins, and sugar) or blood pudding (cakes of millet flour and pig's blood; in certain areas pig's blood was later replaced by chestnut flour in making chestnut cake). Thus, while their choices were limited, they were laden with the same symbolism and prejudice found throughout 15th-century society.

Above right: The Men's Baths, *an engraving by Dürer (probably from 1496). Opposite: Miniature from the codex* Facta et dicta memorabilia, *by Valerio Massimo, from Breslau, around the middle of the 15th century. Public baths were a common institution in northern European cities. At the end of the Middle Ages there were, for example, 11 at Ulm, 12 in Nuremberg, 15 at Frankfurt am Main, 17 at*

Augsburg, and 19 at Vienna. The sexes were not always separated; in 1438 a Spanish nobleman was scandalized by the promiscuity of the public baths at Bruges, which the inhabitants considered "as honest as our going to church." Even so, men often visited public baths to meet prostitutes.

God, the Book, and the Machine

*Opposite: A procession over Venice's Rialto
Bridge, then capable of being drawn open; a
detail of the* Miracle of the Relic of the True
Cross *(1494), by Vittore Carpaccio. Above: A
14th-century print shows man about to explore
beyond the sphere of the fixed stars. Nicolas of
Cusa,* De docta ignorantia: *"It is impossible that
the machine of the world has a fixed, immobile
center, or our earth, or the air, or fire."*

A Christian century

From the point of view of religion and the Church, the 15th century is judged poorly. Two themes are usually emphasized: on one hand, immorality, nepotism, and corruption of the Roman Curia and other prelates, whose abuses would become one of the major causes of the Reformation; and, on the other hand, the growth and spread of interest in magic, astrology, and witchcraft, symptoms of a spiritual world in which certainties were being secularized and ways of understanding reality, nature, and science separated from theology. These tendencies are seen as symptomatic of a world plunging back into ancient pagan prejudices and suffering a disorientation leading to folkloric superstitions.

The reality is actually very different. If it is true that the roots of the Reformation are to be found in the 15th century, it is no less true that the Reformation cannot be reduced to simply a rebellion against the contemporary practices of the Church. It represented, in a certain sense, the continuation of movements begun within the Church itself that were neither disputed not heretical. Humanistic culture — which both speeded the process of secularization in the European intellectual climate and revived ancient superstitions tied to paganism and magic — was born first of all with strong ties to Christianity, in particular the Christianity of the early Church fathers. Humanism was also at first confined mainly to Italy

— particularly Florence, Rome, the Po Valley, the Veneto, and Naples — in a world where the dominant cultural language was still "gothic." Only during the 16th century would Italian humanism — and with it painting, sculpture, architecture, music, and poetry — conquer Europe.

It must be remembered that the 15th century was, throughout most of Europe, a century of relative tranquillity and adjustment: The great conflicts were spent or nearly spent, the areas of friction were localized if not isolated, and political and intellectual tensions were directed more towards reconciliation than division. Without doubt, the stage for the crises of the next age — the European wars, the Reformation, witch hunts, religious strife, the renewed Ottoman offensive — was being set, and the discovery of the New World would lead to new balances of power and new political and economic disruptions. Even if the "blessed" second half of the 15th century displayed at many levels a darker mirror image, for the most part Europe was tran-

122

Above: The mantle of the Mater Dei *protects all humanity—kings and queens, the pope, archbishops, abbots, friars, merchants, and last of all, the people—in this detail of the* Madonna della Misericordia *(ca. 1450), by Enguerrand Charonton. Above right: An example of devotion to the Madonna:* The Virgin Saves a Child from the Devil, *by Niccolo Alunno, from the end of the 15th century. The popular aspect*

of the painting is accentuated by the fact that both the mother's plea and Mary's reply are in dialect (Umbrian). From a song to the Virgin by the Venetian Leonardo Giustinian: "Oh, woman, receive in your beautiful bosom | my bitter tears; | you know that I am close to you and like a brother, | you cannot deny me. | Virgin, do not delay | that charity may be done: | do not wait for the hour | when the wolf eats your sheep."

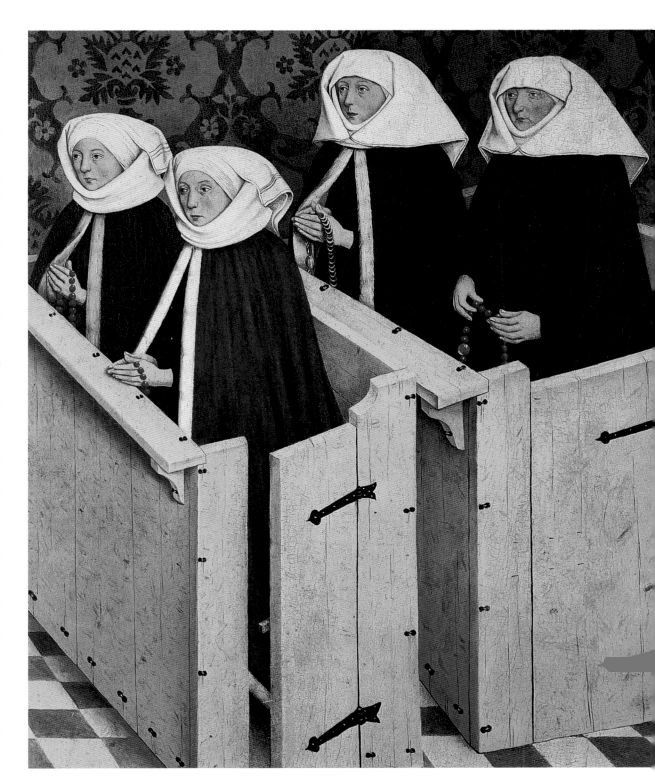

quil. With the exception of the English Wars of the Roses (1455–1485), after the death of Charles the Bold of Burgundy (1477) there were no major wars for at least twenty years; the Turkish expansion seemed to have been contained; and epidemics and famines had slackened and did not impede the ascending demographic curve.

Even the Church, after the noncomformist and heretical crises of the first decades of the 15th century — exemplified by the Lollards in England, the Fraticelli in Italy, and the Hussites in Bohemia — and notwithstanding lingering disputes, was substantially at peace. The era of the many turbulent schisms was over, the popes had been reseated on their historically mandated Roman throne, and the concordatory alliance that they had established with all of the western Christian governments had without doubt greatly contributed to the increased worldliness of the higher levels of the ecclesiastical hierarchy. The latter especially had also sheltered the Church from new disorders and "national" schisms and given the European governments an interest in maintaining the discipline of their peoples. This stability had deterred restless spirits and nonconformists. Spiritual dissatisfaction was directed towards reform, while most desires for dispute were sublimated into mystical and aesthetic aspirations. From this grew the two components that gave form to the religious and spiritual life of the late 15th century: the Observance and *devotio moderna* movements.

The storms of the Reformation were unleashed at the beginning of the 16th century, but its currents had been in the wind for centuries. "Re-formation" properly means returning to its original form something that has been distorted: *reformare deformata* ("reform the deformed"), as it was cleverly expressed. Rather than suggesting new choices, it attempted to bring up to date those whose legitimacy is based on the past.

Hans Memling, from the Triptych of the Judgment. *To the right of the Archangel Michael are the damned; to the left are the chosen. An angel and a devil dispute a soul. "Michael and his angels fought against the dragon; and the dragon fought and his angels, and prevailed not; neither was their place found any more in heaven. And the great dragon was cast out, that old serpent, called the Devil, and Satan, which deceiveth the whole world" (Rev. 12:7-9). The archangel weighs the souls. An enquiring and restless mind, Leonardo da Vinci declared that "the definition of a soul is a power joined with the body . . ." but "the rest of the definition of the soul I will leave to the minds of the priests, fathers of the people, who by inspiration know all secrets."*

The past in this case was that of the Church in its very earliest apostolic period. The Church had distanced itself from its early ideals; "modern" corruption, worldliness, excessive interest in terrestrial goods, and wealth had penetrated the Church and, most of all, the clergy. With the Great Schism (1378–1417) behind it, the time seemed ripe to redirect the Church to new ideals of austerity; and many popes — even the "corrupt" humanistic popes, such as Pius II and the nepotist Sixtus IV — were in agreement with such programs and would have been astonished had anyone accused them of obstructing them.

The conceptual foundation of this reform movement — and the basis as well of humanistic culture in general and Lutheran spirituality in particular — was the extraordinary importance of the rediscovery of Saint Augustine and his tormented soul's search for God. During the 14th century, all of the monastical orders and congregations had been restructured in the name of Augustine, the favorite philosopher and beloved guide of Petrarch. In his name, theology had been renewed, and meditation on Augustinian texts was often at the base of a movement, originally for the most part spontaneous, that took place in many monasteries throughout Europe beginning at the end of the 14th century: in France, where the Hundred Years War had produced moral and material destruction of a frightening order; in Italy, where the movement started in the Benedictine abbey of Cava dei Tirreni, near Salerno; in Bohemia, beginning at the monastery of Brevnov; in Spain at Valladolid; and then again in Italy with the new congregation of Monte Oliveto, near Siena, the reform at Monte Cassino and Subiaco, and in the Po Valley at Santa Giustina in Padua. It was as part of this powerful reform movement in the Benedictine Order that the young Venetian patrician Lodovico Barbo, founder of a canonical community in 1404 and later abbot of Santa

A pious and ancient custom: the ex-voto

This 15th-century tablet is a sign of thanks to the Madonna from a certain Giovanni, son of Francesco. It is part of a large collection of ex-votos (the oldest from the 15th century) in the church of the Madonna del Monte at Cesena.

The term *ex-voto* refers to various types of popular or artisan-made art objects dedicated to shrines and altars or sacred images in fulfillment of a vow (hence, ex-voto), including small paintings, usually to celebrate the recovery from a disease or a danger avoided, and altarpiece paintings showing episodes from the lives of saints from the 14th and 15th centuries. Objects made of silver or other materials (less noble metals, wood, and wax) representing various body parts (here again the ex-voto is tied to the restoration of health) have pagan predecessors. According to religious canons, the voto (vow) is a freely made promise (made obligatory under the penalty of sin) to God, to give or do something; the vows that led to the ex-voto were of the conditional sort in the sense that their fulfillment was on condition of the realization of a certain wish. The ex-voto was soon to become a point of dissension between Catholics and Protestants.

Giustina, introduced the novelty of individual meditation, patterned on the *devotio moderna* movement.

The Benedictine reform movement quickly swept through Germany, thanks to new congregations founded at Melk in Austria and at Bursfeld near Trier. In the convents of the mendicant orders — which originally had been forbidden to own landed property and whose members subsisted on alms — the rules of communal life and poverty were frequently no longer respected. A powerful movement began called the Observance, the aim of which was the reestablishment, in their original purity, of the 13th-century rules of Francis of Assisi and Saint Dominic.

Books are burned before Saint Dominic at the time of the Albigensian heresy (12th and 13th centuries). In 1475 the pope authorized the University of Cologne to investigate books. Sebastian Brant lamented, "With every day the number of entirely false creeds and dogmas grows. The typographers worsen matters; if certain books were committed to the flames, many an error would go with them."

"To lead men to penitence"

The Ferrarese Girolamo Savonarola, imbued with the learning of medicine and philosophy, became a Dominican at the age of 23 in 1475. In 1482 he became scriptural lector in Florence's convent of San Marco, and two years later he began his career as an itinerant preacher. In a ballad composed in 1484 on the occasion of the election of Pope Innocent VIII, he turned to Christ—"sweet comfort and supreme lord"—and pleaded, "Look with pity at the tempest in which your bride [the Church] finds itself and how much of our blood will be lost if your pious hand, which delights in pardoning, does not lead us back to the peace we knew when the church was poor. . . . If this time your hand does not take up arms, since all the perfect lights are spent, without doubt it seems to me, that all of your cults and every good habit will be lost, to our damage, and Rome will be left in great hunger." In 1490 he returned to Florence, by now famous for his preaching. After the Medici were driven from the city in 1494, he became the moral guide of the Florentines. At Pisa, speaking to Charles VIII, he said, "I have never done anything but exhort to lead men to penitence. Proof of this is all the city, all those who are noble or ignoble, men and women, the small and the great, the citizens and the peasants, among whom a few believed, others did not believe, and still others mocked." Excommunicated by Alexander VI, he was hanged and burned in the Piazza della Signoria on May 23, 1498. The xylograph shows the soul of Savonarola being led to Paradise.

126

Franciscan and Dominican Observants became popular preachers par excellence, capable of inflaming those gathered in the squares of Europe by intoning their ideals of purity, poverty, and love of God and inciting their listeners to crusade for the reformation of civil and moral customs. Famous "vanity pyres" were organized at Florence by Girolamo Savonarola in which were burned, helter-skelter, playing cards, wigs, cosmetics, books, and works of art. They also incited the crowds against witches, Jews, and sodomites.

As the fullest expression of the Observance movement, it is instructive to note that Savonarola had gotten his start in 1491 as the prior of the friary of San Marco. Fifty years earlier, Pope Eugenius IV had granted the priorate of San Marco to Antonino Pierozzi — who would later become archbishop of Florence and, in 1523 after his death, Saint Antonino — and instructed him specifically to revitalize the Dominican traditions with the spiritual practices of the *devotio moderna*. The convent of San Marco was given generous gifts and protection by Cosimo I (il Vecchio), head of the Medici family and "crypto-master" of Florence. It

Above and opposite: Probably half a century and certainly opposing views of the subject separate these two paintings, but perhaps they reflect two different ways of living and perceiving the Christian faith. Gay and serene is the tondo with the Adoration of the Magi, *by Domenico Veneziano, painted around 1440; tragic and bitter is the* Pietà, *by Bermejo, from 1490. This last work shows Saint Jerome wearing spectacles.*

Spectacles had been known for some time, and the spread of printed matter contributed to their profusion in the 15th century; the "rebirth of knowledge" is said to be connected with the development of spectacles with convex lenses, which enabled reading to be continued to an advanced age. Concave lenses were introduced at the end of the century to correct myopia.

was built by the same architect who had built the Medici palace in Via Larga, Michelozzo, and its walls were frescoed by Fra Angelico.

Girolamo Savonarola, often cited as a model of the antihumanistic spirit was, in fact, a direct descendant of humanism. It was no accident that he fascinated the philosopher Gianfrancesco Pico della Mirandola as well as the artist Sandro Botticelli.

The idea behind the *devotio moderna*, or "modern devotion," influenced not only the Benedictines, Franciscans, and Dominicans. Towards the end of the 14th century in the Rhineland and the Low Countries, a movement originally composed of spontaneous groups — called the Friends of God — sought renewed spiritual perfection, putting emphasis on the interior life rather than on liturgy or participation in the sacraments. This trend gave way to certain heretical experiences but found its best representative in Ruysbroeck and his "pedagogy" of meeting with the spirit of God. Through his followers, such as Gerhard Groote and Radewin, the practice of the *devotio moderna* developed in Holland — where the Brethren of the Common Life, both clerics and laymen, lived together, praying and meditating in their vernacular tongues — and in the Rhineland, where Thomas à Kempis (or perhaps Groote) composed the celebrated treatise *The Imitation of Christ*. This apologia, personalized and made intimate, freed of inhibiting regulations, became the fundamental tract of the *devotio moderna* and later even inspired Erasmus. In this new way of understanding the experience and expression of Christianity, individuality was given major importance. In response to the restlessness and uncertainty of the new age, the "devout" proposed the necessity of leading a life that was essentially a preparation for death, and the short treatises called *ars moriendi*, expressions of spirituality, enjoyed extraordinary success, which lasted almost until the 17th century. (These tracts

128

also benefited from the art of printing, as the small books decorated with fitting xylographs became more widely distributed.)

The *devotio moderna* movement meshed naturally with the Observance on two points: the necessity of the strict imitation of the life of Christ and the need to communicate directly with the faithful, which made famous the great preachers of the 15th century, such as Saint Bernardine of Siena, James of the March, Saint John of Capestrano, and Robert of Lecce. The sermon was only one way of achieving direct contact with the people: others included a more personal and attentive "care for the individual souls," parish by parish, and the encouraging of more frequent and widespread confessions. The characteristics of modern Catholicism, often attributed simply to the Counter-Reformation, can be found earlier in the *devotio moderna* and in the Observance movement, which also influenced to a large extent the two great fathers of 16th-century Catholic spirituality, Erasmus and Ignatius Loyola.

Arrival of pilgrims in the Holy Land in a miniature from an early 15th-century manuscript edition of the Voyages, *by John Mandeville. "The overseas land known as the Holy Land, or Promised Land, is the most worthy, the most excellent, noble, and sovereign land of all, in as much as it has been blessed and sanctified by the precious body and blood of Our Lord Jesus."*

Merchants and their representatives traveled for business, and pilgrims traveled because of their faith (but a spirit of adventure was probably a strong incentive as well). Apart from the Holy Land, other destinations of this time-honored form of devotion were Rome, Santiago de Compostela—resting place of the apostle James the Greater—Aquisgranum, where every seven years the Veil of Mary was exhibited, and Canterbury, with its tomb of St. Thomas à Becket. Below: Pilgrims traveling to Canterbury in a 15th-century miniature in a manuscript copy of Chaucer's Canterbury Tales: "From every shires ende / of Engelond to Canterbury they wende, / the holy blisful martir to seeke, / that hem hath holpen when that they were seke."

With the growing use of the printing press, increasing numbers of devotional books were directed at the laity, and the religious life of laypersons was strengthened by the development of a religious theater of *sacre rappresentazioni* and "mysteries" (true "living catechisms," as they have been well defined) and by the spreading of the phenomenon of devotional brotherhoods that joined together to pray, to sing the praises of God and Mary, to do penance (often in public flagellations), to perform good works, and to organize sacred pageants, processions, and public prayers. The recruitment of these brotherhoods — by city district, by professional group, by religious inclination — their organization, their characteristic symbols and rituals, and the personal relationships that made and supported them all created a system of strong bonds that united, diocese by diocese, clergymen and laymen.

The same period saw new cults of saints, sometimes tied to political factions — for example, those of Saint Andrew, patron of the house of Burgundy, or the cult of the Three Marys, followed by the romantic "king" Robert of Anjou. But it was probably the new saints, such as Joan of Arc (canonized only later) and Frances of Rome, who best represented the 15th-century religious desire for contact with the invisible world and its need to express itself through a full-bodied, exterior life.

Pilgrimages and reliquary cults con-

Ursula and the 11,000 virgins set off on their pilgrimage (detail of The Reliquary of Saint Ursula, by Hans Memling). The place of the martyrdom of the legendary princess of Britain and her companions is said to be Cologne, also the site of the relics of the Magi brought by Archbishop Reinhard von Dasse from Milan, where he had gone with Frederick Barbarossa.

only Germans who made devout pilgrimages to see the reliquary of the Wise Men of the East at Cologne, nor only the English who made the journey to Canterbury to pray at the tomb of Saint Thomas à Becket.

Pilgrimages, reliquaries, votive offerings, processions, and other acts of faith even more worldly and superstitious seem to be an antithesis of the spiritual and intimate message of the *devotio moderna*. Not without reason was Erasmus, its greater interpreter, a severe critic of any form of external religiosity. However, in actual experience and notwithstanding the contradictions, very intimate devotional expressions can often be found to coexist in 15th-century religious expression together with other more coarse and vulgar expressions.

That which seems contradictory to us did not seem so in the least to the faithful of the 15th century. While they tried to follow as closely as possible the model of Christ and for that reason felt the need to know the Scriptures intimately, at the same they sought — as a tangible experience — the signs of the divine presence in history and in their own lives. Thus, while the intimate ideal of the "pilgrimage of the soul" scorned the pilgrim's voyage as superfluous for the faithful, who knew well that God was omnipresent, it yet lent support to the earthly pilgrimage as well. The faithful who crossed land and sea, traveling great distances to the Holy Land, could, within themselves, travel across time and find themselves together with Jesus in the Olive Garden, on Calvary, or on the road of Emmaus.

tinued to stand in great favor among the faithful and contributed to that mobility, that perpetual wandering, that seems a characteristic of the Middle Ages. People traveled to Rome, of course, to Santiago de Compostela, to Jerusalem, but also popular were the Marian pilgrimages to Montserrat in Catalonia and to Rocamadour and Le Puy in France; and pilgrims went to see the "Veil of Mary," solemnly displayed every seven years in Aquisgranum (where one could also visit the tomb of Charlemagne). The 15th century was also the height of pilgrimages to Mont-Saint-Michel, between Normandy and Brittany. With pilgrims readily traversing national borders it was not

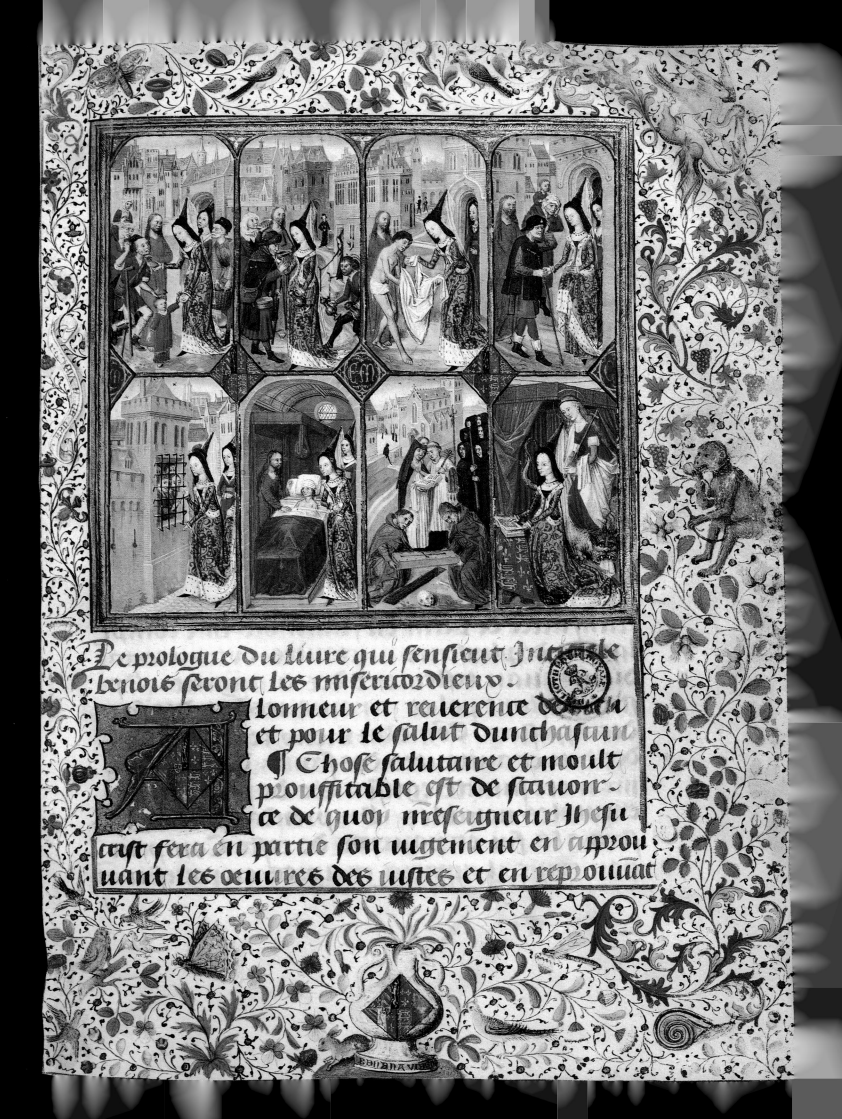

Le prologue du liure qui sensieut Intitule
benois seront les misericordieux.

A l'onneur et reuerence de dieu
et pour le salut dun chascun
Chose salutaire et moult
prouffitable est de scauoir
ce de quoy nresseigneur Ihesu
crist fera en partie son iugement en approu
uant les oeuures des iustes et en reprouuat

"Studia humanitatis"

To read the Scriptures oneself to gain knowledge of Christ, to love him more fully, to imitate him more closely. To reform the Church and, beyond that, to reform the awareness of each of the faithful in order to recreate the perfect form of the original apostolic church. To create a future that was, in reality, the restoration of an ideal historic past. This was the basis of the "modern" Christianity of the 15th century, which, in truth, was inherently conservative if one looked not at the results — which were, without doubt, modern — but at its intentions.

This is precisely the profound connection between this particular way of understanding the Christian message and the humanistic *Weltanschauung*, or view of the world. One can see the first seed and the already perfectly expressed sense of this message — which was, one should not forget, limited to a particular, elite segment of 14th-century culture — in Petrarch's *De sui ipsius et multorum ignorantia*. The work was compiled in 1367 as a response to certain young intellectuals at the university of Padua (usually referred to as Averroists, who were convinced that the basis of knowledge was to be found in mathematical formulas and in understanding mechanical technology) who had accused the author of ignorance. Against that which he held to be, substantially, the basis of knowledge according to his chance adversaries — logical argumentation as an end in itself — Petrarch defended that which to him seemed to be the basis of his knowledge: meditation on ancient science and on the Gospel.

In this somewhat rhetorical, autobiographical self-defense may be found the two basic elements of what would become humanistic culture: on one hand, a backward glance at the paradigms of classical perfection (*reformare deformata*), and on the other hand, reference to the model of Christ. Again and again in his argument, Petrarch returns to the pages of Augustine — espe-

cially his *Confessions*, which inspired the *devotio moderna* hermits and Brethren of the Common Life. Modeling itself on the neoplatonic experience and the writings of the early Church fathers, humanism traces a route analogous to that of the *devotio moderna*: while one sought to hear at close range the voice of God, the other took to heart, in a direct and immediate way, the voice of the ancient texts.

Without doubt, the Middle Ages wanted to know and imitate Christ. At the same time, it profoundly venerated the culture of the ancients from the 12th century onwards. The humanists might see more clearly and further than the ancients, but only because they could build upon the work of the ancients, in respect to whom they believed themselves greatly inferior.

Medieval theology had synthesized the evangelical message without giving much heed to what Christ actually said: Faith in the approved canon, in the authenticity of the divine inspiration of the Scriptures, was enough. In the same way, medieval philosophy had venerated Plato and Aristotle but had treated the truths spoken in their pages in the same way that a Romanesque architect treated the stones and columns of Roman structures: as parts of an established truth to be used in the best way possible to construct another monument, dedicated to a yet higher and surer truth.

Philosophy consoles Boethius: detail from a miniature from the 15th century by the French Maître de Cöetivy. Boethius, a Roman senator, composed De Consolatione philosophiae *while imprisoned in Pavia in A.D. 510 (he was put to death shortly afterwards). The idea is expressed in allegorical form, a popular form in the Middle Ages and beyond. In the text, Philosophy, the Muses, and Fortune appear to Boethius. Printed for the first time in Nuremberg in 1473,* De Consolatione philosophiae *was reprinted another 43 times before the end of the century. Above: Xylograph of the triumph of Fame in the 1488 Venetian edition of the* Triumphs of Petrarch: *"Nihil beatus esse posts quam nominus famam" ("Nothing is greater than a famous name"), as the historian Paolo Giovio was to say.*

Trivium, quadrivium, *and perspective*

The Florentine Antonio del Pollaiuolo made the funeral monuments at Rome for popes Innocent VIII and Sixtus IV and, as Vasari relates, "by mixing with the powerful, and recognized for his virtue and constantly rising, he became very rich." Dated 1493 and commissioned by the pope's nephew, Cardinal Giuliano della Rovere (later Julius II), the monument to Sixtus IV is shaped like a catafalque bearing the lying figure of the pope. The 17 allegorical figures that form the iconography are emblematic of the cultural moment, balanced between faith and *humanitates*, tradition and renewal. Panels on the top of the monument illustrate the three theological (Faith, Hope, and Charity) and four cardinal (Strength, Prudence, Temperance, and Justice) virtues. Ten other figures appear on the sides: the seven liberal arts named by Seneca, which constituted the program of study beginning with the last years of the republic (the first precise definition is in Marziano Capella at the beginning of the 5th century A.D.) and then formed the usual pedagogical program of the Middle Ages in accordance with the teachings of Cassiodorus (contained in *De institutione divinarum litterarum* and *De artibus et disciplinis liberalium*): These are the disciplines of the *trivium*, or the literary level (Grammar, Rhetoric, Dialectics), and the *quadrivium*, or the scientific level (Arithmetic, Geometry, Music, Astronomy). The numerical parallels with the Christian virtues and the repetition of the magic numbers 3, 4, and 7 had profound meaning. Two other figures are Philosophy and Theology. Dialectics took on increasing importance in the *trivium*, considered a necessary introduction to philosophy; and according to the teachings of Augustine, the liberal arts, corresponding to the natural needs of man, had the role of preparing for theology, or the knowledge of God. The tenth figure is Perspective, a young seated woman identified by writing and the meaningful objects she holds. That these are a book and an astronomical quadrant reveal that perspective was interpreted not as a technique but as a general instrument of knowledge.

The humanists pored over the pages of the Gospel and ancient writings intent on gathering the tone and the particular character, the truth and the voice that had spoken it: the voice of Christ, the voice of Plato. It was this spirit, rather than any anti-Curial sentiment, that led Lorenzo Valla to prove to the pope the falsity of the Donation of Constantine, which the Church had been using to support its claims of temporal power, and to investigate errors in the Vulgate, spurring Erasmus to study the Greek New Testament. And it was this same spirit that later led Martin Luther to set about translating the Bible into his mother tongue.

The light of this spirit, too, gave rise to what has been defined as "civil humanism." This was not a matter of exhuming the literary style and philosophic thought of the ancient Romans for archaeological reasons or for purely scholarly interest; rather, facing an early 15th-century crisis of corruption in the Florentine republic, it reflected a desire

133

Top left: Double-faced Janus constructs the ship Argus *in an allegory of human planning ability. The drawing is from the circle of Andrea Mantegna (ca. 1500). Above: Thought, a female figure, inspires the author in a Flemish miniature from the end of the 15th century. Top right: A lady offers the poet the laurel crown in a miniature from the* Admiranda Acta, *by Giovanni Michele da Carrara. Machiavelli later*

wrote (in Discourses on the first decade of Livy*): "Among all men who are praised, those who are most praised are those who have been chiefs and orderers of religion. Close behind them are those who have founded republics or kingdoms. After these, those are also worthy who, placed in the armies, have enlarged either their own kingdom or that of their homeland. Literary men are to be added to these."*

The abacus and Arabic numerals

This woman, who in her appearance and gestures resembles a saint, is Arithmetic. She is comforting and inspiring two souls who are busy counting. The one at the right is using an abacus, the ancient instrument for performing arithmetic. The abacus seems to be a painted design, and the counting is carried out by placing and moving small pebbles—our word *calculate* comes from a Greek word for "pebble." The one at the left is using Arabic numerals. These were spread through Europe with the *Liber abbaci* (1202), by the merchant Leonardo Fibonacci or Leonardo Pisano, considered the most illustrious mathematician of the Middle Ages. He thought these signs to be Indian: "The art of calculating was begun with admirable learning using the nine signs of the Indians." Centuries passed before Arabic numerals and methods of counting did away with the abacus. At the end of the 15th century abacuses came into use in which each movable part on each bar had a value ten times greater than that of the bar below. These saw use until the dawn of the French Revolution. The scrolls above the seated figures bear the names of Boethius and Pythagoras, the latter the author of a work on arithmetic much studied in the Middle Ages.

to renew the morality, the civic sense, and the human dignity that had made the Roman republic great.

Later, these original reasons were, without doubt, lost. Banded together in the retinues following this or that lay or churchly prince, hidden away in the chancelleries of this or that state, the cultivators of literary humanism used their stylistic and rhetorical skills to embellish the Latin of political and diplomatic messages which expressed anything but the ancient virtues. Others retired to the ivory towers of their studies, frequently accepting, however, the protection and patronage conferred on them by the powerful. Still others ended as prisoners of their own illusions, dreaming of heroic tyrannicides and the improbable restoration of ancient cults.

That which solidly remains of the goals of the humanists — despite the errors of evaluation, the weaknesses, and the moral flimsiness of many of them — is faith in the heroic virtues of man and in his ability to reach and conquer any obstacle and thus to enjoy complete liberty, thanks to exertion joined to boldness and knowledge. *Virtù* had always to confront *fortuna*: not to challenge it blindly, which would have been foolish arrogance, but to seize it and possess it. Thus it was necessary to understand the laws that govern the actions of man, on the one hand, and on the other the nature of the universe.

The humanists desired to restore to life the conditions of Adam — those preceding original sin — when man was, by divine grace, knower and master of all things. Giovanni Pico della Mirandola, the canon lawyer turned philosopher, reinterpreted the Creator's words to Adam: "I placed you at the center of the world so that you could more easily look around it and see all that it contains. I made you neither celestial nor terrestrial, neither mortal nor immortal, so that you would be a free educator and

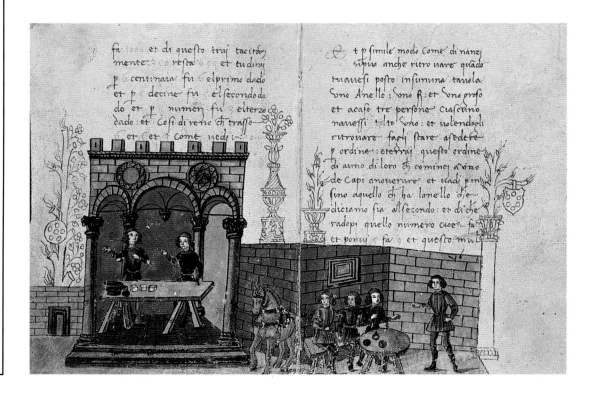

Dedicated to Giuliano di Lorenzo de' Medici (in the margin are the six Medici balls), this Arithmetic, *by Filippo Calandri, was written to teach Florentine youths how to count. It makes use of some rather curious didactic methods: The three dice on the table to the left stand for hundreds, tens, and units; each of the three pupils on the right (the work advises one to "make them stay seated in order") is assigned one of the three objects (to be seen on the round table), and each object assigns for the pupil a place in the sequence; one by one each must double the number at which his companion has arrived.*

Below: Bawdy habits. A drinking session among students from the Directorium Statuum, seu tribulatio seculi *(1489), which contains, among other things, lessons on drunkenness and prodigality held by the students of Heidelberg. Bottom: A professor and his students, a scene often portrayed in illustrations of the time; here it is taken from the* Cathon en François, *printed in the 15th century at Lyons.*

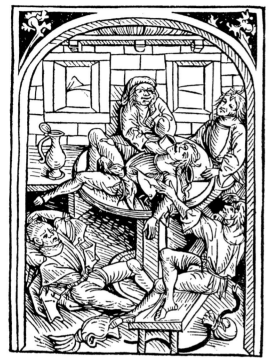

135

It is common knowledge that an artist's school is his master's studio, where he starts with the performance of the most humble tasks. Italian artists, especially architects and sculptors, learned from the study of classical works. Of them, the artist and art historian Giorgio Vasari said, "Their inventions came partly from their own mind, partly from the old curiosities seen by them." One can find these "old curiosities" in their paintings. One of the grand frescoes in the lower part of the Sistine Chapel represents the punishment of Korah, Dathan, and Abiram (who rebelled against Moses in the Sinai; see Numbers 16), by Sandro Botticelli. In the background is a detail of Roman architecture: the ruins of Septizonium, at that time still imposing (the last remains were demolished at the end of the 16th century by Sixtus V).

In one of the frescoes from the choir of Florence's Santa Maria Novella, Zechariah in the Temple *(1490), Domenico Ghirlandaio portrayed some of the intellectuals of his time. The Florentine humanists depicted include the poet Poliziano, to whom Lorenzo de' Medici entrusted the education of his son Piero (though deprived of his post by Lorenzo's wife, Clarice Orsini, who didn't approve of his didactic method); Cristoforo Landino (author of the* Disputationes Camaldulenses, *which concern a hypothetical meeting among learned men in a monastery in which Lorenzo and Giuliano de' Medici, the author, and others discuss the relation between knowledge and action); Marsilio Ficino (translator of Plato); and Gentile Becchi, master of Lorenzo's second son, Giovanni (later Pope Leo X).*

The sense of Opportunity lost

For the Greeks, Kairos was the god of the propitious moment, the moment of opportunity. Lysippos depicted him in a work that, according to a commentary from the Hellenistic age, shows him with "hair that falls across his forehead, alluding to the fact that it is easy to grab him when he comes near, but once he has passed, the right moment for action is gone with him." In this monochrome fresco (below) believed to be the work of a student of Mantegna from after 1490, the figure of Opportunity is placed on a sphere to indicate the speed of its passage and takes from Lysippos's depiction the winged feet and also the long hair (however, Lysippos's Kairos was a boy, not a girl). Opportunity has passed; the youth who has tried to stop her, spreading his arms, is held back by a woman standing on a pedestal. The pedestal recalls the sense of stability in constrast to the movable sphere. The figure is a personification of the virtue of Perseverance. The meaning of the allegory is clear. The natural yearning to grab the right opportunity must be held in check by the exercise of Virtue—that is, with the steadfastness that holds us firm in the face of the caprices of chance. This fresco decorated a fireplace in the home of a noble family of Mantua, and its meaning must have been familiar to its buyer.

master of yourself and so you could make by yourself your own form."

This declaration from the *Oratio, de dignitate hominis* (*Oration on the dignity of man*) becomes even more explicit in the *Heptaplus*, an allegorical treatment of Genesis, which Pico dedicated to Lorenzo the Magnificent in 1489. Pico's later meditations on the cabbala and natural magic — though, like Savonarola, he remained opposed to the popular astrology of the day, which he saw as fatalistic and thus a denial of man's choice in his own destiny — consoled the philosopher in the absolute indefinable and unlimited quality of man's powers.

To many humanists, however, the certainty of man as the maker of his own fortune matched admirably with astrology and with the doctrine of harmony between the macrocosm (creation) and the microcosm (man). Marsilio Ficino, doctor and neoplatonic philosopher, very pious — and very Christian — therapist of bodies and souls, observed that "the doctor must know the other side of man, that which concerns astronomical philosophy; otherwise he will not be a doctor of men, because the sky holds back in its sphere half of the bodies and half of the diseases." The universe was thought of as a giant living body in constant vibration; the stars filtered their energy to men across the heavens. It was up to the wise to understand the astrological laws so as to be able to exploit to the fullest their favorable effects and avoid or mitigate their malevolent influences.

Of course, this complex astro-anthropological philosophy could be used — as it was for many centuries — to serve the cynical aims and substantially irreverent wishes of the powerful. Between the 13th and 15th centuries great lords and cruel tyrants made habitual and constant use of court astrologists: One took the astrological "bearings" before leaving home, before boarding a ship or beginning battle, before making love with a woman from whom one desired heirs, before founding a city or putting up a building.

People awaited with apprehension the

magnus annus ("great year") 1484 and the *annus aquaeus* ("flood year") 1524. The whole Christian world was inundated with a wave of dire predictions (most of them after the fact), and with the new art of printing broadsheets, these predictions passed from hand to hand, were discussed in public squares, and were posted at crossroads. The arrival of the Anti-Christ, the Second Coming of Christ, the End of the World were just some of the crises astrologers promised. Our sense that the end of the 15th century meant the passing of one age and the dawning of another may owe something to this fearful anticipation, the expectant scanning of the sky. "And I saw a new heaven and a new earth" (Rev. 21:1): Columbus would remember those words, facing his destiny alone on the broad expanse of ocean.

The images of this 15th-century astrological science watch over us still from the frescoes with their allegories of the months in the Ferrara palace of Schifanoia or the frescoes in the *salone* in the Palazzo della Ragione of Padua.

Above left: In this enigmatic xylograph from a Roman incunabulum (Anianus, Computus cum commento, 1493), Platonic ideas illuminate the learned. Above right: This miniature is the first page of the Latin translation of Aristotle's Metaphysics *(Venice, 1483), a book both illuminated and printed. "Books are full of words of wisdom, examples from the ancients, habits, laws, and religion." These words are from the* letter Cardinal Bressarione wrote to the Venetian doge Cristoforo Moro in 1468, offering Venice the gift of his library (482 Greek texts, 262 Latin). "If there were no books, we would all be uncouth and stupid, with no memory of the past, without any examples; we wouldn't have any knowledge of human and divine things; the same urn that receives bodies would cancel also the memory of men."

Between dream and technology

Baldassare Castiglione, reevoking in *The courtier* the pleasure and pomp of the Urbino court, recalled that the duke would never add to his rich library anything but manuscripts — and, what is more, only those that were illuminated and bound with gold and precious gems. Not even one of those "books," made of paper from rags and dirtied with ugly inks, would be allowed.

In fact, Johann Gensfleisch zum Gutenberg was himself no humanist. Born in Mainz around 1400 of a patrician family, he became involved in the civil struggles of his city and was consequently exiled to Strasbourg in 1428, where he enrolled in the goldsmiths' guild. If it is true — and it seems probable but not certain — that it was Gutenberg who first invented printing with movable type, he may have been responsible for the first examples of printed works (without dates or exact editorial references). These date from the 1440s and are works that were obviously made to be sold: a poem in German concerning Judgment Day, three editions of the celebrated Latin grammar "by Donato," and a calendar for 1448. Of course, the system of printing with fixed characters was already widespread and remained in use for a long time. It served to reproduce especially images with short texts or playing cards that were then finished by hand. The first works printed with movable type were overwhelmingly religious or devotional: Bibles, lives of the saints, patristic works, liturgical books, and sermons delivered by popular preachers.

The year 1462 is usually given for the export of Gutenberg's press and movable type from Mainz. In that year the city was attacked, taken, and sacked by the troops of Adolfo of Nassau, and typography spread throughout Germany, France, and Italy. For example, at Subiaco, site of a Benedictine monastery, in that same year the arrival of two German clergymen coincided with the setting up of a press that printed Donato's grammar and works by Cicero and

Lactantius. Five years later, the two men moved to Rome, in the care of the illustrious Massimo family, and there they began to produce books evidently directed at a public interested in texts studied by the humanists. The fact that Subiaco was one of the centers of the monastic reform connected with the spiritual development centered around the *devotio moderna* is only a coincidence, one of those coincidences that illustrate the way ideas and culture are spread.

Devotional texts, sacred writings, astrological predictions, and *ars moriendi* were spread by this new technology. They invaded the city squares, and merchants

In 1492, faced with the spread of printed books, the erudite Giovanni Tritemio warned, "Even if we possess thousands of volumes, we must not stop writing [that is, producing manuscript books], because printed books will never be as good." Above: A scribe at his worktable with quill and erasing knife in a miniature from the Catholicon, *by Johannes de Janua, from the end of the 15th century.*

were forced to sell them to the public, who gathered them anxiously and with great interest. For centuries, until the invention of radio, these newly inked pages were the most important way to present news and public opinion. With printing was born a new form of mass media to be allied with the oral tradition of preachers, law courts, heralds, storytellers, actors, and charlatans. It was truly another mark of the new age, our age, that is just now, perhaps, beginning to reach its end.

Naturally, the courts were at first unaware of the disruptive character of this new invention. Sovereigns, princes, and their councillors had long shown great shrewdness concerning their public image and the propaganda regarding their importance, their glory, even their physical good looks — which were perhaps pleasingly "retouched" by the court artist on demand. The portrait, the equestrian statue, the bust in the "ancient" style were born from these conceits. Sometimes princes even acted like Demiurges, emulating the creative power of God. But could the will of a sovereign — united as it was to his own unlimited political power, his economic resources, and the creative inventiveness of his councillors and his architects — compete with a page of the Apocalypse or one of Plato or Hermes Trismegistus, in their descriptions of the perfect abode of man? Could he found and build the ideal city? Here the dreams of power and of knowledge meet: here the prince and the sage reveal themselves, one in the service of the other, in their plans for perfection.

That Europe during the second half of the 15th century was still gothic can be seen in the paintings, in the furnishings, in the works fashioned by goldsmiths and silversmiths, in the illuminated manuscripts of the time. But most of all it can be seen in the cities, with their winding streets and narrow squares and with cathedrals whose great

The first known representation of a typographer's workshop, with a printing press, printer, and typesetter before a typebox; part of a xylograph of the triumph of death, La Grande Danse Macabre *(Lyons, 1499-1500). The various versions of the danse macabre express awareness of the universality of death and form a sort of sociology of the period that constantly changed in response to the realities of the time. Aside from its dramatic impact on the cultural level, the printing industry also constituted a new economic and social reality. At the end of the century, one large Nuremberg typographer had 24 presses and some hundred assistants.*

spires rose to the sky. Only in Italy did the movement change, and most of all in the central area of the peninsula, where, as early as the 14th century, projects flourished that were aimed at applying a certain harmony to the stratified and often "casual" layouts of old cities with the predominance of a polycentric scheme. Buildings and their spaces began to be distinguished according to function: A political area would be characterized by public palaces with a square, a religious area with a cathedral, a business area with a market square.

As early as the end of the 13th century, urban arrangements — even outside of Italy — had been modified thanks to the practice of the mendicant orders that had built their large churches near equally large squares in which they could perform their duties as preachers. Franciscans and Dominicans usually installed themselves at opposite ends of a city, always in neighborhoods on the periphery populated by people of the humbler classes, areas in which the less appreciated and often less pleasant work was done — such as by the port or in its immediate vicinity outside the city, where legal sentences were carried out and the dead bodies of the condemned hung in public view for a certain period as a kind of warning. A few decades later, the mendicants gathered around them the illustrious families who established chapels in their churches and built their homes, later true palaces, in the squares or streets nearby.

The needs for decorum, public hygiene, and production converged to create a kind of urban planning, particularly after the Black Death of 1347–1350, which made available ample interurban spaces and favored the concentration of capital and a flurry of building. The smaller and more coherent ruling classes were able to proceed with greater speed with their new plans, even those that were daring.

The humanistic debate on the "ideal city" — often figured in the painting of the

time and, later, in theatrical stage designs — was without doubt supported by precise, functional rationales, which, however, were not always presented with sufficient clarity. The need for sanitary hygiene and political control would seem to be most important — the events of the second half of the 14th century had demonstrated in a practical way that old, dirty cities with rudimentary water-supply systems were an ideal environment for the rapid spread and dramatic growth of contagions —but wide clean streets, sensible canals, and ventilated buildings were not yet sufficiently recognized as obstacles to the spread of such disastrous epidemics.

The citizens' revolts, particularly of the Ciompi — the lowest orders in the production process for making wool — at Perugia, Siena, and Florence in 1378 had also highlighted the defects in city planning. It had

been made clear how a medieval city, with its narrow and winding streets, favored the rioters and greatly reduced the efficacy of well-armed and organized repressive military responses — in the most obvious example, narrow streets prevented the rapid movement of men on horseback. An orderly and symmetrical city would be much less easy to block with barricades and other improvised means and would therefore be much easier to protect. These were factors that the architect Leon Battista Alberti grasped but then let slip away as he noted the healthiness, the decorum, and the reasonableness of, for example, the urban layout of Cairo: "The wise kings of the very populous city of Cairo divided the city with wide trenches full of water, so that it would be not one city, but many small territories joined together. . . . And in this way they obtained, first of all, a way of not fearing

Artistic and architectural taste and the stylistic "manner" were gothic—centuries old but constantly renewed and vigorously persistent. The choir of Saint Lawrence in Nuremberg was built between 1445 and 1472; the facade of San Paolo in Valladodid was begun shortly after 1486. The chapel of King's College, Cambridge, was begun in 1446, and the work continued at the beginning of the 15th century. The Palais de Justice in Rouen was built in 1508-1509. These are some of the buildings frequently cited as gothic masterpieces. Below: An example of the interior of a gothic cathedral, from the Triptych of the Seven Sacraments, *by Rogier van der Weyden.*

important movements of the multitude and, second of all, of being able to put down with ease such movements should they occur."

And again: "Plato praised those city plans that were divided in twelve parts, in each of which there would be its temple and its minor churches."

And finally: "Some people may prefer having the homes of nobles all together, away from the multitude of the plebeians. Others would prefer that all the areas of the city be so ordered that everyone should be able to find what he needs, and for this reason they do not object that the most humble stores are mixed together with the homes of the most honored citizens."

Symbolic motifs drawn most of all from the Bible and occult lore populated the plans of these ideal cities, as we see in Alberti's use of Plato and the symbolic number 12; and recourse was made to symbolic shapes, such as squares, circles, and stars. The rationale of public order and class decorum cited by Alberti clarify very

Glass and glass masters

"Were they not made of such a breakable material," wrote Vasari, after illustrating the techniques for making "windows of painted glass," "they might last forever. But even so, the art is difficult, cunning, and beautiful." Indeed, because of this fragility, the 15th-century art of stained glass has eluded historians; there are too many gaps, the results of destruction. But the art was certainly not in decline. It is usual to stress that the art of painting on glass approached the refined effects and formal styles of *tout court* painting. Glass masters were inspired by the figurative trends in painting on tablets and miniatures and thus followed first the Gothic International, then the style of the great Flemish artists. Celebrated artists often made designs for stained-glass works on paper, easy to transport and reproduce: Lorenzo Ghiberti made some 20 such cartoons for glass, as did Paolo Uccello, Andrea del Castagno, Donatello, Filippo Lippi, and Domenico Ghirlandaio. Specialized art workshops were numerous and concentrated in the most

important cities; a certain number of these were dedicated exclusively to the servicing of the great glass cycles of cathedrals, by then two centuries old. However, the profession of painting on glass was not without prestige; at the end of the preceding century the king of France Charles V had exempted them from taxation.

Some information exists on the number of masters: Around the middle of the century, about 80 were enrolled in the guild of Saint Luke at Bruges. Similar numbers can be found in corresponding guilds in Paris, Lyons, and Strasbourg, and each master had his group of experienced colleagues and apprentices, the training of whom usually lasted five years. Of significant importance at the time was the appearance of the upper middle class as buyers of stained glass and the movement of the art from cathedrals to its use in decorating castles, public buildings, and private homes. Thus what Guillaume Durand wrote in *Rationale divinorum officiorum*

towards the end of the 13th century remained true, even if not only of churches: "Stained-glass windows are divine writing that bring the luminosity of the true sun, that is of God, into the church and into the hearts of the faithful, illuminating them."

During the 15th century, experiments were made of the new possibilities of silver yellow. Stained glass is first of all a mosaic of colored glass, cut (at that time) with burning iron and set in lead rods; a brush was then used to apply the grisaille (a powder of iron oxide or copper in a solvent), which gave the modelling. Silver yellow—a technical revolution of the early 14th century—was made of a silver salt finely broken up and integrated with burnt yellow ocher and then diluted in water. It changes the color of the glass: Clear glass becomes yellow, while the other colors change according to how they complement yellow (blue becomes green, and so on), thus allowing for the use of less lead filling and a smaller number of glass plates.

The high tower of a gothic cathedral being built in the background of Saint Barbara, *by Jan van Eyck. Critics disagree as to whether this is an incomplete work or whether the artist did not intend to color it. The Flemish master accurately analyzes the architecture (through the three lights in the window we catch a glimpse of a large wheel, probably used to lift heavy materials), and, on the roof, the work of the master* stonemasons who use hammer and chisel to shape and finish the stones. The cult of Saint Barbara, virgin and martyr, began in the 7th century. The fact that she became the patron of gunners—although only in 1529 or shortly before—may be due to the legend according to which she was imprisoned in a bronze tower by her cruel father (who was then incinerated by lightning).*

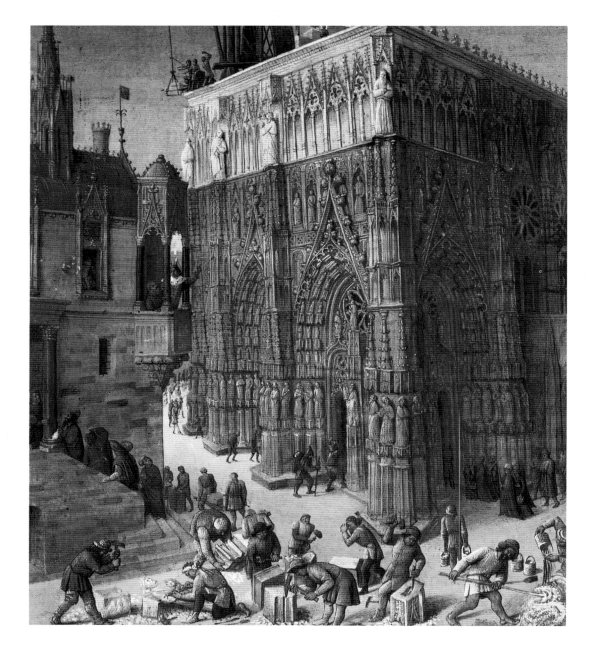

It was in the shadow of the tripartite ideal of peace, stability, and happiness, which justified at least in theory the 15th-century Italian principalities, that was born one of the most complete urban plans of this kind: Sforzinda. It was designed designed by the Florentine architect Antonio Averulino, called Filarete, who had been apprenticed to the sculptor Lorenzo Ghiberti when young and had later worked a great deal in Rome, Padua, Mantua, and other northern Italian centers. Thanks to the good services of the Medici family, he met Francesco Sforza and moved to Milan in 1451, where he dedicated himself princi-

Flaming, perpendicular, flowery: varieties of gothic

well the climate and the sort of political model on which the ideology of the ideal city was based and in which it prospered. It was no accident that urban utopias of a similar character were undertaken with similar references to the Bible and Plato and followed experiences as diverse as those of Thomas More and Francis Bacon: the plans and the creation of the Enlightenment, Masonic architecture, and then the Jacobean and the Bonapartist; the plans of 19th-century socialism; and the new-order urban restructurings of the European totalitarian regimes of the 1920s and 1930s.

Even when describing the Orient as visited by the pilgrim Bertrandon de la Broquière, the illustrator of the Voyage d'Outremer *pleasingly "thinks" gothic. The name given to this style became derogatory because of the classical prejudices of 16th-century mannerism. In contrast to the "ancient style" (the Italian style from Brunelleschi onward), Vasari described gothic as "modern" or "German".*

The Gothic Age

pally to architecture. Between 1452 and 1454 he worked on the construction of the Sforza castle and Milan cathedral; between 1456 and 1465 he planned and worked on the Ospedale Maggiore (the hospital was completed between the 17th and 18th centuries, using his original plans). During the last years of his long life, he drew up a *Trattato d'architettura* in which he related, among other designs, the project for an ideal city dedicated to the Sforza dukes, called Sforzinda.

Filarete had conceived the idea of the city much earlier than the treatise, which dates from 1461–1464, establishing it as the

The 15th-century plan for the tower of the cathedral of Ulm—at 161 meters, the tallest in the world. The fleche was erected at Beauvais early in the 16th century (and collapsed in the same century). Europe continued to build in the gothic, that "cursed construction" with its "many projections, fractures, trusses, and tendrils that make works disproportionate" but were "so many that they have polluted the world." Thus grieved the art historian Vasari in the 16th century. In France, the gothic phase of architecture runs from the beginning of the 15th century to the middle of the 16th and was called flamboyant because of the flaming appearance of the perforations of the windows. In England, the term *perpendicular* was used for the period from about 1360 to the 16th century. Elsewhere, one speaks of "flowery gothic," such as in Italy, where the cathedral of Milan, begun in 1386, presented the technical problems of lanterns. A great intertwining of ribbing in the secondary vaults, ribbed vaults and arches set on columns without capitals, mullioned windows with complicated perforations, a profusion of spires, pinnacles, rosettes, balustrades, and gargoyles: These are some of the characteristics, but this list does not do justice to the breadth of fantasy and the ambitious elegance of this period of European architecture. Local traditions vary with different modulations. The migration of master builders and stonecutters created unique connections. For example, the 15th-century gothic of Cyprus has a certain Aragonese and Venetian accent. Alongside the gothic of the cathedrals was the perfected form of gothic in civil, public, and private architecture.

first instance of a Renaissance city conceived on a uniform design. Sforzinda was conceived in the form of an octagonal star — the result of two squares placed one upon the other following a 45° rotation — inserted within a circle. From a central square dominated by quadrangular buildings radiate streets that link the square to the towers and gates of the city walls and are crossed by secondary, concentric streets. The intersections of these streets form squares devoted to various uses. Porticoes and canals make the city more beautiful and comfortable.

Around 1482, Francesco di Giorgio Martini, in his own *Trattato di architettura*, designed "ideal cities" based on spiral, octagonal, and regular and irregular polygonal plans. At Naples, Alfonso II intended to restructure the city and entrusted the planning of this project to Fra Giocondo (1489–1493). Even Leonardo da Vinci, guest

Brunelleschi and perspective

Of Filippo Brunelleschi, Vasari wrote, "Filippo made a careful study of perspective, which because of all the errors of practice was in a deplorable state at that time, and he worked for a long while until he discovered for himself a technique by which to render it truthfully and accurately, namely, by tracing it with the ground plan and profile and by using intersecting lines. This ingenious discovery made a great contribution to the art of design. It gave him so much satisfaction that he went to the trouble of drawing the Piazza San Giovanni and showing all the squares in black-and-white marble receding beautifully, and he also drew in the same way the house of the Misericordia, with the shops of the wafer-makers and the arch of the Pecori, and the pillar of Saint Zenobius on the other side. What he did was so highly praised by the experts that he grew still more ambitious and before long he started another work; this showed the palace, the piazza, and the loggia of the Signori, as well as the roof of the Pisani and all the surrounding buildings. These works encouraged his contemporaries to continue enthusiastically on the same lines."

Vasari here refers to two perspective tablets, now lost, made by Brunelleschi. Antonio Manetti, the first and contemporary biographer of Brunelleschi, also speaks of these tablets. The first, of the baptistery of San Giovanni seen from a place inside the central door of Santa Maria del Fiore, was "a tablet of about half a yard square." This small work had to be viewed in a special way. Located at the vanishing point of the building's perspective was a small perforation; one held the tablet at eye level and looked through the hole from behind at its reflection in a mirror. Following this procedure, the point of view of the observer coincided perfectly with the point of view of the perspective from which it had been built, thus obtaining the most exact sense of the three dimensionality of the image. The background of the tablet above the buildings was "burnished silver, such that the air in the natural sky was there reflected; and thus the clouds reflected on it were blown by the wind when it blew."

Construction of the Malatesta Temple, from a codex of Epos Hesperis, *by the humanist Basinio da Parma, a poem relating the story of Sigismondo Malatesta. Malatesta, the* signore *of Rimini, commissioned the famous work (it was, in fact, a redesign in a classical taste of the exterior of Rimini's gothic church of San Francesco) and gave the project, around the middle of the century, to Leon Battista Alberti.*

The facade is inspired by Roman triumphal arches, its sides by the arches of an aqueduct; the cupola that was supposed to complete the building was never made, construction work being interrupted by the decline of the prince's political fortunes. The building is one of the most noble incunabula of classicism: "With harmony and sure proportion in all parts," Alberti, De re aedificatoria.

1486. Fieravanti had been earlier in the service of Francesco Sforza, working on the hydraulic projects extremely important to Milan's urban order.

Later, in pontifical Rome, in the Florence of the Medici, and in the Ferrara of the Estes, architects in the service of princes created systems of palaces and gardens joined by corridors, bridges, and overpasses in such a way that the "cities of the masters" duplicated the cities of the people, superimposed over them. In a certain way, the "city-palace" was an ideal addition. The urban ideas contained in the *De architectura*, by Giovanni Suplicio da Veroli, printed in Rome in 1486, came to legitimize urban development that was princely — whether utopian or not and whether actually executed or left at the planning stage — but whose intentions were far distant from those of their inspirer.

We have traditionally perhaps looked a little too harshly at the symbolic, philosophic, and hermetic intentions of the urban planners of the 15th century. Their notions of the ideal city — with their references to the cross, the circle, the star, and the labyrinth, on which many modern scholars have with reason insisted — seem to bring to mind something else: cogs and gears, which

in Milan of Lodovico il Moro, worked out urban designs such as his celebrated plan completed in 1497, which proposed a city with streets "on two levels" — one for "representation" (for the aristocracy) and a lower one "for services" (that is, for the plebeians).

These brilliant, often ingenious follies were never realized except on paper. The plans for these ideal cities reveal their true nature as smooth political instruments when

we compare them to the creations they resemble most: the fortresses of the 15th and most of all 16th centuries.

At the same time, thousands of miles from Italy, a "forbidden city" was being built whose towers and red walls closely resembled the Sforza castle: it was the Kremlin. The Bolognese Aristotile Fieravanti worked on the building (and the drawing up of the plans for the beautiful church of the Assumption) and died in Moscow in

144

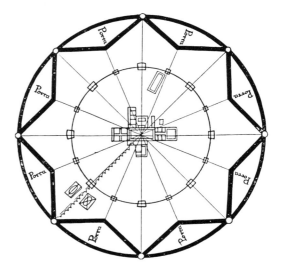

The star-shaped plan of Sforzinda, the "ideal city" as imagined by Francesco Sforza, duke of Milan, from Filarete's treatise on architecture. The fantastic conception of the plan contains some curiously minute details. Filarete calculated that executing the plan would require precisely 103,200 workers from various guilds.

". . . a new form to architecture . . ."

While all the rest of Europe continued to build following the gothic structural system and style, in Italy, particularly in Florence and other areas of central Italy, a formal lexicon derived from classical antiquity was being perfected that later gave a new visual image to "construction" throughout Europe. Ancient theories of architecture were studied along with the precepts of the "orders" in the manuscripts of Vitruvius (the first printed edition of *De architectura* was made in Rome and edited by Giovanni Sulpicio da Veroli and Pomponio Leto in 1486; the first printed translation was made in Como in 1521 by Cesare Cesariano). Roman ruins were measured. To give a few examples, Brunelleschi ("We can surely say that he was sent by heaven to give a new form to architecture, which for hundreds of years had been neglected," wrote Vasari) began the Cappella Pazzi in 1443; Bernardo Rossellino built the Rucellai palace in Florence following a design by Leon Battista Alberti between 1446 and 1451; in 1465, Federico da Montefeltro employed Luciano Laurana to enlarge and change his Urbino palace. The architect from Dalmatia began with the marvelous courtyard (in the drawing): measured columns, capitals, arches, cornices, and pilasters, all of it, as expressed by Vasari, "arranged with the greatest conjunctions" and with an outcome of "gracious beauty."

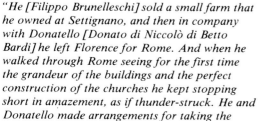

"He [Filippo Brunelleschi] sold a small farm that he owned at Settignano, and then in company with Donatello [Donato di Niccolò di Betto Bardi] he left Florence for Rome. And when he walked through Rome seeing for the first time the grandeur of the buildings and the perfect construction of the churches he kept stopping short in amazement, as if thunder-struck. He and Donatello made arrangements for taking the ground plans of the buildings and measuring the cornices, and they set to work regardless of time or expense." So Vasari described the journey to Rome by Filippo Brunelleschi and Donatello— one of the great symbolic events in the renewal of the arts. The journey may have taken place between 1402 and 1406, but there is some doubt as to whether it actually took place at all. Examples of ancient architecture were also to be *found outside Rome; nor was their study and imitation an entirely new phenomenon. Above left: Classical ruins in a detail from the background of Andrea Mantegna's* Saint Sebastian *(1485).*

Vocal polyphony, renewed and spread by
Flemish masters, had established firm roots in
sacred and lay music by the end of the century.
At the same time, the humanist spirit triumphed
in secular songs, while music for the single voice
gained in popularity and impressed itself upon
the circle of Lorenzo the Magnificent. From
there, it spread into the courts of the nobility.
The predominant instruments included the lute,

used both for accompanying voices (see below, in
the Concert, by Ercole de' Roberti) and for
dances, and the positive organ, "the king of all
instruments," according to Guillaume de
Machault (14th century), which was heard in
churches. The fortunes of the small "portable"
organ, which could be hung around one's neck,
also continued. Opposite: Painting from an
organ flap by Hans Memling, 1465.

rest of Europe had much in common: aesthetic and cultural forms slowly passed
from one to the other, but the technological
discoveries of the age circulated much more
rapidly.

The affinities between such Italian en-
gineers and German technicians are note-
worthy. Perhaps the fact that the many-
sided and extraordinary genius of Leonardo
touched on such an array of technical subjects has made us forget that he was not at
the base but at the apex of this movement,
and that his intuition would have been
unthinkable without the tradition that pre-

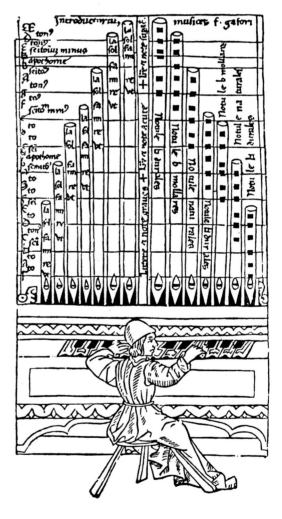

reflect the "mechanical" passion of many of
the city planners.

During the 15th century, the cityscape
was conceived of as a machine, and many of
those whom we call "artists" (a term that
was originally technical and that we have
loaded with aesthetic and emotive values
unknown to the 15th century) were seen,
and in fact were, first of all artisans and
technicians. In this sense, the humanistic
spirit of Italy and the gothic culture of the

The spread of string, wind, and percussion
instruments began the liberation of instrumental
music from vocal music. This long process was
completed only in the 17th century. The period
saw the generalized use of black and white notes,
the foundations of the contemporary system of
notation. Above left: A 15th-century songbook in
the symbolic form of a heart, illuminated by Jean
de Montchenu. Theorists were very active in this

period, among them the Fleming Johannes
Tinctioris and the Milanese Franchino Gaffurio,
who printed the Theorica musicae in 1492. This
was a fundamental work for the development of
the harmonic aspects of music. Above right: In
this print from the Theorica musicae, an organist
is seated at a so-called positive organ (positive in
the sense of "to be positioned").

ceded it. Which is not meant to detract in any way from his originality but, instead, to increase the meaning and the weight of his creations and his plans.

Fifteenth-century painting might not ever have reached the heights it did without the introduction of painting with oils, which spread from Flanders around the beginning of the century. The building of canals and dikes capable of controlling internal waters owed much to the 14th-century experience of the Dutch (the locks of Spaarndam, near Amsterdam, are the oldest in Europe). Printing shops multiplied at a dizzying rate, numbering fewer than 400 presses in 1480 to more than 1000 20 years later. Glassmakers, particularly those on the island of Murano

— the Venetian government had ordered them distanced from the city center — benefited enormously from the fall of Damascus to Tamerlane in 1402, which had been until then the principal producer of glass in the Mediterranean. Progress made in the art of majolica and in development of the manufacture of enamels from tin opened the way for the process invented by the Frenchman Bernard Palissy, who, during the 16th century, began using ceramics for domestic and technical uses (they had previously been used only to make artistic works).

The bustling late medieval cities had long felt the growing need for a way to quantify and measure time: thus clocks

were introduced, though frequently very expensive. The medieval masterpiece of this kind was the astronomical clock constructed around 1350 by Giovanni de' Dondi, perhaps with the help of his brother Jacopo, which required 16 years of work. It was set up in the library of the Viscontis at Pavia, but when Giovanni died no one else could be found capable of maintaining and operating this remarkable machine. In the middle of the 15th century a Frenchman, William of Paris, was hired for this task, and he successfully repaired the clock; but it was then destroyed around the beginning of the 16th century.

The architect Filippo Brunelleschi was also interested in clocks, and clockwork mechanisms were found from around the middle of the 15th century at the Burgundy court. In 1481 King Louis XI of France had a clock made for himself that he took with him everywhere; and at the turn of the century the first pocket watches appeared. It is interesting to note that (as is seen around the beginning of the century at Lille and Fribourg and in 1455 at the Genoese colony of Caffa on the Black Sea) clock-makers were usually also cannon makers, a fact that throws an interesting light both on the range of knowledge of these mechanical experts and the extent of their competence. At the end of the century, Noel Cusin,

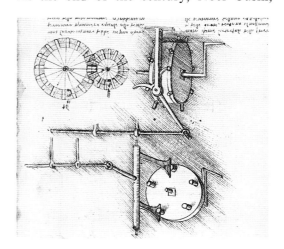

Study of a clock (the cylinder escapement). The idea of making money was not totally absent from Leonardo's interest in mechanics and its applications to machines of various types: A note of his calculates the rate at which a certain machine could produce needles ("400, 100 times each hour") and the attendant hypothetical profit: 61,000 ducats a year, working at a rhythm of 20 days each month.

custodian of the clock in the cathedral of Autun, also made cannons and organs.

The similarities among these mechanical objects — clocks, cannons, and organs — should not be surprising. As can be seen in the Italian *ars nova* and in the grand Burgundian and Flemish experience of the 15th century, musical instruments, particularly the first portable organs were, objects with a certain precision, and their construction and upkeep required great technological skill. At the same time, music involved a keen knowledge of mathematical and acoustical rules, highlighting the close connection between art and technology that is often overlooked by scholars accustomed to underlining a dichotomy between the two talents.

In Milan, the great Leonardo was architect, engineer, plumber, painter, sculptor, and cannon maker in one. His mechanism for the festival "of Paradise" in 1490 was described thus: "The Paradise is made to resemble half an egg, with the inside all covered in gold, with a great number of lights like stars, with certain slits for the seven planets, according to their level higher or lower. Around the edge and hung over this half circle are the twelve signs, with certain lights in glass that make a gallant and beautiful sight; and in this Paradise was much singing which sounded very sweet and gentle."

149

Below left: This crane (from a 14th-century Flemish miniature) was used in the port of Bruges to hoist loads and functioned by the walking action of men setting its great sidewheel in motion. Evidence exists of a similar device used in Roman times. In the 17th century, Francis Bacon wrote, "The use of mechanical devices handed down to us is, among all the other factors, the most innovative and fundamental for a philosophy of nature, that philosophy of nature that cannot disappear in the mists of subtle, sublime, or idle speculation but must make itself useful for the progress and advantage of human life."

Writing to Lodovico il Moro in 1482-1483, Leonardo had promised, "again, if I can, to work on the bronze horse that will be the immortal glory and eternal honor of the kind memory of your father." It seems that this horse was never cast, perhaps because — among other things — the use of bronze to make cannons may have made it difficult to furnish the 200,000 pounds of alloy (80% copper and 20% tin, according to the usual proportions for the castings of monuments) that Fra Luca Pacioli, the Franciscan mathematician on whose calculations Leonardo depended, estimated would have been necessary for the statue. For his part, as is revealed by his sketches, Leonardo tirelessly designed pieces of artillery.

Statues, church bells, and cannons all came out of the same workshops from the hands of the same artists and were products of the same technology. Without the development of the great artillery — of which certain Italian princes, such as Alfonso d'Este, were so fond — perhaps we would never have had Donatello's *David* or the *Perseus* of Benvenuto Cellini.

150

Above right: A waterwheel (detail of Encounter of Christ and Mary, *by Filippino Lippi). Opposite: A foundry for casting cannons in a drawing by Leonardo. One can breathe the technological atmosphere of the period in Filarete's description of an ironworks (1466): the bellows "are about six yards high and four yards broad. Each one has a window for taking in air, a yard in size . . . when they blow, they make a noise like a seastorm . . . made of hide, they are indeed very large and decked out with good ironwork of huge dimensions. The men who practice this trade are no striplings, and one's impression is that of those of the house of Pluto, the tormentors of the soul, black, dressed in shirts."*

The stars and planets

This zodiacal man (1) is one of the xylograph tables in the *Fasciculo de medicina in volgare*, printed in Venice in 1493. The engraving shows the influence of the signs of the Zodiac on various parts of the human body. "At the beginning of the creation of the world, Aries began to come into view and be visible: and this is the sign said to control the head of man." Taurus "controls" the neck and throat, Gemini the arms, Cancer the chest and lungs, Leo the stomach, Virgo the liver and intestines, Libra the kidneys, Scorpio the genitals, Sagittarius the thighs, Capricorn the knees, Aquarius the legs (from the knees to the ankles), Pisces the feet. The practical implication of this astrological anatomy lesson is that "when the moon is in the sign under which falls the member of the ill patient, no medication should be applied to that member."

The first edition of this work, in Latin and also printed in Venice, appeared in 1491; in that same year, the 17-year-old Nicholas Copernicus enrolled in the university of Krakow, where he studied astronomy and mathematics. Copernicus later made his living practicing medicine, but, in an attempt to construct a model of planetary movements that would be simpler than that of Ptolemy and more in accord with the information gathered from personal observation, he formulated his theory of heliocentric movement.

This theory was first made known in 1540 in a preliminary commentary by Georg Joachim, better known by his Latinized name, Rheticus (*Narratio prima*, "A first narrative"). Controversy over whether Copernicus's theories could actually describe with precision the movements of the planets led to increased observation of the heavenly bodies.

Using an armillary sphere and other instruments in his observatory at Uraniborg, the Dane Tycho Brahe—an opponent of Copernicus's theory of an earth in motion around the sun—carried out observations on the basis of which Johannes Kepler formulated his laws of planetary motion—which, however, rejected Brahe's criticisms of Copernicus's system.

Brahe's instruments were those commonly used during the 15th century, but they were larger and thus more precise, and it was by obtaining greater and greater levels of precision that astronomy advanced. The mingling of astrology and astronomy continued, however, and to many scientists of the period the two presented no incompatibility: Kepler himself was an astrologer and worked out Wallenstein's horoscope.

The astrolabe (3) is an ancient instrument for determining the position of heavenly bodies. The version that has come down to us was perfected by Islamic astronomers from the 9th to 11th centuries; it arrived in Europe a few centuries later and remained more or less unchanged. The edge of the reverse face of the instrument (2) is graduated and has a hinged alidade to sight through. Holding the instrument suspended by its ring, one can use the alidade to measure the height in degrees of a celestial object with respect to the horizon of the observer. The astrolabe can also serve as a time-keeping device. A projection of the celestial sphere is engraved on its front face (5), up to the Tropic of Capricorn, with the azimuths or arcs of great circles (a great circle is the maximum diameter of a circle traced on a sphere: the plane on which it lies passes through the center of the sphere itself; the equator and the meridians are great circles). Around this is a scale divided into hours. The so-called rete, or grid (4), was mounted on this face; the eccentric circle represents the elliptic, and each of the points stands for one of the more luminous stars; a hinged ruler was attached to the center of the rete (4, above). Having measured the height from the horizon of one of the luminous stars indicated on the rete, one moved the rete until the pointer for the observed star aligned with the great circle corresponding to the measured height of the star. One then moved the pointer along the elliptic corresponding to the position of the sun (a position that had to be noted, as the sun moves on the elliptic daily). At this point the ruler gives the precise hour on the scale on the border.

Another interesting instrument used during the 15th century was the *torqueto* (6), also an Arab invention. The oldest known European example seems to be one conserved in a museum at Trier that was acquired in 1444 by Nicolas of Cusa. The *torqueto* is used to establish the elliptical and equatorial coordinates of a celestial body. Its description requires a short introduction. The position of a star in the celestial sphere is indicated by lines of longitude and latitude, just as one measures an object located on the earth's surface. The two measurements are angular distances with respective planes of reference (for a point on the surface of the earth, the plane is that which passes the

1

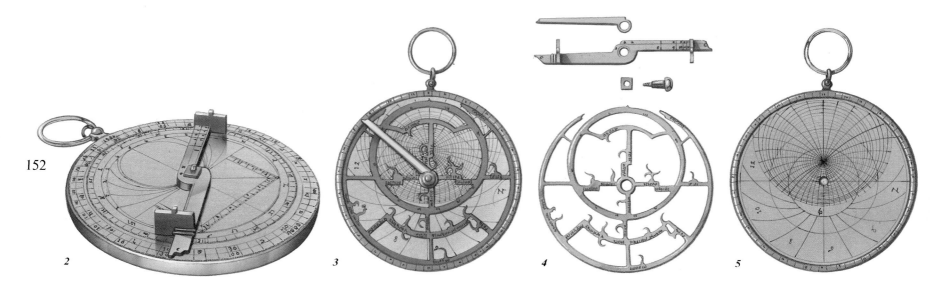

2   *3*   *4*   *5*

6

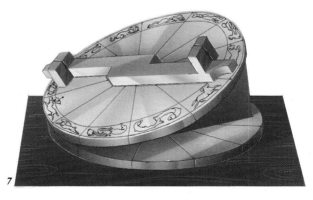

7

tion of the sun on March 21—the vernal equinox—is used as a starting point for measuring the longitude of celestial bodies with both the second and third systems. The longitude with respect to the first point of Aries is the ascension line.

In practice, the positions of astronomical objects are catalogued using the second system; the calculations permit the translation of data from one system into another. These are, however, relatively long and complicated calculations: hence the utility of the *torqueto*. The representation of the instrument given here is based on a description in a treatise by Petrus Apianus from the early 16th century. One can see that it is composed of two graduated disks, each with an alidade and sight attached to the center; one is more or less vertical (D) and the other is more or less horizontal (C). These two disks serve to measure angular distances—the first latitude, the second longitude. The vertical disk is paired with a second auxiliary semi-disk fixed to a bar (E) matched to the sight of the alidade. Beneath the more or less horizontal disk is another structure that determines two dif-

observer (angle A plus the latitude equals 90°). The angle shown in the figure is about 38°; the instrument is thus positioned to be used at more or less the latitude of Amsterdam. To use the instrument in a location with a different latitude, the inclination of the equatorial plane would be changed accordingly. The plane immediately above (C) that on which rolls one of the sighting alidades is the elliptical plane (7). The elliptical plane forms an angle of 23 $^1/_2$° with respect to the equatorial plane. Incised along the edge of the disk of the elliptical plane are the houses of the zodiac or constellations of the elliptical and a scale in degrees; it can be turned on the equatorial plane. It is necessary to align the first point of Aries on the elliptical plane in the direction of the same point in the sky—that is, a star that is found in the first point of Aries. (Thus the equatorial plane of the instrument is parallel to the equator; the star in the first point of Aries—which is at the intersection of the celestial equator and the elliptical—is also found on the elliptical plane of the instrument.) Thus the instrument is oriented and

equator and that of zero meridian, which today corresponds to the observatory at Greenwich). For celestial coordinates, one uses three different planes of latitude and two of "zero meridian."

Thus there are three systems of navigation. The first system makes reference to the plane corresponding to the horizon of the observer and a cardinal direction (the altazi-

muth system); when one takes the height of a star using the alidade of the astrolabe, one is determining an altazimuth coordinate. Another system uses for the latitude a plane parallel to that of the earth's equator (although the latitude of the angular distance from the equator is called the declination). With this system, the rotation of the earth does not affect the measurement of lat-

itude, which remains constant in time (it does, however, change with the first system, as the stars "rise" in the sky). In the third system, latitude is taken from the elliptic plane—the plane on which the sun appears to move. The elliptical is inclined at the celestial equator at about 23 $^1/_2$° and intersects it at two places. One of these points of intersection, the first point of Aries or the loca-

ferent planes at different angles (A and B) with respect to the base. The base plane must be perfectly horizontal; it becomes the horizon of the viewer, the reference plane for latitude in the altazimuth system. The other plane (B), fixed in position, represents the equatorial plane, which is to say a plane parallel to the earth's equator. Angle A is equal to the geographical altitude of the

the zero of the longitudinal scale coincides with the first point of Aries. Establishment of the coordinates of a heavenly body is then easy: It is sighted through the alidade on the elliptical plane and its longitude is read on the elliptical, which also gives the ascension line. It is then sighted through the alidade of the upper disk and one reads its latitude on the elliptical plane.

153

The Other Face in the Mirror

Opposite: The external part of the doors from the Haymaking Triptych *(probably 1485-1490), by Hieronymus Bosch, an edifying interpretation of the "path of life." This detail, showing cutpurses assailing a traveler, an allegory of worldly evil, has the appearance of being a not infrequent incident. Above: A danse macabre from the* Liber chronicorum, *by Hartmann Schedel.*

"On plague, famine, and war..."

To the world when it was half a thousand years younger, the outline of all things seemed more clearly marked than to us." When he wrote that phrase during World War I in his important *The Waning of the Middle Ages*, Johan Huizinga could not foresee the violence that was yet to come. Even so, rereading the phrase many decades after it was written, his judgment still seems in many ways valid.

There is no doubt that the guise of moderation and respectability that contemporary Western culture imposes on feelings and their expression (with a reserve and modesty not demonstrated in other circumstances) still shapes a certain attitude. The overly direct expression of feelings or the recounting of events in their actual disturbing brutality is judged unseemly. Not even the culture of "free expression" of the 1960s has succeeded entirely in shattering the remains of that gloomy Victorian composure — we often still hide or disguise feelings that might appear too "strong."

The preindustrial age, in contrast, wept, laughed, screamed, swore, and pleaded much more loudly than our own. It was a more violent age than ours. Of course, during that period the expression of emotion was perhaps a cathartic ritual: Every great event — even a riot, execution, or funeral — was immediately transformed into a pageant

Leonardo draws a hanged man

On December 28, 1479, with a spirit of cool observation, 27-year-old Leonardo da Vinci sketched a hanged man, carefully noting on the margins of the page the colors of the man's clothing. The dead man was more than an ordinary criminal. He was Bernardo di Bandino Baroncelli, one of the "bold youths bound to the de' Pazzi family," as Machiavelli described them, who had taken part as executioners in a celebrated anti-Medici plot 20 months earlier; Bandino had been the plot's leading protagonist. On April 26, 1478, in the cathedral of Santa Reparata, "full of people at the beginning of divine services," Bandino, "with a short dagger brought for the purpose, stabbed in the chest Giuliano, who took a few steps and then fell to the floor." The conspirators who were supposed to kill Giuliano's brother, Lorenzo de' Medici, were less prompt, and "seeing that Giuliano was dead, Bernardo Bandini killed Francesco Nori, because he was a great friend of the Medicis', or perhaps because Bandini hated him or because Francesco had tried to help Giuliano. Not content with these two murders, he ran to find Lorenzo to use his own spirit and promptness to make up for what the others, late and weak, lacked; but finding him taking refuge in the chapel, he could not do so. . . ."

Is punishment carried out in public to provide an example or because the public enjoys the spectacle? This depiction is from the Auto-da-fé Presided over by Domenico di Guzman, *by Pedro Berruguete from the end of the 15th century.* Auto-da-fé, *"act of the faith," was the public proclamation of the inquisitor's sentence. A procession reached a platform in a square, the sentences were read, and abjuration pronounced.*

The condemned were handed over to secular justice, which carried out the executions. Even though this could occur in the same square as the auto-da-fé, the execution was a separate act and was carried out in the presence of a notary when the Inquisition judges had left. The common language did not, however, follow this important but subtle distinction, and auto-da-fé *was used mostly to refer to the burning of heretics.*

The tortured man: detail from the cycle of frescoes dealing with the Life of Saint Ambrose (1490), by Bernardino Butinone and Bernardino Zenale in the Grifi Chapel at San Pietro in Gessate in Milan. Bishop Ambrose lived in the 4th century, but the details of the painting clearly record contemporary usage. People were moreover aware of the uselessness of torture as a method of inquisition: "I am not content with confessions torn out by torture, as I know that the fear of such torments can induce the accused to confess things that do not correspond to reality." This consideration was spoken by Archduke Sigismund of Austria in the dialogue De lamiis et phitonicis mulieribus (Concerning female sorcerers and soothsayers), by Ulrich Molitor (1489).

157

In the foreground of this 15th-century miniature from De Sphaera mundi, by the English astronomer John of Holywood, an execution is about to take place. Hooded monks comfort the condemned; the executioner has already lifted his sword. In addition to houses and agricultural details, the landscape is dotted with wheels to which a condemned may be tied to die of starvation and gibbets from which swing the hanged: "We are dead, let no one taunt us / But pray God that he absolve us all. / The rain has washed and cleansed us / The sun dried and turned us black / Magpies and ravens have pecked out our eyes / And torn away our beards and eyebrows / Never are we at rest / Now here, now there, as the wind shifts / At its whim, it keeps swinging us," François Villon, from the Epitaph.

The distribution of bread and wine to the poor, as depicted in 1422. The economy was fragile, and the step from a bad harvest to famine was short. Social institutions inspired by Christian charity did what they could, but they were certainly not able to tackle the problem of poverty at its roots. All in all, the spirit of the times was severe, as the English poet Robert Crowley commented, "For officers and all / do seek their own gain / but for wealth of the Commons / not one taketh pain. / And hell without order / I may it call / where every man is for himself / and no man for all."

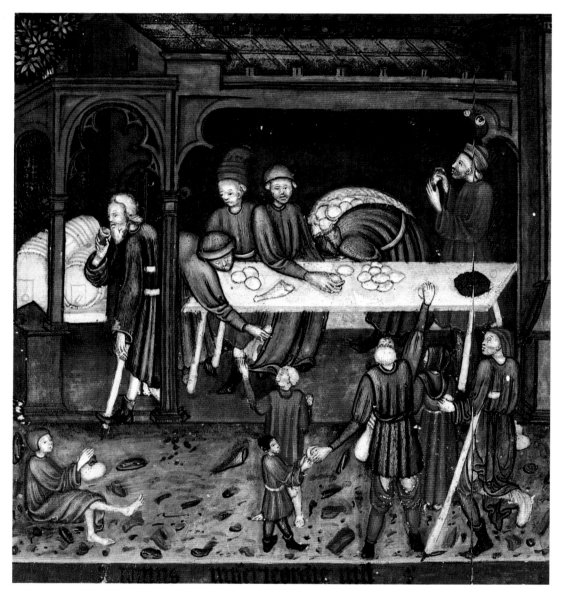

France, companion in arms of Joan of Arc, a national hero and benefactor of the poor — was executed for heresy. In the eight-year period from 1432 to 1440, he had killed or ordered killed — after they had been raped — hundreds of children. He had become involved in black magic, had invoked the devil, and had used the alchemist's art to try to create gold.

Gilles de Laval died like a saint. Having consoled two of his servants — who, having been his accomplices, were to be executed with him — he turned to the crowd that had come to watch — among whom were undoubtedly many parents of the children he had killed — and prayed for his soul. In the end, he asked Saint Michael not to abandon him in his hour of need. *"Sancte Michael Archangele, defende nos in proelio."* En-

and the occasion for both a holiday and a collective psychotherapeutic session. For at least two centuries, our military academies have taught — in the manner of the Spartans or Romans — that it is wrong to reveal anger, compassion, pain, or fear. But medieval heroes — like those of Homer before them and of Shakespeare after them — split their sides with laughter, burst into tears, tore their hair, trembled in fear, and fell victim to fits of dark anger or deliriums of panic. The chemical pollutants of our industrial age were unknown during the 15th century, but modern social historians have shown us that organic aromas and odors of every sort were sharper. In the words of Johan Huizinga, life then smelled, literally, of blood and roses.

On October 26, 1440, at Nantes, Gilles de Laval — baron of Rais, marshal of

158

Above: Beggars of all sorts made up part of the urban landscape. This drawing by Hieronymus Bosch presents a sorrowful catalogue; most of them are physically deformed. Opposite left: This engraving from the Ship of Fools *shows a certain intolerance towards beggars; few are honest, few are truly poor; they are fools who give birth to more children than they can care for and invent tricks to live off the labor of others.*

Below right: The frescoes in the hospital of Santa Maria della Scala at Siena show Foundlings Being Taken in and Nursed *and the* Marriage of the Foundlings (Domenico di Bartolo, 1440). *The figures are known for Siena, and they may indicate a general tendency: The number of illegitimate children seems to have increased tenfold in the century beginning in 1420, arriving at a proportion of one out of ten.*

couraged by his example, his servants followed him in their turn, exhorting him as a valiant knight in the name of God and the memory of the passion of Our Father. The crowd, including the parents of his victims, wept and prayed for him. Gone was the murderer of children, the sodomite, the necromancer. In his place stood the hero of Orléans, the companion of the martyred Joan of Arc. Saint James and Saint Michael, knights like Gilles, waited for him amid the clouds in their shining tournament armor to accompany him to the Highest. Now that he had known the sorrow of death, the children he had massacred would come to greet him, spreading their wings like van Eyck angels and singing for him in the heavens.

Though easily moved to compassion, repentence, or forgiveness, the 15th century was nevertheless a world of cruelty. Thirteen years before the edifying execution of the baron of Rais, a young knight-brigand was hanged in Paris. As he was climbing the gallows, a high functionary — perhaps one of those personally offended by the con-

demned — rushed forward to prevent him from confessing and, so, repenting. He struck him, then used threats and blows to force the executioner to hang the brigand immediately. Frightened, the executioner bungled his job. The rope broke, and the condemned fell, breaking his legs and ribs; he was obliged to crawl back up to the gallows for a second time.

Two years earlier, again in Paris, the rabble had rushed to enjoy a "tournament"

of blind men who, wearing armor and supplied with clubs, swung away at one another for the prize of a pig. On April 14, 1488, at Forlì, Girolamo Riario, nephew of Pope Sixtus IV, was assassinated in a conspiracy. His body was thrown out the window of his palace into a square, where it was stripped, mocked, and torn to pieces.

Cannibalism, in fact, may not have been infrequent at the time. The stories of hosts who chopped up unfortunate guests

159

and served their flesh — perhaps in meat pies, the tastiness of which is applauded before the terrible truth is revealed — are rather common.

Hunger gnawed at this society, and even if famines were less frequent during the second half of the century — though there were several years of bad times, especially the "great hunger" of 1436–1450 in Normandy, which one modern historian has compared to the bombing of Hiroshima in its destructive power — they were still one of the spectres that haunted the people of the time. The tales of enormous feasts in

folklore reveal an obsession with hunger. The excessive abundance at banquet meals and the lack of moderation in stuffing oneself whenever presented with the opportunity betray a chronic and general hunger. Bread was made of every sort of flour, obtained from cereals, plants, and even herbs, some of which had remarkable properties: It has been suggested that such herbs might have been responsible for the visions and hallucinations that seem to have perpetually tormented the population.

These circumstances, however, are true to much of the preindustrial age, and hunger

was not the exclusive problem of humans. In February, wrote François Villon, "wolves live off the wind," and it often happened that one of those poor beasts, driven by hunger, would venture too near the homes or sheep pens of its age-old enemy. Only rarely did wolves attack humans. Even so, substantial bounties were offered in the statutes of rural communities for each hide or head delivered — with a bonus if the hunter could prove he had killed a female with her young. More than representing a particular danger, the wolf, as seen in many legends, became as much a metaphor for

"Many travelers, who were wont to go from town to town with trained bears, were found dead in the streets. The bears, driven by hunger, left the woods and raided the villas and impetuously entered the houses. The country people took flight from their violent presence, and outside in the cold they perished miserably" (Moscovy, described in the Commentarii, by Sigmund von Herberstein, 1549, reported by

Ramusio). How could one provide for the cruel realities of winter, even in the more temperate areas, in a pretechnological age, when heating was both scarce and limited in its efficiency? The cold in the west drove the wolves inward: In 1438, a year of famine, Parisians were terrorized by wolves from the forests of Boulogne and Vincennes. Fourteen people were torn to pieces in the area of Montmartre.

The sense of winter's snow is masterfully depicted in this miniature from the Très Riches Heures *of the duke of Berry (1413-1416). In the house the women are seated in front of a fire with their skirts drawn up so that the warmth can reach their legs. The history of the fireplace began in the 12th–13th centuries; the 15th century saw its widespread use in the homes of the well to do, where it became the principal decorative element.*

death as the Ancient Adversary or as the gaping jaws of hell.

One might also fear the cold, a time when food grew even scarcer, fresh footprints in the snow, muffled howls in the distance, the troubled sleep of children, a husband late in returning from the woods, the faint scurrying and the shining, slanted eyes in the dark. Secure in the comfort of our world, it is difficult for us to imagine the profound effect of nature — the black of night, the absolute silence, the intense cold — and its impact on the senses.

Famine, Plague, War, and Death were the horsemen of the Apocalypse, proclaimed by the prophets and astrologers towards the end of the century. The fifth horseman was Fear — and it ruled the age. Aside from fear of hunger and fear of violence, fear of illness was widespread. Diseases came in all forms: Some were sudden, deadly, and spread inexplicably; others were slow, insidious,

and chronic; all were accepted as one accepts the dark of night, the rains of autumn, or — for the lucky — old age.

Without doubt, plague was among the most feared scourges of the age. There were many rather widespread epidemics during the 15th century: in 1399, 1412, 1427, 1438, 1456, 1464, 1472, 1478, 1482, and 1494.

A man, perhaps having just returned home, warms his bare hands and feet at a hearth. This touching image illustrates the month of February in a German calendar (Augsburg, 1485). The hearth was without doubt the only source of heat in most houses, although some of the higher classes had begun to have a fireplace in at least one room other than the one where they did the cooking.

Epidemics did not strike all social classes equally (better hygienic and sanitary conditions provided a certain defense for some); nor did they rage throughout the year (summer months were the worst) or uniformly across the land. The contagion of 1399–1400, for example, hit hardest in central and southern Italy. For Venice, the

worst outbreaks were those of 1311–1313, 1478, 1486, and 1498; Perugia suffered long periods of pestilence in the years 1429–1430, 1447–1450, and 1475–1479; Florence suffered between 1448 and 1450 and then again in 1464.

Even if the term *plague* is generic and does not always refer to the true Black

161

Below: A procession to invoke the end of the plague in Rome. This miniature, from the Très Riches Heures, transposes to the 14th century what was recounted about Pope Gregory the Great and the epidemic of 590. Some of the people taking part in the procession are seen falling victim to the contagion. The bacteria responsible for plague was discovered in 1894 by Alexandre Yersin, who proved the connection between the human affliction and that of the rat; four years later, Simond discovered the role of the flea in transmitting the virus. The decline of the plague beginning in the 17th century has been partially attributed to the introduction of the nightshirt: The alternation of day and night garments and the resulting temporary deprivation of body warmth from the garments prevents the fleas from multiplying.

162

Above: In the Croniche delle cose di Lucca, *by Giovanni Sercambi (1347–1424), angelic archers inflict death by plague. In the* Iliad, *Apollo in the guise of Smintheus, the destroyer of rats, inflicts death by pestilence on the Achaeans ("taking aim at the men, the sharp arrow was fired and the pyres of the dead burned thickly"). Sebastian, traditionally martyred with arrows at the time of Diocletian, became the patron saint of archers*

Death of 1347–1350, so called from the black spots it produced on the body, one can nevertheless speak in basic terms of a pandemic, contagious, and recurring disease. The period's medical science and therapeutic practices were impotent and could neither prevent the disease nor cure it. It was believed that the disease was connected with heat or humidity, and it was spread by the "corruption of the air"; other than burning the household furnishings of the infected and isolating the sick, there was little that one could do. The medicines that were used — mostly odoriferous preparations or the famous theriac cure-all (a pasty Venetian compound of 64 drugs mixed with honey, it was popular also as an antidote for poison) — were totally useless.

According to the Veronese physician Girolamo Fracastoro, everyone suffered smallpox at least once; and provided one did not die of the disease, one was usually granted future immunity. The face of almost every European during the age of Columbus showed, more or less clearly, scars of the disease. Unhealthy, low-lying swampy areas with stagnant water were the home of malaria — a disease sometimes spread with the

aid of man, as happened in 1472 around Ferrara, when the Venetians broke the dykes of the Po River and flooded the countryside. The celebrated and quite widespread scrofula, a tubercular disease involving the lymph glands, was believed curable by the touch of a king's hands; during a campaign in Italy in 1494–1495, Charles VIII of France "touched" its victims at Rome and Naples.

Leprosy — as early as biblical times, a disease feared and abhorred as a sign of sin and corruption — may have been in regression in northern and continental Europe, but it raged on in the Mediterranean. A leper hospital was built at Trieste in 1414, and one is known to have existed at Catania in 1482. Although it was believed that the disease was not very contagious, it terrified   163

and was chosen as a protector from the plague. Top right: A medical consultation in a 15th-century Hebrew manuscript of the Canon of Medicine, *by Avicenna (980–1037), an Arabic philosopher and doctor. Avicenna, whose authority was unquestioned towards the end of the Middle Ages, combined the explanations of Hippocrates and Galen on the outbreak of epidemics with astrology:* "Et principium

ommium horum sunt formae ex formis coeli facientes esse necessarium illud, cuius adventus ignoratur" *("The origin of all this—epidemics—is forms, astral configurations, resulting from the form of the heavens, which renders them necessary, although their origins are unknown to us").*

Below: A hospital ward in a 14th-century illumination from the Manuscript Gaddiano 2470. *One doctor takes the pulse of a patient, a nurse brings a meal, another doctor assists a patient with an arm in a sling, and a third medicates a sore. Below right: Xylographs from the* Hortus sanitatis, *printed at Mainz in 1491, showing "alternative" modes of healing. Top: A woman subjects herself to a form of beauty*

treatment consisting of the facial application of toads; contrary to what is shown in the illustration, the toads were supposed to be minced prior to use. Bottom: This man is undergoing a treatment with stag's tears, regarded as a form of aphrodisiac.

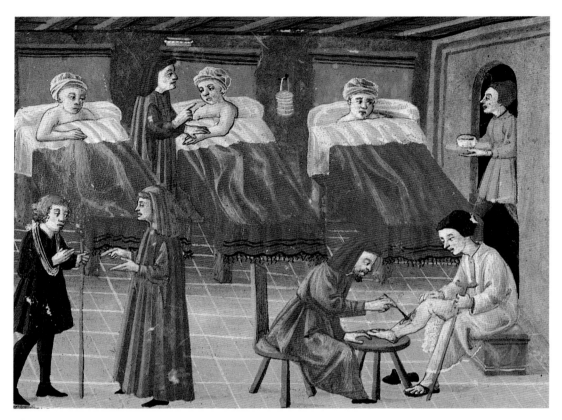

nevertheless, both because it was considered incurable and because lepers were isolated, their public life ended. They were forced to wear certain dark colors (usually gray or black), to carry in full view special badges — "marks of infamy," like those of Jews and prostitutes — to live isolated outside the city in a leper colony, and to announce their approach with the chilling sound of a bell or rattle. Everyone fled from the sound of these bells; and the healthy person who had relations with a leper was severely punished, according to city ordinances.

The symptoms of the disease — shiny, taut skin and areas insensitive to pain — were well known and dreaded; and the supposed wicked character of lepers, their evilness, and the blind anger they harbored for the healthy became proverbial. Pogroms would be directed against them; for example, when epidemics broke out, the lepers

were accused of having caused them or of having spread them by poisoning wells. The unfortunate lepers may well have greeted the plague with a sort of sorrowful pleasure: In a certain sense, such diseases shortened their dramatic distance from the healthy.

Syphilis reached Europe around the end of the century. The disease is popularly considered a gift from the New World, a form of revenge wrought by the conquered, as the Saracens had bestowed leprosy on the crusaders and the Tartars had given the plague to Europe. Cases of syphilis may have occurred earlier, but the disease became common beginning in 1495, when an outbreak was reported in Madrid. The rumor spread in Italy that the contagion had been brought there by the armies of Charles VIII, armies that may have excited the imaginations of those who saw the number of prostitutes bringing up the rear.

Opposite: A doctor and his students in a pharmacist's shop in another miniature from the Hebrew codex of Avicenna. *One of Avicenna's observations concerning the plague has already been noted. To Marsilio Ficino, who wrote an "advice" on the occasion of the plague in Tuscany in 1478, "pestilence is a poisonous vapor conjured in the air that is the enemy of the vital spirit; the enemy not because of elementary*

elements, but because of specific properties." Since the plague was a poison, other poisons could be used as antidotes. "As soon as you can, smear your body with scorpion oil, your wrists, temples, hands, feet, nostrils, neck, throat, and chest with tiriac." The poisonous nature of the plague was refuted by the Veronese doctor Girolamo Fracastoro in 1546.

Thus the Italians called syphilis the "French pox." For their part, the French baptized it the "Neapolitan disease"; the Spanish called it the "German disease"; to the Flemish it was the "Spanish disease"; in Russia it was known as the "Polish disease"; and the Turks called it the "Christian disease." The ancient and truth holds that the origin of a disease — particularly a disease with infamous connotations — is always attributed to the enemy. However, it is worth pointing out, particularly with this disease, that hostility has never prevented fraternization.

Disease was frequently spread by war. The conflicts of the second half of the 15th century — from England to the Rhine-Moselle area, to Spain, to Italy, and to the Danube basin — were usually localized and were conducted by professional soldiers and mercenaries. Conflicts were usually more or less military promenades, and because mercenaries were less willing to risk their lives, battles were often conceded as soon as one army gained a tactical superiority. Thus, though the battles were rarely bloody for the combatants, they were a tragedy for the populations of the war zones.

It should come as no surprise that the 15th century found — in its painting and sculpture, in its literature and music, in the collective sensibility of its folklore — one great protagonist: Death. It has been noted that death was much less feared during the Middle Ages than it was later; at least it does not seem to dominate the individual and collective consciousness as much as it does from the Black Death onward. There are various and opposing interpretations: Did the people of the last years of the Middle Ages fear death more than had their parents because, after the plague of 1347–1350, it was a greater presence in their world? Or was it because life had become for them (despite all those circumstances that would have seemed to us unbearable hardships) more tolerable — sweeter, even — than it had once been, so that death appeared more bitter?

The macabre is one of the distinctive characteristics of the period. The frequent repetition in art of the personification of Death is, without doubt, sign of a sensibility — perhaps even an obsession — that is somewhat new. Three iconographic patterns are representative: the theme of the encounter between the living (usually three elegant and joyous knights) and the dead (three corpses in three different phases of decomposition); the danse macabre , or "dance of death," in which Death (or, better, a dead person) dances with representatives of various ages and social classes (a king, bishop, knight, usurer, peasant, merchant, elderly man, young girl, and so on); and, finally, the "triumph" of Death, in which Death, armed and crowned, rises victorious over a supplicating and trembling humanity (a theme that seems to be a despairing analogy to the Last Judgment).

It has been pointed out that these are ancient themes: The first two seem to go

166

*Encounter between an army of the living and an
army of the dead. These panels are from the
inside faces of the doors of an altar; the outside
doors illustrate the mass for the dead. The work
is by a Bernese master (1505). The weapons,
clothing, armor, and tents are those of the
period. The weapons of the dead are prevalently
pikes and pitchforks while an armored skeleton
on horseback bears a gravedigger's shovel.*

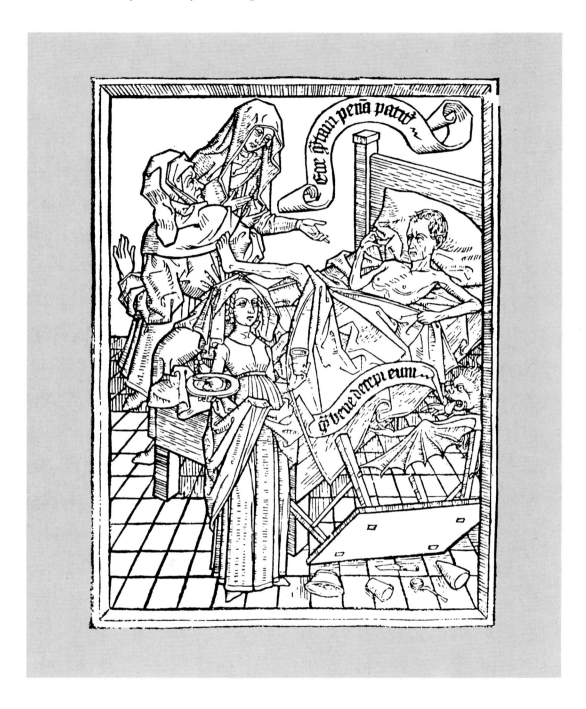

back to Hindu-Buddhist ascetic concepts, and the earliest great painting of a danse macabre was that of the Paris Church of the Innocents, made in 1424. (It no longer exists, but corresponding literary texts were widespread as early as the end of the 14th century.) In the sequence of the "triumphs" — which, beginning with the work of Petrarch, became common subjects of paintings and dramatic performances — one of the victors is Death. What messages do these images convey?

There are two standard responses. One tends to stress that the obsession with death corresponds to a growing attachment to life, suggesting that the late Middle Ages were more secular, less certain of the world beyond this one, less believing than the peoples of earlier ages. One can cite the celebrated verse "Be merry who would like to — for there is no certainty of tomorrow" from a carnival song written by Lorenzo de' Medici, which in truth is not a radically new world view but only a translation, in terms suitable to the occasion (in this case, a carnival celebration), of Horace's *carpe diem*, or "seize the day." A contrary line of reasoning claims that the image of "conquering" death was an element of ascetic propaganda spread by the Church to reassert control over a society too much affected by lay agitation on one side and heretical agitation on the other. The Church thus provided a dark and gloomy *memento mori*, a grim reminder that glory, wealth, and the joys of this world are useless because death conquers all. Finally, there are others who have stressed a political component in the danse macabre : An "egalitarian" Death dances with everyone, from prince to peasant — the perfect starting point for an antihierarchical discussion.

In reality, the frequent representation of death indicates a much less pessimistic and frightened outlook than is characteristic of Western culture in our century. True, an obsession with death can certainly contain

These are the themes of the *ars moriendi*, the themes worked out by the great popular preachers who insisted on the the last things (Death, Judgment, Heaven, Hell), the aims of the *devotio moderna* and the Observance movement. It is, for example, significant that one of the most frequent literary and iconographic themes was the death of the miser, vainly clutching his sacks of gold coins, which Death forces him to leave behind. This theme was reaffirmed when, thanks mostly to the Franciscan Observants, who had reimposed on their order strict adherence to their original rule of poverty, the prohibitions against loaning money at interest and various other credit activities — harshly condemned by the Church as usury — began to give way. A more moderate attitude that permitted one to enrich oneself, while at the same time remaining in peace with one's conscience, arose, but on condition that one serenely accept separation from one's wealth — and that implied restitution of ill-gotten gains

elements — more pastoral than truly ascetic — that urge us to reconsider the joys of life and earthly pleasures; but it also reminds us of the positive elements of life. There is a *memento mori*, yes, but there is also a *memento vivere* in the face of a death that is not an end, but only a passage, a change in circumstances. The encounter of the three living men with the three dead corpses can be seen as an invitation to reconsider the human condition. And, consistent with a society that was discovering individualistic elements of life but still thought primarily in terms of the group (city, family, social class, guild), it can also be seen as an invitation to live better, each according to the duties appropriate to one's station in life.

Thus is confirmed the fully hierarchical character of Christian society: Death dances with everyone, but with each the dance is different. It has a special significance for the emperor or the prelate, the wealthy man or the beggar, the young girl or the old man; it can frighten or console, be severe, ironic, or even compassionate.

and charitable donations to the Church. The image of the cold, clawed hands of pale Death tearing the dying miser from his treasure was not meant to frighten or convince the sinner to convert; rather, it was a plea that part of the wealth be redistributed.

For their part, upright merchants opened a column in their account books under the name of the Lord Almighty and noted as His debt and to their credit every sum offered to charity. On the other hand, everyone knew that a little money spent on masses and prayers could help the needy in the here and now as well as the souls in Purgatory in the hereafter — a kind of saintly accounting supported by a saintly insurance plan for the uncertainties of eternal life. A sinner who feared his heirs would eat up his money and leave him in Purgatory without benefit of a prayer could join a confraternity of lay brothers. He could do a little good, pray for the dead of the brotherhood, and when he had passed on to the Other Side, his brothers and those he had benefited would pray for him, too. 169

In Sebastian Brant's Ship of Fools, *no folly is greater than man's consideration of the afterlife, the eternity for which the earthly existence of every Christian, with death as its inevitable conclusion, is merely preparation. Above left: This illustration (from a Latin edition) shows the folly of a man who, even confronted by the tomb, does not stop trampling the scriptures (the metaphor is made clear by his*

gestures). Above center: The warning in this illustration is that the sinner will continue for eternity to drag along difficult paths the cart that he so improvidently let run riot amid earthly vices. Above right: Human folly is manifested by using the same scale to weigh earthly and heavenly goods (the scales indicate that the former weigh more); foolhardiness lies in believing this illusion.

Old practices and new fears

It has recently come to our ears, and not without being for us the cause of great pain, that in certain regions of upper Germany — such as in the provinces, cities, territories, districts, and dioceses of Mainz, Cologne, Trier, Salzburg, and Bremen — many persons of one or the other sex, who have forgotten their salvation and deviated from the true Catholic faith, have voluntarily offered themselves to demonic incubi and succubi; by means of enchantments, spells, charms, and other superstitious, infamous, and reprehensible magical procedures they decay, suffocate, and extinguish the progenitors of human beings, the young of animals, the harvests of the land, the shoots of vines and fruits of trees; and not only this, but also men themselves, and women, the beasts, whether large or very small, the other animals of all species, the vines, the orchards, the fields, the pastures, the grains, the corn, the vegetables. These persons distress and torture men, women, beasts of burden, herds, and flocks with ills and cruel tormentations, both internal and external. These persons prevent men from fecundating women and keep women from conceiving; they keep spouses from performing their legitimate conjugal duties. And these persons go so far as to renounce, with sacrilegious mouth, the very faith they received with their baptism. These, further, do not fear to commit and perpetrate infamous excesses, instigated by the Enemy of humanity, at the cost of putting in peril their own souls, to offend the divine Majes-

This may be the earliest representation of witches on broomsticks (in Le Champion des Dames, *by Martin Le Franc, ca. 1440). The devil "transports witches from place to place... and sometimes makes them pass through doors and gates, which open so quickly that the witches seem to enter through closed doors, which, however, is not so,"* Jordanes de Bergamo, Quaestio de strigis *(The question of witches), ca. 1470.*

Devils, Hell, witches, and the angels of Paradise. Above: A detail from Hell, *part of the* Garden of Earthly Delights *triptych (ca. 1510), by Hieronymus Bosch. There are varying interpretations of how the chastised in Hell are symbolized. The lute, the harp, the hand organ, and other musical instruments used as means of torture for the damned can be seen as pre-Freudian sexual symbols alluding to carnal sins; as Biblical instruments used for praising the Omnipotent, from whom the sinners had broken during their lives; or as a reminder, horrifying in Hell, of the harmonies of Paradise. To the right, Satan, with a bird's head, swallows the wicked.*

ty, and to create a scandalous example for all the pernicious."

The tone of this pontifical bull, promulgated December 5, 1484, by Pope Innocent VIII, clearly signals an emergency, the urgency of which was underscored by the fact that Innocent had taken office only three months earlier, and this was one of his first official acts as pope. Across wide areas of the German world — from the Alpine arc along the course of the Rhine to the North Sea — a conspiracy, at once heretical and criminal, was in progress, one that was causing death, abortion, epidemics, famine, and, in fact, the disintegration of the social and religious fabric of those regions.

The pope's bull authorized the Dominicans Jacob Sprenger and Heinrich Kramer to undertake, with inquisitorial authority, an investigation in those areas affected by the heresy. Since the authority of the inquisitors came directly from the pope, the actions of the two Dominicans would — for the term of the investigation, and in relation to the object of the inquest — deprive the local churches of their ordinary powers. This was no small matter, for most of those churches were directed by prelates who were also princes of the empire, and the bishops were always jealous of their privileges in relation to the Holy See.

Note that the bull attributes the "reprehensible magical predecures" to "persons of one or the other sex" — a witch, in other words, could be either male or female. Since antiquity, however, it had been women to whom were attributed magical practices aimed at infanticide, the creation of impotency, the sterility of animals and fields, or the stimulation or extinguishing of erotic attraction. These practices might be performed out of wickedness or for revenge, but they were usually for pay.

Beliefs of this sort had been treated in depth by such poets as Lucretius, Horace, Tibullus, Ovid, and Lucan, whose works were widespread in the humanist culture

171

The distinction of three orders of angels, each divided into three choruses is found in De caelesti hierarchia. *Until the 16th century this was considered the work of Diogenes Areopagita (a member of the supreme tribunal of Athens), converted by Paul, but then it was considered the work of a theologian (Pseudodiogenes) from the 5th century. During the same period the iconographical image of the winged angel appears, derived from the classical Victory. From the 16th century, angels are increasingly depicted in sacred art. This detail is from the* Triptych of Judgment, *by Hans Memling. The work was commissioned by Angelo Tani, an official with the Medici bank in Bruges. Having embarked for Italy, the ship carrying it was captured by a pirate from Danzig who gave the painting to his city's cathedral.*

and who were already well known to the Middle Ages. Such beliefs, supported by corresponding theories provided by Hellenisic culture, found clear confirmation throughout the ancient Mediterranean world and were also confirmed by passages in the Bible and the Koran. The Celtic, Germanic, Slavic, and Ural-Altaic folklores each preserved such beliefs and added enrichments and complexities of their own. The belief, for example, that at night certain women could turn themselves into nocturnal birds of prey, such as owls, and suck the blood of humans, particularly children, was widespread in the Roman and Hellenic worlds, and it survived in the Slavic-Balkan legends of vampires. During the 10th to 11th centuries, certain canonical texts discussed a popular "new" belief, the "flight" of certain women following a nocturnal hunting goddess (dubbed in the ecclesiastical Latin of these texts "Diana"), probably based on the folklore inherited from ancient Germany.

The Middle Ages had been Christianized rapidly, but the faith remained superficial. The Church had not been overly troubled by superstitions and witchcraft but had limited itself to discouraging the spread of such beliefs by forcing penitence from those who declared themselves believers. With the spread of heresy during the course of the 13th century, however, had come a greater concern for general religious instruction. More attention was given to the spread of folkloric beliefs that could become the roots of heretical opinions. While scholastic theology specified the limits of the demons' power on the visible world and thus the possibilities for their collusion with humans, the old pagan superstitions began to worry the Church authorities. The increasing Christianization of the European world brought with it a diminished tolerance for growing folkloric cults tied to the pagan past, and the Church began to seek out, using inquisitorial instruments and methods, wizards and witches to determine at what point these magical practices might take the form of outright heresy.

What made witchcraft a crime, as far as the Church was concerned, was the pact with the devil that each witch supposedly entered into: This demon idolatry was heresy, of course, since worship and adoration are due only to God. Of less importance — and at first only at a purely theological level — was the question of whether wizards and witches might actually believe themselves in possession of the powers attributed to them or if they were simply victims of diabolic deceptions. Roman law accepted that certain crimes could be committed by means of magic but punished the guilty according to the crime and not according to the choice of instruments by which the crime had been committed. The Church thus found itself caught up in a tradition — both biblical and Greco-Roman — that accepted the reality of magical powers, the objective necessity of safeguarding the principle of divine omnipotence and of the subordination to God of all creatures (which made necessary the precise detailing of demoniacal powers), and the need to protect orthodoxy from heretical thrusts.

All of this helps to explain the attention, at first essentially disciplinary, given to witchcraft. It does not explain, however, how this madness reached its height between the 16th and 17th centuries, as the Church began to furiously persecute heretics, both those who supposedly made a profession of being wizards or witches and claimed for themselves magical powers and those who were only accused of doing so. It is probable that, aside from the crisis presented by the growth of heresies between the 12th and 14th centuries that had alarmed the Church, the demographic decline begun during the first half of the 14th century put in motion a series of sociocultural mechanisms that spread throughout Europe and had a major impact on the history of witchcraft.

The high degree of infant mortality, hunger, and disease that had disturbed the demographic equilibrium had powerful consequences on the socioeconomic level, devastating entire communities and causing the rise and fall of fortunes, the transfer of real estate, and the movement of sometimes quite numerous groups of people from one region to another or from the countryside to the city. As people moved they naturally brought with them their ideas, including their prejudices and superstitions. Calamities, particularly those affecting a collective group, demand explanations, both direct and indirect, and often the search for their causes involves the hunt for a scapegoat.

For centuries the collective life of the Christian in Europe had remained unchanged, at least from outward appearances. But then, in the period of a few generations, everything was thrown into confusion. Particularly in the more isolated areas — but there was no city whose population was not composed of people from the countryside or children whose parents had moved to the city from the countryside, bringing with them their rural traditions — people were accustomed to making use of both men and women whose healing practices followed a traditional cultural syntax that, though adapted to the Christian faith, was far more ancient than Christianity. Witches were perhaps more common than wizards, since much of their magic or medicine concerned female problems, especially infanticide and abortion. The 15th-century witch was often also a healer, a doctor, a midwife, an abortionist, a keeper of the community's "dark secrets." Alone, and not infrequently "marked" in some way (by age, ugliness, or some particular physical characteristic), the witch performed an uncertain role: Although poor and lacking the support and protection of a family, she was also believed to possess valuable "powers" that of themselves were neither good nor evil but that she alone was capable of using.

172

A wizard travels to the sabbat mounted on a wolf, from the De lamiis et phitonicis mulieribus *(Concerning female sorcerers and soothsayers), by Ulrich Molitor (or Müller). This treatise was requested by the Archduke Sigismund of Austria, who was worried by the developments in an important trial for witchcraft at Innsbruck in 1485, which had implicated and falsely accused various nobles, even touching on the consort of* the prince. *It is written in the form of a dialogue among Molitor, a professor of law at Constance, the Archduke Sigismund himself, and Konrad Schatz, master of rhetoric and jurisprudence at the University of Fribourg. Their conclusion concerning the witches was that "because of the corruption of their will, since they have distanced themselves so far from God, these wicked women must be punished with death."*

The reasonings of witch burners

As related in the *Malleus Maleficarum (Hammer of Witches),* by the Dominican inquisitors Jacob Sprenger and Heinrich Kramer, it sometimes happened — thanks to the devils' work — that witches either confessed their crimes or persisted in silence. "Experience taught us, as was clear from the confessions of all those we burned, that many witches had become involved in witchcraft against their will. They did not make this claim to free themselves, for it was clearly the truth, and one could frequently see on their swollen and bruised faces the blows and lashes given them by the devils when they refused to obey orders. In the same way, after confessing their guilt, these witches tried insistently to kill themselves by hanging; a truth brought by our practices. Thus, after the confession of the crimes, they were always given guards with hourly turns to watch over them: even so, every so often, due to negligence on the part of the guards, they were found to have hanged themselves with belts or veils. It was therefore the enemy who caused this, since they could not obtain pardon with either contrition or the sacrament of confession. That part of the heart that the enemy was never able to seduce and that thus would most easily have obtained divine pardon the enemy tried, in a last act, to bring to desperation by means of earthly woes and a horrible death. In truth, with the great grace of God, each could obtain, as we must religiously believe, pardon with a true contrition and a pure confession, provided they had not participated in those filthy practices voluntarily. All of this is proven by events that took place just three years ago in the dioceses of Strasbourg and Constance and in the cities of Haguenau and Ratisbon. In the first city, a witch hanged herself with a torn and fragile veil. Another city, called Walpurgis, became known in a surprising way for its witchcraft of silence (which makes the witches not confess their crimes) that, according to information from other gossipy women, the witches are supposed to have made by cooking in a stove a young male child, a first born. Other acts and episodes that have happened are available. . . ."

Witchcraft is born of weakness, fear, suffering, disease, and anger. Recourse to witchcraft — which usually serves only as the ritualized revenge of the powerless and the unfortunate, vulnerable to reverses of fortune or the abuses of the more powerful — represents in its own way a means of maintaining social balance, an outlet for a unified culture. The witch consoled the afflicted. She took upon herself the sins of the community, she assumed responsibility for the deaths of children and unfortunate marriages, she soothed as best she could wounds and suffering using herbs, roots, and psychotherapeutic rituals (a wisdom distant from the haughty chatter of doctors in ermine coats but empirically more effective). The witch knew the secrets of nature but also those of the heart, during a period when — as evidenced by the *devotio moderna* — priests were still very far from their parishioners.

But the power a witch held in relationship to the community was extremely fragile. One strained personal relationship, one dissatisfied client, and the witch would find herself at the mercy of her former friends, former clients, and former accomplices, who would now seek explanations for their misfortunes and revenge for their frustrations. After every epidemic or calamity of the 14th or 15th century, people would look for answers and, if possible, seek retribution. They would ask themselves: Was this scourge the vengeance of God? Was it some evil alignment of the stars? Had someone made signs in the air or murmured profane words? Or did the evil furtively enter the home at night, in the guise of a bat or a black cat?

In 1458 the Dominican Nicholas Jacquier published a treatise titled *Flagellum haereticorum fascinariorum* (*Flagellation of heretics*), an attack on what at that time was the major hurdle standing in the way of a vigorous prosecution of witchcraft. The official and accepted Church position had

been that the acts attributed to witches were pure illusion and fantasy. Essentially, there was no such thing as witchcraft, and the only heresy consisted in *believing* in such pagan superstition.

Jacquier was one of many who refuted this position. Witchcraft, he said, had been foretold in the Bible and was a very real phenomenon. Through such arguments, the Church gradually came to accept that acts of witchcraft — nocturnal sabbats, transformations into animals, intercourse with demons — did in fact occur. In what amounted to a complete about-face, Rome decided that *disbelief* in witches — and not just witchcraft itself — was now a heresy.

Meanwhile, instances of collective psychosis continued to occur, as at Arras and Lyons between 1459 and 1460. With increasing frequency, witches were here and

174

From the De lamiis*: A witch commits an evil act, splintering a branch into a man's foot. An extract from the end of the dialogue: "Although such cursed women cannot cause anything actually to happen, even so, if because of devilish instigation, desperation, poverty, hate of their neighbor, or other temptation they have distanced themselves from the true and most pious God, then they have fallen into heresy."*

there burned at the stake: Heidelberg in 1446 and Cologne ten years later. In Italy, the Franciscan Observants expressed growing concern and a real fear of witches.

By 1484, the phenomenon had reached maturity and the stage was set for full-scale persecution of witches as heretics. The papal bull of Innocent VIII linked illicit traffic with demons and magic practices to the deaths, poor harvests, diseases, and accidents that had been suffered during that period in certain areas of Germany. Two years later, Sprenger and Kramer, the two inquisitors appointed by Innocent, published the results of their investigation in the form of a treatise, the celebrated *Malleus maleficarum* (*Hammer of witches*). Their work stressed the "feminine" aspect of witchcraft (from then on, people spoke of "witches" and only rarely of "wizards"), which was explicitly sustained by way of

uniting that particular form of heresy with the nature of women. In describing witchcraft, the two Dominicans brought together all the forms — ancient and recent, biblical and classical — of misogyny and a fear of sex spread by previous literature. The *Malleus maleficarum* is the source of the first rationalized and nearly canonized description of the pact with the demon (a pact usually sealed by sexual union), the flight of witches, and the witches' sabbat. This first comprehensive handbook for witch hunters also provided detailed instructions for prosecuting witches, including their arrest, imprisonment, questioning, and torture.

The *Malleus maleficarum* was reprinted nine times before the end of the century; it was then reprinted again and again, almost without interruption, until 1669. Without doubt, it is the most widespread and authoritative of the early tracts on demonology. It is also a monument to one of Europe's most regrettable and shameful follies.

Another scene from the De lamiis*: the carnal union between the devil and the witch. An excerpt from the dialogue:* Sigismund: *"What should we think about the question of whether devils can lie and join with such women?"* Konrad: *"These women confess to having consummated the carnal act with nightmare spirits who behave like real lovers."* Sigismund: *"A foolish trust induces the women to talk of*

things that only they give credit to." Konrad: *"In truth, some of them persist in such confessions even at the moment when they are being led to the gallows. . . . Moreover, Saint Augustine says, 'It is well known that sylvans and fauns, commonly called incubi, have existed, and often they have exerted an evil influence on women, they have desired and possessed them.'"*

The witch of Todi

On March 20, 1428, Matteuccia di Francesco was burned at the stake following legal proceedings in Todi's square. The court's verdict defined her as a *feminam male conditionis vite et fame, publicam incantatricem, facturiarum et maliarum et stregam* ("woman of evil life and ways, a public enchantress, doing evil, wickedness, and witchcraft") — that is, a witch. Her crimes were recounted in 30 detailed indictments, each joined to the next by the formula *item non contenta predictis set mala malis addendo* ("furthermore, not content with the aforementioned, but adding evil to evil"). Matteuccia specialized in amorous concerns: To a wife who complained of being mistreated by her husband, she had recommended an egg and horsegrass; to another beaten wife she gave a wax image to place under her husband's bed. To a servant who complained that her master, a priest, no longer wished to have sexual relations with her, Matteuccia gave a wax image to be melted on a heated brick. For another woman with a similar complaint, she directed that the woman burn a few swallows and have the man in question eat them and drink a liquid with their ashes; in another case, to help a wife obtain greater amorous warmth from her husband, she directed the woman to have him eat a small swallow fed on sugar and drink a mixture of wine and the water in which she washed her feet. On the other hand, a blessed candle — lit, bent, and hidden — would prevent carnal relations as long as it was tended. Then there were her "voyages" to a walnut tree at Benevento. She greased herself "with an unguent made of the fat of vultures and the blood of bats" and then pronounced the formula "O Lucifer, demon of hell, cast out as you were, come to me or send me your servant." This servant was a goat, and Matteuccia would change herself into a fly and ride on the goat to the walnut tree and there meet other witches, enchanted spirits, infernal demons, and Lucifer. Matteuccia gave a "spontaneous and true confession" of all this. A cowl was put over her head, her hands were tied behind her, and, riding on a donkey, she was led to the place where justice was administered.

The Other among us and against us

Witches are only one example — perhaps the most spectacular — of a general phenomenon that occurred during the course of the 15th century and took root again in modern Europe and — alas — even in contemporary Europe: the hunt for the Other on whom to heap guilt and responsibility. It seems that a collective anguish — the growing discomfort caused by epidemics, famines, demographic crises, political changes, and social and religious instability — led to a fevered search for a metaphysical Enemy responsible for the ills of the world. This malaise, often implicit rather than explicit, was buried just beneath the surface throughout the 15th century, even during the long decades of apparent calm and more or less satisfactory circumstances — it was a condition that would explode in full force during the Reformation. In the meantime, storm clouds grew thicker on the horizon, but at the time no one suspected how violent that storm would be. The religious disquiet, the anticipation of the end of the

world or at least of great changes announced by the heavenly bodies, the spreading malaise that was a sign of the times, all were symptoms of — as well as, perhaps, contributing factors to — a building tension.

During the course of the century, and most of all during the period between 1453 and 1480, anxieties and fears were focused on the new Muslim peril, caused by the advance of the Ottoman Turks, who had toppled the Byzantine empire and were threatening the Aegean, the Adriatic, the Balkans, and the Italian peninsula.

"Lord, will the Turks come to Rome?" Dionigi il Certosino speculated during one of his mystical visions. "Do you believe the Turks will reach Italy this year?" asks one of the characters in Machiavelli's *Mandragola* (*The Mandrake*). About 70 years separate these two speculations, and both demonstrate the distress that seized all of Europe during the second half of the 15th century.

No one became truly aware of the danger until the banners of Mohammed II were waving over the golden cupolas of Constantinople. After that fateful April

The advance of the Ottoman Turks across Europe. Above right and opposite left: The city of Constantinople from the Liber Chronicorum, *by Hartmann Schedel (1499). In 1366, Murad I made Adrianople his capital. In 1389, in one of the bloodiest and most desperate battles of the times (even Murad I lost his life), the Turks defeated a coalition of Serbs, Bosnians, Bulgarians, Rumanians, and Magyars at*

Kossovo. Ottoman expansion was halted by the invasion of Tamerlane, who inflicted a crushing defeat on the Turks at Angora in 1402, and then resumed under Mohammed II. After taking Constantinople, he unsuccessfully laid siege to Belgrade (1456), took the Peloponnesus (1460) and Trebizond (1461), and attacked Negroponte (1470). In 1480, the Turks took Otranto but evacuated it after Mohammed's death.

When Mohammed II attacked Constantinople in April 1453, the Eastern emperor Constantine XI did not have enough soldiers to man the city's walls. When the city fell on May 29, Mohammed immediately took possession of the cathedral of Hagia Sofia in the name of Islam. Then, strolling through the rooms of the imperial palace, he is said to have recited verses from a Persian poem: "The spider spins his web in Caesar's palace, / the owl hoots in hours from the towers of Afrāsiyāb." The sultan allowed his soldiers to sack the city for a few hours; the damage they did is said to have been less than that done by the crusaders in 1204. Below: Constantinople in an illumination from Voyage d'Outremer, by Bertrandon de la Broquière, a Frenchman who returned from a pilrimage to the Holy Land by way of Constantinople (1432–1433).

and May 1453, when the sultan laid siege to New Rome and then entered it as a conqueror, the West seemed to rouse itself from a deep sleep that had lasted much too long. And the first act after the awakening was to lay the blame: Genoese, Venetians, and Florentines set about accusing one another of having assisted the Turks. They were themselves engaged in the most intense exploitation of the Byzantine markets and thus felt most damaged by the Turkish conquest. They felt the urgent need, without being able to declare it, of coming to an agreement with the new ruler of the Bosphorus.

Christian princes hurled at one another the charge of cowardice and complicity with the infidels. For his part, Pope Nicholas V issued a bull on September 30, 1453, proclaiming a crusade against the sultan, who was seen as a precursor of the Anti-Christ, the Red Dragon of the Apocalypse.

For his part, Mohammed energetically exploited his success. Well aware that the West would have difficulty finding the unity necessary to move against him, he pursued his conquests, trying to enlarge his territory

177

The Turks besiege a Christian city in a miniature from a 15th-century Latin codex. The fall of Constantinople aroused great emotion but inadequate response. In Burgundy, Philip the Good held a banquet in Liège, and there knights made holy vows on live pheasants, appropriately adorned, to God, the Virgin, the saints, and the women they loved. This was the voeuz du faisan ("vow upon the pheasant"), an example of the chivalrous, proud, and boastful rituals that were in use at that time. Many such vows were made during the Hundred Years War. Knights swore to abstain from a certain food or drink, not to undress, to wear a hair-shirt, or to undergo some other privation until completing a gallant deed. In the voeux du faisan a knight swore not to touch food from animals on Fridays until wresting the banner from the Great Turk.

"Those damned Turkish dogs"

Count Gabriele Capodilista of Padua went by galley on a pilgrimage to the Holy Land in 1458, leaving, as was then the custom, from Venice. On June 11 he reached Rhodes and enjoyed a "wonderful dinner" at the table of the bishops. "And on that day we had news that a galley of crusaders and one from Rhodes had taken three small Turkish galleys and were due to arrive in a few days. The Turks were to be cut into pieces and then impaled following the custom of those knights of Rhodes because the Turks did the same and much worse to them."

In 1480, the Milanese Santo Brasca, a Sforza official, made the same voyage, stopping at Rhodes on the return trip, where a Turkish siege had recently failed. His visit to the battlefield and the description he was given of the furious combat, the outcome of which had been much in doubt, seemed to the traveler emotions not to be missed, and he shared them with his readers: "I went to see the destruction that those damned Turkish dogs had done to that poor city, from the tower of San Nicolo to the sea, where at first those pigs had tried to destroy the tower, damaging it in many places and also the houses and churches all around it with their big bombards." The Turks had then assaulted a breach opened in the walls by their artillery, "and the Rhodians, numbering about six hundred, having repaired the break in the wall with casks and bundles, came forward in a procession with a crucifix, believing that they would that day loose the field and die; and when the Turks came to the walls they stabbed them and killed so many that the dead bodies formed stairs for the others to climb to the walls, but as soon as they climbed up they were pushed back by the Rhodians, but they attacked again and did so six times, each time being pushed back. Thus, one can say that that land was lost and retaken many times that day and that it was God who defended it, not the mind or force of men. About two hundred of the Rhodians were killed, and of the Turks about twelve thousand." Santo Brasca saw the bodies in a lagoon, "piled one atop the other like eels in a barrel."

before the Christian princes could succeed in reaching an agreement and form an effective counterstrategy. In the spring of 1455, he attacked Rhodes, effectively defended by the Knights Hospitalers of Saint John. The following November he occupied New Phocaea, an important center for the production of alum, used in the textile industry. By June he had conquererd part of Serbia, including the silver mines of Novo Brdo, and from there he moved up the Balkans toward Belgrade, the key to Hungary and the upper Danube. The task of organizing Christian resistance to the Turkish onslaught fell to the elderly regent of Hungary, John Hunyadi, and an aging brother of the Franciscan Observants, John of Capistrano. In July of 1456, Mohammed II was forced to lift the siege of Belgrade, and that event coincided with the last great explosion of crusader enthusiasm in medieval Christianity.

Riding the wave of that enthusiasm, Pope Pius II tried to organize a great expedition against the infidels. Though practical support never materialized, the humanist pontiff deserves credit not as the leader of an improbable crusade but for having argued the theory that the Turks were in some way connected with the Trojans (an opinion that had circulated since the Middle Ages): The danger they constituted, therefore, should be interpreted as Asia's umpteenth attack on Europe, the last of a series that began with the 5th-century Persian wars against the Greeks. His policy reveals an interesting shift of the crusade ideology from an exclusively or at least principally religious view to one that could be called geopolitical. It was the beginning of the secularization of the confrontation between Christians and Muslims, a redefinition of the relationship between Europeans and Asians. It also laid the foundation for a new political age that would distance the concept of "Christianity" from that of "Europe."

We have noted that Pius II's polemical-

179

Devils leaving the possessed (they visibly depart the small figures standing at the sides of the church) during a sermon by John of Capistrano (painting by Sebastiano di Cola da Casentino). This celebrated Franciscan is a revealing character: Already well known as a jurist and involved in court politics, he became a monk after having been made a prisoner by Malatesta. By the middle of the century he had a rising career in the order (he worked hard as an inquisitor against the Jews). Nicholas V sent him across the Alps to oppose the Hussites and preach to the Turks. Three years after the fall of Constantinople in 1453, when a Christian army led by John Hunyadi defeated an army of Turks that was greatly superior in number at Belgrade, John of Capistrano commanded the left wing of the ranks.

rhetorical "Letter to Mohammed" can be
interpretated not as a threat to the sultan
but as a reprimand to the Western princes
guilty of being both unwilling and unable to
confront the infidels. The crusade continued
to rule, at least in theory, the themes and
diplomacy of European courts and was
used at the popular level by many preachers,
most of all the Franciscans. Renewed fear-
fulness followed in 1477–1480, when Turkish forays against the Venetians in the
Balkans, the Aegean, and the Adriatic
brought the Turks' half-moon banner as far
as Friuli, Carniola, and Puglia. In that year,
the humanist Anio da Viterbo preached on
the subject of the imminent Apocalpyse,
surely occasioned by the Turk, the Anti-
Christ, and the astrological prophecies of
the *magnus annus* awaited in 1484.

When the great sultan died in 1481, the
Turkish peril seemed to have passed. With

apparent sincerity, Charles VIII of France
still talked of a crusade, but in 1494 he
invaded, instead, the Kingdom of Naples.
The subject of a crusade had been one of the
arguments proposed to the Catholic kings
by Christopher Columbus while trying to
convince them to finance his transoceanic
undertaking; his cause was not just a rhetorical argument but a plea consistent with
great seriousness and profound conviction.
But the era of united action by the Christian
West against the Muslims had passed.

For many years, the abstract idea of a crusade had guided, at least in theory, the moral and political decisions of the ruling classes; irrefutable and even unquestionable in principle, by this time the concept had become, in practice, only a pretext for sterile rhetorical argument. The simple fact was that the European economy needed access to the Levant and the Black Sea, and the Turks, though infidels, were happy to provide that access to Christian merchants.

The sultan Bayazid, successor to Mohammed II, was in constant contact with the Papal Curia: Among other things, Rome did him the favor of holding hostage his brother Djem, who had contended with him for the throna. Bayazid was well aware that the leaders of the Christian nations were quite vocal about their crusading duties, although, in reality, they were willing to accept or even to solicit the friendship of the

Above left: A Turkish prince held prisoner on a galley of the Knights of Saint John. This is Djem (or Zyzymy, as his name is given on the miniature), who failed in an attempt to take the throne from his brother, Bayazid, and fled to Rhodes (1482), having received promises of help from the grand master of the knights. The grand master, however, sent him off to France as a prisoner, receiving in exchange peace and 45,000 *ducats from the sultan. Djem was then held prisoner in Rome (1489–1492), and he died at Naples, where the French king Charles VIII had brought him. Above right: Turkish costumes from the* Preaching of Saint Mark, *by Gentile and Giovanni Bellini. After a peace treaty was signed with Venice in 1479, Gentile Bellini was sent to the court of Constantinople, where he painted a portrait of Mohammed II.*

182

infidels under the table: Christian sovereigns, Bayazid quietly explained to his collaborators, incited one another to battle the Ottomans, but in truth they sought allies for making war among themselves.

There were other cracks in the facade of a united Christendom that was presented to the Turks. Until the 12th century, the crusades had occasionally given rise to criticism from contrary voices — from mystics, the occasional, less-aligned thinkers, the merchants. The same year that Constantinople fell, Nicolas of Cusa drew up one of his most fascinating works, the *De pace fidei*, a hymn of love to the God who speaks to all peoples and a song of praise for everyone who, each in his own language and according to his own traditions, adores God. A pacifist Christian, vigorously relying on prophetic scriptures and the pentecostal message, he agreed with the critics of a corrupt Christianity that before taking up arms against the infidel it would be better to restore the Church to the true path of the Gospel.

Girolamo Savonarola insisted on the uselessness of victories against the Turks when the structure of the Church was collapsing from within. And Erasmus, for whom war against the Turks was always preferable to fratricidal war among Christians, placed crusades and pilgrimages among the great follies of mankind and bitterly reflected that many Christians behaved worse than Muslims. It would be better for them to truly love one another in fraternity, he said, than to constantly invoke the unity of their arms against the infidels.

These pacific, conciliatory attitudes were symptoms of a highly complex reality, full of agitation and contradiction. They hid conflicting impulses and grave dangers and, what is more, they had much more dramatic consequences on the western world than any crusade would have had. One of the strongest arguments of those who held that a war against the Turks was futile, if

not contrary to the fundamentals of the Gospel, was that it was neither useful nor wise to look for battle elsewhere, against external enemies, when Christianity itself was home to many adversaries. The leitmotif "worse than the Saracens" continually circulated in the political and religious propaganda of the time. And, more than a hyperbolic slogan, it served as the rationale for a harsh program of persecution.

Fifteenth-century Europe eagerly sought out internal enemies; and there were many, battle-ready, in guilty league with the devil. Unlike the Turks, they did not threaten the borders but corroded from within. In the past, such enemies had been identified most of all in heretical groups, which had been defeated or isolated. A new internal enemy had been found in the wizards and witches, as we have seen. During epidemics, some found their scapegoats in the chronically ill, those exiled from society and believed to be evil and envious of the health of others: Lepers, for example, who carried on their bodies the stigmata of divine punishment for sins, were blamed for having poisoned wells to spread the contagion.

But the increasingly urban society of the 15th century—which had lost the characteristics, if not of the truly nomadic life, of that mobility typical of the medieval world and that had by then become a fundamentally fixed society — began to display certain characteristics of a collective mentality — above all, a distrust for the "Other," the "Different," those on the fringes of society. Something of this can be seen in the treatment of foreigners and pilgrims, who had been more or less welcomed or at least easily tolerated in medieval cities but were now looked upon malevolently and with curious suspicion. (This process had begun earlier: It is enough to remember the many hagiographic legends in which the devil appears disguised as a traveler or pilgrim.)

The 15th century was obsessed with the

Opposite: Page from the Arba'ah Thurim *("the four orders"), rules of life by Jacob ben Asher. This codex was written at Mantua in 1436, and the few splendid illuminations that decorate it are by a Lombard artist. This illustration represents marriage, and the two words in capitals signify "It is not good," a quotation from Genesis ("It is not good that man should be alone; I will make him an help meet for him"). The scene shows the*

*first phase of the marriage ceremony (*qiddushim, *or consecration): In front of witnesses, the groom puts a ring on the right index finger of his bride, pronouncing the words by which he declares her his wife. The ceremony is to take place in a synagogue or in the home of the bride and is celebrated by a rabbi or another person in authority, such as the bride's father.*

לֹא טוֹב

בראשית בר בן מיוכבד הלוי וה גדול ובנני ד שטוטרל
אב [ ] ו לאליישמיס וחדי פירות ובעים הבן לי יושמ
כ סמ כלל וישת דיליד רתו הש ומל מ וו לי יוצתר ומד כ
וה וכל שלו מיתרן ולרהמ נקר ישו רומ מכו היופנר ל הייתי
שפ ו ול ע הל לי לה טובג וני רומ וכיב גד פומן ורו וק
לשטר ל ומ ירו שומ מ ברב וביתו רבמ ביהי כד טוי אימ
ל רתוה פוו אש ויני וינו יורי רמ פותר בטטה בל לשון
הלו שטל מול מבט ואקמ בהוו והדו יי מתורר שקזל
מטר שה ירומר בהורתה וכרכשה ובתורה טורר להרר
והמטמ המלי קמ מטור רן הריטווט בש שוטי ורתמ ברל
בי יהירך מלינו נרס בתורה תרי בן שן שוטי ורחמ ברל
פורה מיל כרה שלהולרמו מל מר וקטר ל להות
מיה מורתר יתמ ורויין ישל ו לותכר ל הטוך לקתל
וני ויומ ומ יתר מ ירל מרר ושקר וטרל אשמ ללי
רו יכין רלו מרה ולרהם ורה וילרר רל רמתר בהכ
וט מ רלת ורו ת מ בוה רי וברלה רלה בטים הכמים
ולך ובט רו טר הוה שמו

 היתה המוכלך בן ומיוחי ל ועור נכבר ובשבן ומוי
כל הבל פרוח מה וך ומכטר גרל אמרל מן כי מפיתהם
לנורם שנורחה לחורו מל מן ינבו לו וכר ב בכטר ורטר כ
כנר הכרתימוב בהור וערכה לריבמ וחך מרי מוידהוחל
פריתמ ולט בר שוכמ ל רמי מכבליר לך הרינהם
מרת ויכך ארי ורברו ומ למכר מכליום שמנומו נטחמ
שומר ורה בל דל רומים וניר ולן ומוסי חרל חשהרל ב
שחבל ושיני אשר ווך הוריד מור מ וריל קריו רבמ וחמל
וישכ פמ וברו בטל ו בשונ ורה חך ל בשומ הרל ולויב
רב בב יהר ורמ בהיתור אלור וחר מפל הרז פרל כל מ
ומ יכין שומו מיטם כטוכה חמפטלק רר מק מתה ולמן
מטר ע קרלהיט ופ ירתתר ברכטלוחה רחל מלי וחרק
לרין פל ל רי מר ולמיר וחז ים חלינור בל ורמ לא רחרל
למוכ מילו שמ רכובה לחני בטרה ורן כיר שלו חל בשומ
הכמרך הרומ רבטם ומון היר פ מהטלתי ליל ול ה בל
ישר ול רם רמ מיר ווריל רוליל מ רומל ומ ויחרל וריר

"enemy within," who could be readily identified.

Most easily recognized was the Jew. Although the category of ideological and pseudoscientific antisemitism was not born until the 19th century, preindustrial Europe had without doubt known antisemitism, partly due to religious prejudices, partly explainable in the light of various social circumstances. There were already strong signs of this antisemitism in the Roman world and the High Middle Ages — the writings of the early Christian fathers are not without their *contra Judaeos* volumes; however, this attitude showed signs of increasing gravity beginning with the first crusade and became worse during the course of the 12th and 13th centuries.

The Jews, often referred to hatefully as "god-killers," were already disliked for their wealth. Many of them practiced — usually with great scrupulousness — the career of banker and thus, in the mentality of the time, were usurers (though their rates of interest were generally lower than those asked by their Christian colleagues). The Jews were accused of having poisoned wells during the various epidemics, and they were sometimes blamed outright for the pestilence. They were said to have profaned sacred images from which blood often miraculously squirted. They acquired from unfortunate women consecrated hosts for the sacrilegious pleasure of using them in every kind of wickedness, confirming their role as the crucifiers of Christ and defying the reality and holiness of the transubstantiation. (In a painting by Paolo Uccello, Jews are shown being burned at the stake for having profaned the host.) Their sacrilegious fury drove the Jews even to terrible murderous parodies of the Easter sacrifice: They were said to abduct Christian babies and, after having horribly tormented them, kill them and use their blood to make the unleavened Easter bread.

Despite the clear absurdity of this infamous tale of the "ritual murder," it was spread throughout Europe. The first case of the kind was registered at Norwich, England, in 1144; from then on it is difficult to say how many unresolved crimes, how many cruelly murdered babies, how many accidental deaths of innocents were regularly blamed on the Jewish community. During later medieval times, the Jews played a role surprisingly similar to that of the witches and lepers: The accusations directed against them had been directed against the other two groups as well.

Neither the Church nor temporal authorities lent an ear to these slanders — for one thing, the Jewish bankers were too useful for both groups. The Holy Roman emperors, in particular, were generous with signs of respect and protection for the Jewish communities, as was the Holy See. But the

184

pressure from those interested in destroying the power of the Jews increased with the growth of European malaise, and it finally joined in a cruel unity of popular "voices." As early as the fourth ecumenical Lateran council in 1215, it had been established that the goats should not mix unpunished with the sheep. Jews were ordered to wear in full view on their clothing a badge, or *rota* — that is, a small disk made of yellow cloth. In that period, and in the mentality of that time, wearing a sign of one's station was not unusual: knights, doctors, and pilgrims were marked as well. The yellow *rota* (yellow was an infamous color used for fools, lepers, and prostitutes) was, however, a badge of discrimination to be compared to the sign ordained by God in Genesis after the fratricide of Cain.

From this beginning, the situation of

Both Christian and Islamic creeds forbade usury, one of the reasons money-lending became a chief occupation of the Jews in Europe; they were also encouraged in this by the authorities. This engraving from Ship of Fools *reflects popular resentment toward Jewish usurers. The text adds though that their Christian counterparts equalled them in every way.*

the Jews got only worse, a result also of the social tension — noticeable in the mass psychology of the time — typical of the 14th to 15th centuries. The popular preachers of the Franciscan and Dominican Observance spread antisemitic feelings, frequently using them as a starting point for institution of special organizations to give credit to the most humble classes — the Monti di Pietà (pawnbrokers) — and thus tear them from the "influence" of the Jewish usurers. In 1475, at Trent, a great furor exploded following the sermon of the Franciscan Bernardine of Feltre: The Jews were accused of having killed, on Holy Saturday, a baby named Simon and were driven from the city. (The cult of "San Simonino of Trent" lasted, without any true ecclesiastical sanction, until 1965.)

In Milan in 1488, a lawsuit was begun against certain members of the large local Jewish community, charging them with having books containing injurious judgments against Christianity. Among the members of the commission assembled to judge the case was the Franciscan Bernardino de Bustis, cochampion of the Monti di Pietà. The Jews had already been expelled from France as early as 1394 and from England in 1290; they were expelled from Spain in 1492. In Germany, the hatred of Jews grew — as is shown by the celebrated *Narrenschiff* (*Ship of Fools*), by Sebastian Brant — and led to the notorious *Judenspiegel* (*Jewish mirror*), by the converted Jew John Pfefferkorn, and the pamphlet *The Jews and their lies*, by Martin Luther. Even in Florence, urged on by the preaching of Savonarola, another organizer of the Monti di Pietà, a Jew was lynched who had, it was said, dared

The "men," as they defined themselves in their original language, or the gypsies, spread across Europe in the 15th century from the Balkans. This may have been due to the advance of the Turks or it may simply have been a continuation of a nomadic tradition. (The name gypsy is simply a shortening of Egyptian, where they were believed to have come from.) Having left India, they settled for a time in Greece and Asia Minor.

Below and opposite right: These two small canvases are by Bernardo Parentino, who worked mainly in Padua. They can be dated to around the end of the century. They show traveling players, probably gypsies, in Oriental costume, accompanied by dogs and monkeys. In the painting below, a keg, probably containing wine, is kept cool in the basin of a fountain that was originally a sarcophagus.

profane the beloved image of the Madonna of Orsanmichele.

Meanwhile, however, other "different" peoples were facing the xenophobia of Europe. It was not merely the Jews, who were so little "different" that it was necessary to make them wear special badges to distinguish them; nor was it only the Tartars, the Russians, the Circassians, or the Slavs (from whom is derived the word *slave*), who were frequently used as household servants, particularly in Italian cities. They were all without doubt "different" and were therefore accused of theft or enchantment, but they were still somehow familiar. It was possible that they might become integrated into society, and all might be subordinated.

The new targets of wrath were the gypsies, who called themselves *Rom* ("men"), a group of nomads originally from India. Their language was a western Indo-European, and at first they were called *Romani*, perhaps because of the homophony of this term with the word *Rom*.

186

"Head of Negroes"

The commerce in black slaves carried on by Arabs and Portuguese on the Atlantic coasts of Africa was described in detail in an account by the Venetian Alvise da Cadamosto. This merchant, born into a noble family, entered into relations with the circle of the infante Henry (the Navigator) in the port of Cape Saint Vincent (Portugal) during a commercial voyage to Flanders, and in the service of the Portuguese prince he made two voyages of exploration (1455 and 1456).

"And the aforementioned infante has made this island of Argin [Agruin, in the gulf protected by the peninsula of Cap Blanc, Mauritania] a monopoly for ten years and in this way no one can enter the gulf to trade with the Arabs except those with a contract, and they have homes on this island and administrators who buy and sell with the Arabs who come to the shore to buy various things, such as clothes, fabrics, silver, and *alchizels*, that is, coats, rugs, and other things, but most of all wheat, for they have a terrible hunger. And these Arabs give in exchange head of Negroes, which they take from the lands of the Negroes, and pure gold. The infante has made a fortress of this island to protect this traffic forever, and all year Portuguese caravels come and go to this island. These Arabs also have many wild horses, with which they trade, and they take them to the land of the Negroes and sell them to the leaders, who give them in exchange head of slaves; and they sell these horses for from ten to fifteen head each, according to their value. Likewise, they take there items of Moorish silk, made in Granada and Tunis and Barbary, and silver and many other things; and in exchange for these they get more head and a certain sum of gold. These slaves are taken to the port and then to Hoden, and there they are divided up, and part go to the mountains of Barcha and from there to Sicily, and part go to Tunis, and part go to the Barbary coasts; and another part go to Argin to be sold to the Portuguese, and in this way every year seven or eight hundred leave Argin for Portugal."

Above: Head of a Negro, a charcoal drawing by Albrecht Dürer. For the entire period of the Middle Ages, Negro slaves—though not all slaves were black—came principally from the markets of Alexandria and Damietta, Tunis, and Tripoli, where caravans of Arab merchants arrived after crossing the desert. During the second half of the century, the Portuguese brought them directly from the Atlantic coasts of Africa.

Furthermore, *Romani* referred to the Greek Byzantines, and *Rum*, for the Arabs, was the empire of the *Nea Roma*, or Constantinople. After the gypsies had been pushed from India across Persia, Armenia, and Asia Minor, they halted for a long time in Greece and the Balkans. There, from an area called "Little Egypt," they acquired the name "Egyptians," which would accompany them henceforth and linger in such terms as *zingaro*, *gitane*, *gitano*, *zigeuner*, and *gypsy*, all of which are still used in Europe and elsewhere. Voltaire, in the 18th century, believed them to be Egyptians, none other than descendants of the priests of Isis.

Early in the 15th century, groups of gypsies, driven from the Balkans by the advance of the Turks, and, perhaps, by the rhythms of their own nomadic life, arrived in Hungary, Germany, and Switzerland. They moved on to Burgundy, where their appearance was noted in 1419, and then to Paris, where they arrived in 1427. It was said that they were from Bohemia; the word

bohémien has remained as the French for "gypsy." Meanwhile, they had also established themselves in Italy and moved into southern France and then to Spain, where the word spread that they had come — like the blacks — from northern Africa. At the same time, they crossed Hungary and Romania and reached Poland and Russia. In the 14th century, they had already been made slaves in Romania. Ragged and picturesque, feared and disliked, the gypsies dragged along with their wagons their reputation as prophets, tinkers, metalworkers, fortune tellers, wizards, and thieves of horses and children.

Like the Jews marked with the *rota*, the prostitutes and fools with their infamous badges, the lepers announced by the sinister sound of their bells, the pilgrims with their capes covered with seashells, palms, crosses, or other symbols, other irregulars crowded the European cities of the 15th century: wandering actors, vagabonds, beggars, charlatan hawkers of miraculous salves. To gain

187

Here the Moor appears in a Venetian context in one of the large canvases of the school of San Giovanni Evangelista, the Miracle of the Cross at the Bridge of San Lorenzo. *The painting depicts the recovery of a relic of the True Cross that fell into a canal during a procession (an event said to have taken place during the late 14th century). Even the Moor seems to want to dive into the water to recover the sacred object.*

Below: Preachers filled the squares; they alone knew the topics and words that reached the people. Savonarola: "In order to make chalices, our prelates take from the poor people that which they need just to live. You know what I have to say about that? In the original church, the chalices were of wood and the prelates of gold; today, the church has wooden prelates and golden chalices." Bernardine of Siena knew the value of his preaching technique: "When I go about preaching from place to place, when I arrive in a place I contrive to always speak in their words." Shown here is a sermon by Vincent Ferrer, a Spanish Dominican (painted by Bartolomeo degli Erri, 1467–1477). Another of the popular preachers, he began in 1399 after a mystical vision and continued until his death in 1419; he was canonized in 1455.

hospices were abolished or transformed, precisely because of their inability to respond to the new needs or to contain the problems brought about by these crowds of indigents. Hospitals would soon be seen as places for the ill; and madhouses, reformatories, penal institutions, barracks, or hospices would contain the old and mutilated. The practice had begun of putting into ghettos all those who, for one reason or another, modern society wished not to see wandering the streets. Enforced confinement had become the order of the day.

But the paradox of the 15th century and early 16th century lies in the fact that the anxieties and fears that were the cause of the growing intolerance towards the marginal members of society were, in part, caused by these marginal persons themselves, and not merely because of their social behavior. Traveling among the vagabonds, storytellers, and charlatans were the prognosticators of alarm and redemption, those who performed the "revelations," the "prophecies." Their predictions could be found in tracts like "Saint Brigida" (twelve editions were printed from around 1478 to 1525), the psuedo-Joachimite *Vaticinia pontificum*, the *Diluvio di Roma del MCCCLXXXXV*, by the Florentine Giuliano Dati, the *Iuditio sopra tutta la Italia* (*Judgment of all Italy*), by the storyteller Notturno Napoletano. These were works of varying quality and of diverse provenance, but all were characterized by a popular diffusion in print or even in manuscript, accompanied by a rapid and feverish circulation through the city squares, where they were read, commented upon, and summarized. The arrival of the Turks, plagues, famines, floods, as well as profound revivals and great final acts of justice were foretold (sometimes after the fact), often in the form of gossip. Together with the preachers, these soothsayers constituted the great mass media of the Middle Ages and sent up a voice that was difficult to ignore.

pity from passersby, many unfortunates displayed their amputated limbs, the result most often not of congenital malformations or accidents but of corporal punishments — following the cruel habits of the time — for various crimes. Former soldiers left as invalids on the roadways and without means of subsistence round out our by-no-means-complete catalogue of the penniless.

This rabble of the down-and-out invaded squares, streets, and the halls of churches and sanctuaries. They brought disorder and infective diseases. According to circumstances, they could transform themselves into a wailing and insolent crowd appealing to the generosity of a wealthy man, or into a more or less manageable mass to be manipulated during riots. City authorities gave them humble and repugnant chores; in other cases they merely expelled them without remark.

The marginal, aimless, homeless person was no longer accepted in an increasingly fixed society. In a short time, the medieval

Opposite: The fears of the age led to prophetic rumors, and printing fanned the flames of the deepest anxieties. Detail from Daughters of Lot, by an anonymous Flemish painter (16th century). "And the Lord rained upon Sodom and upon Gomorrah brimstone and fire from the sky, and he overthrew those cities and all the plain, and all the inhabitants of the cities, and that which grew on the ground" (Gen. 19:24-25).

The Color of
the Ocean

The ocean is finally crossed. Opposite: A detail
from a ship's log, 1561. The number of ships that
left Spain for America in the first half of the 16th
century, even just for a few years, is significant:
22 in 1506, 33 in 1512, 60 in 1533, 86 in 1542, and
101 in 1549. Above: A xylograph from an edition
printed in the first years of the 16th century of
the Mundus novus, by Amerigo Vespucci.

Spices and sails

When they closed their eyes, the people of Christopher Columbus's age dreamed of the Terrestrial Paradise. It existed, isolated and inaccessible, in some part of the Orient or Africa — which in their minds were connected geographically (Ethiopia was then called *India maior*). High walls of crystal, diamonds, or fire enclosed it, and sometimes a horseman following the tracks of Alexander the Great succeeded in making out its splendor in the distance. All the great rivers of the world had their source in that Terrestrial Paradise: the Nile, Ganges, Tigris, and Euphrates. Over the springs of these rivers hung the branches of precious plants and wonderful trees: balsam and cinnamon, myrrh, cardamom, and benzoin. Miraculous leaves and marvelous berries fell into those waters and were carried towards the lands inhabited by men who had lost Paradise.

Jean de Joinville, marshal of France's Louis IX and his companion in arms during the unfortunate crusade in Egypt (1249), explained in this way the influx of spices to the markets, such as Alexandria and Damietta, at the mouth of the Nile. Whether he actually believed this cannot be known. Without doubt, however, the merchants — Arab, Pisan, Venetian, Genoese, Provençal,

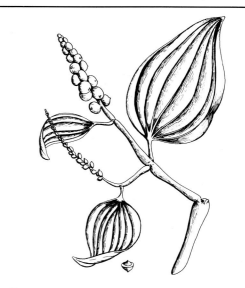

Pepper

"In the territory of Calicut (southern India) there are many pepper trees," wrote the Bolognese Lodovico de Varthema, who traveled adventurously during the first decade of the 16th century. The pepper tree "by itself cannot stand upright, just like a vine . . . and is treated like ivy and grasps and climbs as high on the wood or tree as it can cling." It has many branches, each with "five, six, or seven clusters a bit longer than a man's finger" with fruit like "small raisins, but drier, and they are as green as unripened grapes. During the month of October they are gathered when they are still so green, and gathered again in the month of November, and then they are exposed to the sun atop certain reed mats and left in the sun for three or four days, and become as black as they are when they arrive here." The immature and dried fruit of *Piper nigrum* gives black pepper; the same fruit, mature and without its pericarp, gives white pepper. The consumption of pepper seems to have increased in Europe up to the 16th century, when it declined until the middle of the next century. The profits from the importers, always high, grew even higher with the arrival of the Portuguese in the production areas. According to a Venetian ambassador, the prices at the piazza of Lisbon during the first years of the 16th century were seven times higher than they had originally been.

A spice-seller's shop in the 14th-century frescoes at Issogne castle (in the Valle d'Aosta, Italy). The Venetian monopoly of the European spice trade was on the verge of ending. Duarte Barbosa (companion of Magellan and author of one of the first descriptions of the Indian Ocean known to the Portuguese) wrote (1517–1518) that at Suez "the Moors of the seaport of Zidem [Mecca] transport all the spices, herbs, and precious stones, pearls, ambergris, and other costly merchandize from the Indies. From there they are loaded onto camels and brought to Cairo overland, and at Cairo other merchants bring them to Alexandria, where they are taken away by Venetians and other Christians. This traffic has now ceased, mostly due to the Portuguese, who use their fleet to prevent the Moors from sailing the Red Sea."

The harvest of pepper in a miniature from the Livre des Merveilles ("Book of Wonders"), based on the writings of Marco Polo. Curiosity concerning exotic herbs was intense. John Mandeville, the rather doubtful English traveler, wrote of the coast of Malabar: "In that country pepper grows in a forest known as Combar. It grows in no other part of the world. . . . I have been told that during the pepper harvest they light bonfires and fires in the area to keep away snakes and crocodiles. But pay no heed to those that tell you this. If they really lit fires around the trees, the pepper would burn as well, and all its virtues would dry up along with all other things. . . . In actual fact the natives smear their hands and feet with a paste made of snails and suchlike things that has a smell the snakes and poisonous animals detest."

and Catalan — who crowded the Egyptian docks were well aware that, in truth, those precious commodities were transported by river from the upper Nile after being unloaded on the African shores of the Indian Ocean. Even so, the legends asserting that these goods — essential for medicine, gastronomy, the preservation of food, the manufacture of textiles, and many other uses — came from a Paradise have a great deal to say about the importance they had in the medieval imagination, an importance that corresponded to their economic and commercial roles.

Even Columbus, on his voyage towards what he believed to be Asia, dreamed of plantations of incense and forests of pepper trees. But by then, Europe already desired other kinds of merchandise, perhaps less fragrant, that called for ships with larger holds. During the preceding decades, a few sacks of spices had been enough to warrant such a voyage and even to make a good profit, but by the time of Columbus's trip, the far-reaching markets and various activities being developed called for bulkier and

simpler merchandise, less precious but more essential: grain and wine, primarily, then sea salt, cloth, dyes, and sugar (used more in medicine than cooking, for which honey was less rare and less costly).

The Hanseatic League brought Baltic and Polish grain to western and southern Europe and imported from Saintogne and Portugal the salt it used to carry on, at an almost "industrial" level, the manufacture of salted herring in barrels. By land, sea, and river, wine traveled from the Mediterranean, the Rhone, and the Rhine to northern Europe (which did not affect the consumption of locally brewed beer, which was also increasing). Wool and fine-quality textiles at good prices came from England, with its manufacturing centers at London, Bristol, and Southampton. In central Europe, these goods competed with the cloth   193

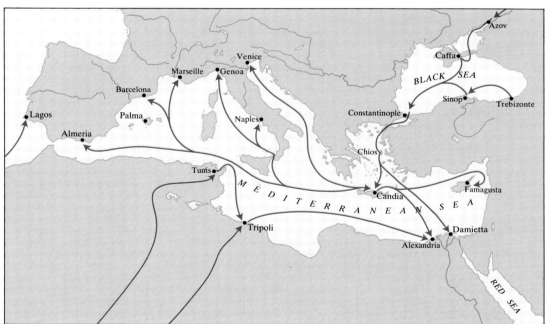

The route taken by the slave trade in the Mediterranean in the 14th and 15th centuries. Slav, Tartar, and Caucasian slaves from Tana were sent toward Egypt; black Africans arrived from the Maghreb coasts. By the second half of the 15th century, Portuguese vessels were carrying on a flourishing slave trade. A popular saying of the time held that a voyage to the lands of the blacks was the best cure for poverty.

from Flanders and Brabant and reached as
far as Russia. In 15th-century Florence,
cloth that was most costly but of a very
different quality was made with Castilian
wool from the celebrated merino sheep,
which had begun to reach the Mediterranean
by way of Bruges, in Belgium. Among the
coloring materials most in demand, with
the valuable brazilwood and cochineal from
the Orient, were saffron from France and
the Abruzzi, as well as Catalonia, and woad
or pastel (which gave cloth a not very
intense blue color and was widespread because inexpensive) produced in Picardy,
Normandy, Tuscany, and later also in Languedoc.

The Turkish conquest of Constantinople in 1453 dealt a fierce blow to European
commerce with the eastern and Egyptian
coasts of the Mediterranean. The Genoese
and Venetians immediately tried to reestab-
lish the trade, which proved difficult. Venice
had to continue its importation of spices
and Chinese silk through the Moslems at
excessive prices. For their part, the Genoese,
no longer able to exploit their bases in the
Black Sea, tried for some time — until 1458
— to purchase their raw materials in Asia
Minor. They concentrated, on the Aegean
island of Chios, their stores of alum, indigo,
lacquers, wine, timber, and above all Turkish cotton, which they then exported to
Lombardy, where it was used in competition
with the Syrian and Egyptian cotton pro-
cured by Venice.

The Ottomans had no intention of
blocking imports to the west, but they
imposed on European merchants their conditions, which meant a general increase in
prices. Genoese, Neapolitans, and Catalans
were forced to restrict themselves to the
development of their business prospects in
the western part of the Mediterranean. Sub-
stitutes were found for goods that were no
longer available from the Orient or were too
expensive: sugar from Granada, Algarve,
and Sicily; silk from Granada, Valencia,

Perhaps because he painted in a sea town—
Venice—and for a public acquainted with marine
paintings, Vittore Carpaccio's paintings of ships
always have a striking realism. Here below is a
detail from one of the large canvases of the
Legend of Saint Ursula. Six ships are represented
with a great wealth of detail. To the right, a ship
has been "keeled over"—that is, placed on its side
for a periodic cleaning.

The anchor

One could imagine navigating without an
anchor, but one could not "arrive" without
an anchor. Even in the ports — by the
15th century almost always supplied with
piers and wharves — ships anchored and
even more so in the unknown waters of
exploration. With the vicissitudes of
navigation, anchors got lost, so at least
four were usually kept on board. Even so,
Columbus once found himself with only
one anchor for two ships. Fifteenth-
century anchors are no longer in use, but
the so-called admiralty anchor — the
surest, capable of holding on any bottom
to which an anchor might hold — is their
direct descendant. These were made of a
strong iron bar (the shank) with a hole at
one end through which passed the anchor
ring, to which was tied a hemp rope (iron
chains were later used). At the other end
of the shank were spread, from a diamond
point, two curved extensions, at the ends
of which were the flukes. On the side of
the shank was fixed the stock, a strong
beam of wood made of two parallel pieces
(through which the rope passed), bound
together with rope. If one looks down on
one of these anchors, suspended by its
shank, the flukes and the stock can be seen
to form a cross. Thanks to this
arrangement, no matter how the anchor
arrived on the bottom, pulling on the rope
would allow the flukes to settle in and take
hold.

196

Sicily, and Calabria; alum from central
Italy; wine, cochineal, and wax from Liguria
and Naples. Aside from obliging them to
produce certain goods themselves, the loss
of the Oriental markets led the Europeans
to wonder whether India, distant homeland
of spices, might not be reached more directly, thus avoiding the difficulties of traffick-
ing with the Moslems.

The increasingly frequent shipment of
large, heavy, and bulky goods led to the
design of larger and heavier ships. The
members of the Hanseatic League and the
merchants of northwestern Europe, obliged
to confront the climate of the Atlantic, were
forced to use ships that were particularly

*In another painting by Carpaccio, a galley that
has entered a port is lowering its sails. The galley
was quicker in navigating the Mediterranean
than rounder vessels of Atlantic origin, most of
all because it could use its oars in times of calm,
though navigation by sail was preferable,
particularly with carrying winds. Gabriele
Capodilista, a pilgrim who traveled by galley to
the Holy Land, recalled the arrival of a favorable
wind: "Up to that time we had had no wind
astern, and everyone leapt with joy and
jubilation, not only the pilgrims but also the
seamen, who in celebration" climbed up the
rigging and "standing on each other's shoulders
even touched the foresails."*

heavy and strong. Thus came into use, as early as the 14th century, the cog, a large, rounded ship originally build in Flanders and capable of hauling tonnage of over 300 barrels (one "barrel," a unit of measurement for tonnage, was equal to about 900 liters). These ships could carry about three times the amount of cargo carried by the ships that worked the Mediterranean. Venice had meanwhile begun to replace the old galley (a narrow oared vessel most suited for war) with the merchant galley, which used sails and reached a tonnage of between 200 and 300 barrels. Following the example of the Hanseatic League, the Genoese and Venetians began to make increasing use of the carrack, which, during the final third of the 15th century, had reached a capacity of 1,000 barrels. During the second half of the century, the caravel came into use, a ship with three masts (the other ships had two) and smooth planking on its sides instead of overlapping planks; the tonnage of a caravel could reach 400 barrels, but its chief asset was speed.

The shipyards of the 15th century worked at full speed. In the maritime cities, these were the installations that most resembled modern "industries," with centralization of the various phases of production.

197

During the 19th century, Adam Smith, having analyzed transport by land and by sea, observed: "Six or eight men, with the help of a craft, can deliver and carry back in the same time the same quantity of goods between London and Edinburgh that can be carried by 50 large carts driven by 100 men and drawn by 411 horses." The historical importance of marine transport (and also the later predominance of the round ship over the galley, which also had a far greater crew) arises from considerations of this kind. Above: In this illustration from a French miniature in a 15th-century Roman de Troyes, a round ship prepares for sea. Once again, this is the ship of the Argonauts, from Greek myth. The crew and the shipwrights prepare the ship for sea while Hercules and Jason amuse themselves.

These shipyards employed large segments of the turbulent city "preproletariat" and made use of enormous quantities of timber. Venice imported its wood from the forests of the Dolomites by way of the Adige River; Pisa got its timber from the forests of the Appenines by way of the Arno; Genoa, because the surrounding mountains were without trees with large trunks, imported timber from Nice, Dauphiné (this wood was floated down the Rhone), Corsica, and even Turkey.

With technical changes, sea travel had become safer. Changes in sails, the use of the Catalan rudder, which was mounted on the sternpost (instead of the two side rudder oars), compasses, trigonometric tables, nautical charts, and pilot books had become important aids that allowed the beginnings of navigation across open seas, eliminating the need for constant visual contact with the

On making hawsers

Navigation required wood for ships, masts, yards, blocks, and the barrels in which to stow water and provisions; iron for nails and the pintles of the rudder; cloth for the sails; and pitch to make the ship watertight and protect it from the sea's salt. On January 14, 1493, shortly before beginning his return voyage, Columbus noted that his two surviving ships were taking on water because of the caulkers who "at Palos had done a poor job, and when they saw that the admiral was aware of their shoddy work" and wanted to ask what could be done about it, they disappeared. Also needed was hemp for making rope, standing rigging, running rigging, shrouds, stays, halyards, ties, sheets; ships were machines that ran on ropes.

Cable-laid rope is a wonderful human invention, made of yarns of plant fibers that join together when

twisted. Hemp was well suited to this because its fibers are long. A certain number of yarns are joined in strands; the yarns are twisted to form strands, and three or four strands twisted together make a rope. From stage to stage, the direction of the twisting is changed.

This drawing shows how rope was made in the Casa del Canevo or Corderie of the Tana annexed to the Venetian arsenal. It is taken from the precise "iconographic projections" with which Giovan Maria Maffioletti documented the state of the arsenal before and after its sack by the French at the fall of the republic. At the end of the 18th century, the same methods were still being used. The twisting of the yarns required long areas in which to work; the Venetian Casa del Canevo measured 300 meters. Visible are the support on which the three strands were twisted using winches, the little carriage that controls the advance of the twisting of the strands to form the rope, one of the supports that were located strategically to hold the rope as it formed, and the guide, weighted with stones, that held taut the system and from which the strands were twisted.

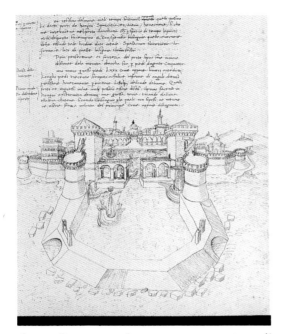

shore. It was no longer necessary to sail before the wind, and ships could navigate even under cloudy skies.

These technical advances offered little protection against privateers and pirates, which were numerous. In the Mediterranean, they ranged from the Catalans to the Genoese, from the Turks of Asia Minor to the Barbary pirates of Maghreb (to which city came the gold of the Sudan). In the Atlantic, Basques, Bretons, the English, and the Dutch preyed upon merchant vessels. In theory, while pirates were considered full-fledged outlaws, privateers operated under special authorization: Sovereigns issued letters of marque, which allowed the bearer to legitimately prey upon those ships flying a certain flag, in most cases the banner of a state with whom the sovereign was at war. In practice, however, these distinctions were difficult to implement. In 1495, a treaty between France and England sought to establish a minimum of clarity in this matter, but abuses and ambiguities continued and were destined to increase after the discovery of the new lands on the other side of the Atlantic.

A large proportion of the representations of ships and ports occur when depicting the subject of the Magi. They seem to underline the distant origins of the kings who made their homage to the Christ child and therefore the universal nature of the event. This city-port—in the Crucifixion *(1503), by the Milanese Andrea Solario—is therefore an exception. This port also seems to be imagined in an estuary, protected, of course,* *as many important European merchant ports were and would be also in the future: Bruges, for example (although it was overcome by sand in the 15th century), Antwerp (which replaced Bruges in importance), Pisa (which was to be succeeded as a port and landing place by Leghorn), Hamburg, Lisbon, Venice (which was later to have problems with its foundations), Seville, London, and Amsterdam.*

The Great Khan
or Prester John?

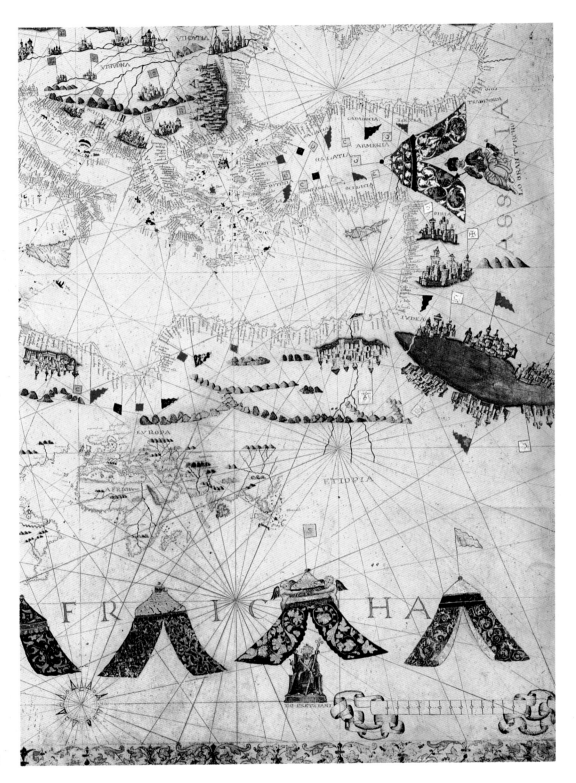

Between the 13th and 14th centuries, under the orderly if brutal peace imposed by the Mongol conquerors, Asia had seemed to open itself to western merchants and missionaries. The Silk Road, which ran from China to Constantinople and the ports of Asia Minor, was regularly traveled by caravans, and a Catholic archbishop had succeeded in setting himself up in Peking. Substantially reputable travelers, such as Marco Polo — as well as those more imaginary, such as John Mandeville — had succeeded in reaching areas south of the Silk Road and had visited (or claimed to have visited) the Indian peninsula. Certain Mongolian tribes were believed to be Nestorian Christians — Byzantine dissidents and followers of Nestorius, a 5th-century bishop of Constantinople — and during the second half of the 13th century attempts were made at diplomatic if not military alliances between westerners and Tartars, based on their common interests in attacking the Islamic powers (the first of these being the Mameluke emirate in Egypt). For a long time there was hope of an alliance with the masters of Asia that would have allowed a crusade strong enough to return Jerusalem to the Christian powers, and between the late 13th century and the 15th, the authors of theoretical treatises on the crusades considered — even if finally to refute it — the possibility of an alliance with the Tartars.

Such hopes had little basis in reality. As early as the middle of the 13th century, the empire of Ghengis Khan had been broken up into a series of independent realms, and a national revolt in the Chinese empire in 1368 had removed the Yuan dynasty from the throne of the Son of Heaven. It was replaced by the Mings, who brought with them a powerful xenophobia that considered — and not without reason — the western merchants and missionaries as supporters of the "barbarian" Mongols who had imposed their will on China. From then on, the empire was closed to western pene-

Under a tent trimmed with gold, "the preacher Iani" is depicted in this map of 1561 somewhere in the unknown regions of Africa. The merchant Girolamo Sernigi reported of the voyage of Vasco da Gama: "In that city [Calicut, India], they have had news, but not much, of Ianni the Priest by way of ships traveling to Mecca . . . it is very far from Calicut to the other side of the Arabian Gulf. It borders on the kingdom of Melinde and with the Ethiopians, or Negroes, and also with Egypt. . . . This priest called Ianni has a following of clergymen that make sacrifices and observe the Gospel and the decrees of the church as other Christians do; indeed, there is not much difference between the two." Opposite: The taste for the exotic. Cheetahs in a detail from The Procession of the Magi (1459), by Benozzo Gozzoli.

Even the sea was full of omens. Below: The shipwreck of a ship caused by a magnetic mountain pulling out its iron nails, from the Hortus sanitatis *(1491), an almanac from Mainz. The legend appears in the "Thousand and One Nights"; John Mandeville repeated it: "I saw in the distance something that appeared like a large island with many trees and bushes, shrubs and brambles. The seamen explained to us that they*

were all that remained of the ships attracted by the stones to calamity because of the iron contained in them."

Seville

Work on the cathedral went on from 1402 to 1498. It is located on the site of a mosque, of which remains the minaret, the Giralda, a square brick tower from the end of the 12th century. In 1568, its second shaft was replaced with a Renaissance crown. The city was surrounded by Roman walls restored by the Arabs. The narrow and tortuous streets opened into small squares and branched off into blind alleys. During the summer, following Islamic custom, curtains were hung across the streets to provide shade from the Andalusian sun. The homes enclosed square courtyards in which fountains gurgled and oranges ripened, overlooked by patios of Moorish design but derived from the Romans. The Gold Tower, last work of the Almohade dynasty, already rose over the profile of the city. Located on the left bank of the Guadalquivir, the Iberian and Roman city of *Hispalis* became the Arab *Ishbilyah* before becoming *Seville* (all these names being derived from a Phoenician word).

Ferdinand III of Castile entered Seville on November 23, 1248, but the city's great season began with the discovery of America. It benefited from its location at the mouth of the Guadalquivir at a point where the tide arrives (thus all the ships of the period could reach its port). It also benefited from having the ports of Palos and San Lucar de Barrameda. Many of the expeditions to the New World set off from those ports. Just as Seville depended on commerce with the Americas, the bishops on the other side of the ocean were suffragans (assistant bishops) to the church of Seville. During the period of Philip II, the city is believed to have arrived at a half million inhabitants. Beginning in 1509, the Casa de Contratacion of Seville was the only agency through which men and merchandise could travel to the "Indies." The principal reason for this monopoly was fiscal: The officials of the crown placed a tax, first of one-half the value and later reduced to one-fifth, on the merchandise and precious metals unloaded in the port. But the concentration in Seville of transoceanic commercial activity aided local development. The monopoly lasted until 1718.

tration. Even so, European literature continued to think of a crusade of reconquest and placed its hopes in another Great Khan who for decades no longer existed.

In the same way, Europeans continued to search for "Prester John." As early as the 12th century, western sovereigns had received letters said to arrive from a mysterious Christian preacher king of eastern Asia, the ruler of a kingdom as rich and powerful as it was just and peaceful. After describing, in the most alluring tones, the marvels of Asia (following themes already known from Pliny, Solon, and the apocrypha known as the "letter from Alexander the Great to Aristotle"), these documents urged the western princes to reach an accord so as to prepare for the new crusade.

Prester John was believed to be related in some way to the Apostle Saint Thomas, reputed to have converted the Indian subcontinent. The seat of his kingdom was sometimes said to be India, sometimes *India maior* (that is, Ethiopia). During the course

of the 15th century, the "Ethiopian" theory eventually prevailed over that of the "Indian," and Prester John came to be identified in the Negus of Ethiopia.

The closing of China led to the abandonment of the land route to Asia. In exchange, however, it led to plans for the circumnavigation of Africa to reach the Asian continent from the south, between Borneo and the Red Sea. For example, the merchant adventurer Niccolò dei Conti left his homeland as a youth, remained in Damascus between 1410 and 1414, and reached Hormuz by caravan, where he boarded a ship. He visited the Indian coast to the mouth of the Indus at Malabar, Ceylon, the gulf of Bengal, Sumatra, the Malaccas, Java, perhaps even Borneo, and returned to Italy in 1440.

Although the continental mass of Asia was closing itself to the west and sea voyages seemed to hold the only promise of permitting exploration of its distant shores, the continent of Africa was slowly being opened. The gold of the Sudan, which dazzled Christian Europe in the storehouses of the pirates operating between the Pillars of Hercules

Fabled monsters

The study of geography was enlivened by tales of bizarre monsters. This small sample is from the illustrations from a German edition (1481) of the *Travels*, by John Mandeville, a very popular book from the 14th to 16th centuries. Nearly 250 manuscript copies of the book are known, and these were followed by many printed editions. The author claimed to have gone on a pilgrimage to the Holy Land, and that trip served as the inspiration for a general description of the fabulous Orient in 1322. He also claimed to be an English knight from St. Albans, Hertfordshire. As it happens, the actual existence of this person is questionable; the name may be a pseudonym. The text was written in French, shortly after the middle of the 1300s. The "monsters" are, in order, sciapodes, monoculars, cynocephalus, and acephalous. The sciapodes "have only one foot yet walk so quickly they are a wonder. That foot is so large that with its shadow they shade all

A monkey, from the Triptych of the Passion, *by Hans Memling. From the* Description of Africa, *by Leone Africano (the Lion of Africa), a learned Muslim captured by Christian pirates in 1517: "Not only do they have feet and hands, but their faces are also similar to those of men, and they are naturally gifted, astute, and intelligent. . . . Those that are trained can do incredible things; but they are also savage and cruel."*

and Tripoli, soon captivated European explorers. In 1447, the Genoese Antonio Malfante undertook to cross the Sahara in Algeria and made his way far to the south, and it is possible that the rather boastful Florentine explorer Benedetto Dei may well have arrived in 1459–1460 in Timbuktu, the fabled destination of the caravans described in the extraordinary diary of the Arab traveler Ibn Battuta.

Ethiopia was the most alluring destination of all. Its name recalled stories from the Bible in which it seemed to be full of rich stores of incense, gold, and ivory. It exerted the powerful attraction of the mysterious and inaccessible source of the Nile and remained an enigmatic Christian empire inexplicably isolated from the rest of Christianity, cloaked in vague legend. A few Italians reached the court of the Negus, following an Abyssinian legation that, in 1402–1403, had traveled to Venice. The Franciscans, especially Alberto da Sarteano, were intrigued. An Ethiopian legation from Jerusalem arrived in 1441 for the Council of Florence, and in 1480 the Franciscan Giovanni di Calabria was sent as ambassador

their body from the sun when they lay down to rest." (Mandeville locates these in Ethiopia.) The monoculars are giants with "a single eye that is in the middle of their forehead, and they eat nothing but meat and raw fish." (These were from an island, perhaps in the Adamane archipelago.) The cynocephalus "are very intelligent and gifted with great intuition, except that they worship an ox as their god. Thus, each of them wears a gold or silver ox on their head for devotion." Finally, there was a people "with bodies so horrible and of natures so wicked that they have no heads and have their eyes near their shoulders. Their mouth is twisted like a horseshoe and is located in the middle of their chest." This amazing ethnography originated with Ctesia of Cnido (4th century B.C.), a Greek royal doctor who wrote a description of India.

The Canaries, Madeira, and the Azores were "discovered," "lost," and then "rediscovered" many times during the course of the 14th century. Their importance grew during the next century with the increased demand for sugar cane throughout Europe.

An essential chapter in the story of the exploration of the coast of the African continent was written in 1433–1434 by the Portuguese Gil Eanes, who rounded the the celebrated and terrible Cape Bojador, the "Bulging Cape," which marked the end of the torrid zone to the south. According to the wisdom of the geoanthropologists of the time, the climate caused men there to be born black instead of white. In 1447, the Portuguese reached the mouth of the Senegal, from where it was possible not just to make contact with the Arabs who led the black slave trade but even to reach the legendary city of Timbuktu. A few years later, between 1456 and 1457, the Genoese Alvise da Cadamosto, Antoniotto Usodimare, and, later, Antonio Da Noli reached first Cape Verde and then the islands of the same name. In 1488, Bartolomeu Dias rounded the Cape of Good Hope.

to the court of the Negus. It was hoped that the Christian emperor of Antioch would attack the Mamelukes of Cairo or cause the cataracts of the Nile to dry up or flood Egypt, thus forcing the infidels to return Jerusalem to the Christians.

Thus Africa, like Asia, was seen as the source of precious goods and as a land that might, when more clearly understood, play an important role in the organization of a crusade. The gold of the Sudan, which had been marked on Catalan maps as early as the 14th century, held an increasing attraction, to which were added new riches, among them ivory and slaves. Catalans, Majorcans, and Portuguese — following the lead of the Genoese—explored beyond the Pillars of Hercules in the stretch of water between northwestern Africa and the Canary Islands.

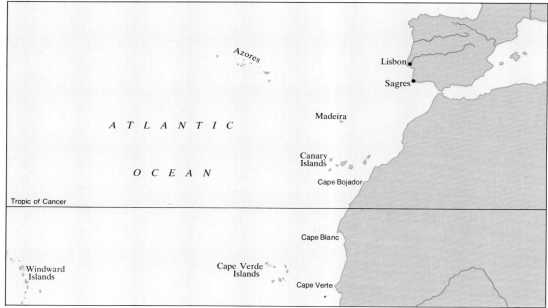

The Atlantic archipelagoes and the African coast up to Cape Verde. The Portuguese settled Porto Santo and Madeira, then the Azores (1427), and rounded Cape Bojador (1433). Around 1445, using a route that described an arc on the ocean in order to take advantage of the southwest trade winds, they solved the problem of returning home (circumventing the chief obstacle of the northern winds off the African coast). Once past the desert, they came across the surprise of the tropical lands. There was Cape Blanc, also passed by the Italian navigator Alvise da Cadamosto: "The Portuguese, who were the first to discover it, saw that white, sandy promontory without the merest sign of grass or vegetation." Cape Verde "was given its name because the first to discover it, the Portuguese, found everything covered with the green of tall trees."

205

In this detail from the Saint Vincent *triptych (ca. 1465), by Nuño Gonçalves, the kneeling figure is Henry the Navigator, fourth son of King John of Portugal and famous for his pioneering navigation (the boy at right is the future King John II). On Henry the Navigator's death in 1460, the Portuguese had reached the Cape Verde Islands. In 1475, from the fort of São Jorge da Mina on the Guinea coast, large quantities of gold began arriving. Henry's horoscope was written in the contemporary chronicle of Gomez Eannes d'Azurara: Aries is ascendant in the house of Mars, and Mars is in Aquarius, house of Saturn. "It is clear," the author explains, that the prince "is called on for great conquests and especially to discover things that as yet remain hidden from other men, since Saturn is the protector of secrets."*

With the Jacob's staff

Until the nautical chronometer was perfected (during the 1700s), there was no way to determine longitude (the distance from 0 meridian) with precision. It was reckoned by taking the direction (given by the compass), the time (measured with an hourglass kept on board and turned over each half hour), and the speed of the ship (determined by the captain's nautical sense; the log chip was invented around the end of the 16th century). Latitude (distance from the equator) was established by measuring the height of the Pole star (the angle between the horizon and the star, with the observer at the vertex) or of the sun at the meridian (that is, at noon or when it is directly south). The height of the Pole star is the latitude; to derive latitude from the height of the sun calls for calculations and the use of special tables (ephemerides). South of the equator, the navigator no longer had the help of the precious Pole star. The instruments of measurement were quadrants and simplified astrolabes. These astrolabes were less refined than those used by astronomers and gave less precise measurements. Their use on ships was rendered difficult and inaccurate by movements caused by waves and thus, as soon as possible, latitude was measured on land. More practical was the Jacob's staff or rod, also known as the cross-staff (*bastone di San Giacomo* to the Italians, *baculo de Santiago* to the Spanish, *belestilha* to the Portuguese), which came into use in the 15th century. Looking down one end of the graduated rod or arrow, the observer slides the chaser until its edges match the horizon and the star. Even at the end of the next century, the great sailor John Davis stated that no instrument "was the equal of the cross-staff for the use of mariners."

Thus was opened the "eastern route" to the Indies. The continent of Africa had revealed itself to be much longer, in terms of latitude, than the cartographers of the time had suspected, but the western coast was by then more or less under control and dotted with "farms" and Portuguese docks. In 1497, Vasco da Gama set sail from Lisbon to repeat the voyage of Bartolomeu Dias and continued across the Indian Ocean as far as Calcutta, on the Malabar coast.

The epic story of the Portuguese adventure in Africa bears the mark of the great organizer and charismatic figure Henry of Aviz, son of King John I of Portugal and brother of the future King Edward, of Peter, duke of Coimbra, and of the Isabella who wed Philip the Good.

Born in Oporto, Portugal, in 1394, Henry played an important role from an early age in the Portuguese contribution to the Reconquista and in the idea of a western crusade. Once the Moors had been almost completely expelled from the Iberian peninsula, the Catalan, Aragonese, and Portuguese sailors were free to take control of the Mediterranean "channel" that divided the Andalusian coasts from those of Maghreb so that they could eliminate the Barbary pirates, a task at which they failed.

In 1415, Henry participated in the Christian conquest of the city of Ceuta. He then undertook a series of nautical, cartographic, and oceanographic studies directed at, among other goals, locating the source of the Atlantic current. Governor of the Order of Christ, a religious-knightly order born in Portugal from the disbanded Order of the Temple, Henry established himself at Cabo de Sagres in the Algarve, the southernmost point of Portugal, and there he set up a true office for naval and cartographic studies. To him is owed the impulse of the Portuguese discoveries.

Henry's ultimate aim was without doubt the capture of Jerusalem, and towards this end he hoped to make contact with Prester John of Ethiopia. But following an unfortunate military expedition against

Geographers measured distances with the compass. The navigator Diego Gomes noted: "From Ptolemy we have inherited many beautiful things about the divisions of the world, but in one instance he reveals himself to be badly informed." In the tropics, supposedly uninhabitable due to the heat, "one finds the opposite. Innumerable populations thrive, and the plants grow to an enormous size."

The first greeting Vasco da Gama received at Calcutta seems to have come from certain Tunisians who spoke both Spanish and Italian: "Cursed be he who cast you up on these shores!" The coasts of Malabar were under the sovereignty of the "lord of the seas," known to the Portuguese as Samorin. "In my land there is cinnamon, cloves, ginger, and pepper in great store; I possess the same in pearls and precious stones," runs Samorin's message to the king of Portugal. The fabulous India that the Portuguese had finally reached is ably conjured on this page of the atlas dedicated to Manuel I (1519) by Lopo Homen and the Rynel brothers. The scroll beside the archipelago and south of the Deccan reads "Hic lapis gignitur herculeus . . ." ("Here is to be found the stone of Hercules, and here are pulled those ships that have iron nails").

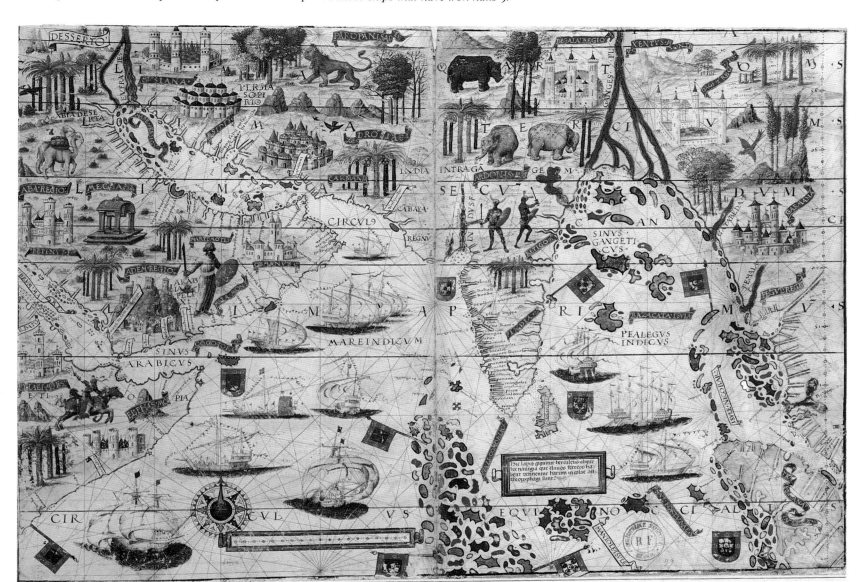

Tangier in 1437, his activity — which remained focused on the realization of the holy crusade — was dependent on the conquest of the sea. If the Portuguese could succeed in bringing the spices of the East to Europe by way of their trading stations in Africa, they would effectively overcome their disadvantage in not having ports on the Mediterranean; the Mediterranean, in fact, would become irrelevant to their commercial interests. The conquest by the Ottoman Turks of Constantinople would be revealed as a hollow victory, for the Christians would be able to circumvent the overland trade, which was not only expensive but also helped fill the coffers of the infidels.

In 1460, in his beloved Algarve, Henry the Navigator died, while Mohammed II was in his seventh year at the Golden Horn of Constantinople. Having failed at the congress of Mantua, Pope Pius II was still trying to organize a new crusade, but Cape Verde had been reached, and much activity was directed towards attaining the southernmost point of the Asian continent, which was expected rather soon.

Instead, another 37 years would pass before Asia would be reached. During that time, cartographers and sailors, cosmographers and geographers, would ask themselves if, on the basis of ancient scientific texts, it might not be wiser to point the prows of their ships towards the west and voyage across the unknown waters of the Atlantic to gain, in that way, the Indies and the empire of the Great Khan.

207

Homage to the admiral

A long, historical tradition attributes to the learned men of Salamanca the odious role of stern and obtuse custodians of righteous, dogmatic, and superstitious beliefs against which the heroes of new and free thinking had to battle.

The truth is much different. The Spanish commission that, between 1486 and 1487, met at Salamanca and Cordoba to consider the proposals of Christopher Columbus and to report them to the Catholic kings was anything but a rabble of incompetent fanatics. Rather, it was a select group of sage theologians and wise professors who countered the claims of the enterprising admiral, who mixed with impunity the knowledge of ancient geographers condemned by Ptolemy, pages of the Bible from the Prophet Esdras, and deductions based on fragile evidence (such as the writings of Marco Polo) with the official scientific reasoning of the time. Scientific commissions have always been skeptical; this is their role, and they cannot be reproached for having performed it scrupulously.

Columbus was certain of the existence of "Cipangu," Marco Polo's name for Japan, but his inquisitors argued that Polo was not a reliable source and that Ptolemy had never mentioned that marvelous land. Columbus held that the distance between the Canaries and Hangchow was no more than 5,000 nautical miles, while the calculations of the commissioners, based on Ptolemy, indicated twice that distance. The commissioners were closer to the actual distance of 11,766 nautical miles. The more accurate speculations of the wise men of Salamanca make Columbus look wrongheaded indeed. The result was that the commission calculated that, to reach Asia, one would have to navigate towards the west for one hundred days, more than fourteen weeks at sea, without seeing land. An undertaking of that length of time was absurd.

Their refusal was reasonable, well founded, and blameless. And yet, notwithstanding his errors and the better judgment of the wise men of Salamanca, that obstinate and presumptuous admiral was in a sense right, for halfway between the Canaries and China there lay another continent, and no one — with the technology and knowledge of that time — could have suspected its existence. Least of all Columbus.

There was a certain logic, however, in Columbus's calculations. Aristotle had maintained that the Atlantic Ocean was nothing more than a short arm of sea separating the Iberian peninsula from eastern Asia; this opinion, accepted by Seneca and Pliny, had been repeated throughout the Middle Ages. However, until the 13th century, it had had little practical weight, both because of the doubts concerning the roundness of the earth and because the instruments and nautical knowledge of the time would not have permitted a challenge to that dark ocean, clouded in frightening legend. Meanwhile, the Arabs had spread as far as the west the geographical ideas of Ptolemy, based on the Latin translations of the *Almagest*: Ptolemy advanced the notion of a world divided into

A 15th-century Catalan map of the world. This is one of various maps showing geographical ideas as they were at the beginning of the age of discovery: As well as the Mediterranean, the coast of western Africa as far as the gulf of Guinea is shown with considerable precision. There is, however, an imaginary continental mass, curiously shaped, attached to Africa.

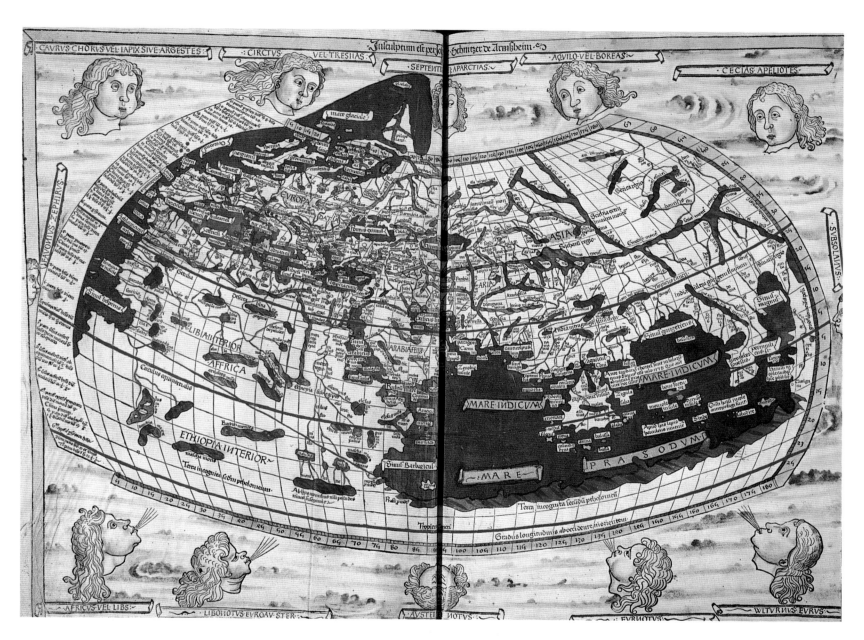

areas above and below water and of equal size: The globe was half covered by water and half dry. The triumph of Aristotle's ideas was secured by Scholastic philosophy. Nevertheless, the possibility of crossing the great ocean was not easily considered.

Around the beginning of the 15th century, a sort of regression took place. Because

of increased cartographic skills and nautical experience, many mistaken ideas concerning the formation of the globe had been changed. The conclusion had been reached, for example, that the African continent extended in latitude far beneath the equator, which defied previous speculation, and Pietro d'Abano had gone to great trouble to

prove the possibility of human life in the torrid zones of the globe, refuting yet another myth. Then, in 1410, Jacopo Angelo made a Latin translation of the *Cosmography*, by Ptolemy. In the growing humanistic climate, it was immediately granted enormous authority, with the result that a kind of "return to the ancients" mentality

209

Toscanelli's map

"To Christopher Columbus, Paolo Fisico [Toscanelli] salutes you. I share your noble and great desire to travel there to where the spice trees grow; thus, in response to your letter I send you a copy of another letter that a few days ago I wrote to a friend, the cultivated and serene king of Portugal . . . and I send you another navigational map, similar to that which I sent him." This letter and another to Columbus that the admiral's son inserted in his *Historie* are looked at with suspicion by many scholars. The celebrated map sent by the Florentine geographer to the king of Portugal and then, as stated in the contested letter, a copy of which was sent to Columbus, has been lost. Reconstructions have been made, such as the map here, which shows the fabled island of Antilia. On the world map of Martin Behaim (1492), son of a nobleman of Nuremberg who took part in the *junta dos mathematicos* in Portugal, under the representation of that island is written: "In the year 734 from the birth of Christ, as it was calculated, when all of Spain was occupied by infidels from Africa, the above indicated island of Antilia, called the Seven Cities, was colonized by an archbishop of Oporto in Portugal, together with six bishops and other Christians, men and women, fleeing Spain in a ship with cattle, goods, and baggage. In 1414, a ship from Spain navigated near to it." Beyond Antilia is Cipangu, which, as Toscanelli — following the description of Marco Polo — says "is very fertile with gold, pearls, and precious stones. . . and one can reach it easily."

set in concerning geographical knowledge, and its acceptance was a highwater mark for classical authority in its long conflict with experience. An indication of this attitude can be seen in the works of the theologian and thinker — not without intelligence or a scientific bent as an experienced encyclopedist — Pierre d'Ailly. In his celebrated geographical work *Imago mundi*, he expressed, based on his reading of Aristotle and Bacon, beliefs close to Aristotle's. But in the following *Compendium geographiae*, he hurriedly changed arguments, agreeing instead with Ptolemy's balance between land and oceans.

Whether Columbus was born at Genoa or, as others would have it, in Catalonia, there is no doubt that the discovery of the New World was the child of four circumstances. The nautical, cartographical, and cosmological revolution of the 14th and 15th centuries, and the closing of the path to the Orient following the Ottoman advance — and thus the need for new trade routes — both played a part. So, too, did the spirit of rivalry between Spain and Portugal after the papal bull of Calixtus III that, in 1456, had assigned to the Portuguese a sort of monopoly on new discoveries, an act that was modified, in 1493, by the Bull of Demarcation, created by another Borgia pope, Alexander VI. Finally, the Florentine humanistic culture offered the conceptual basis for exploration and in such men as Amerigo Vespucci and Andrea da Verrazzano later furnished its most audacious discoverers. The name *America* — derived from a proposal in the *Cosmographiae introductio*, by Martin Waldseemüller, edited in 1507 — has immortalized the memory of Vespucci. Perhaps this is only the last injustice — among the many, real and imagined — suffered by Christopher Columbus; it has certainly been the most long lasting. Nevertheless, it acknowledges that Florentine humanism without which Columbus's voyage

might never have taken place or would have taken place in a different time and under different cirumstances.

Representative of this humanist intellectual atmosphere of 15th-century Florence is the astronomer and geographer Paolo dal Pozzo Toscanelli. Unfortunately, we know relatively little about his life. Indeed, it is not even certain that the works attributed to him — under his name in a manuscript preserved today in Florence's Biblioteca Nazionale Centrale — were actually written by his hand. Among these works is a treatise on comets based on observations made in 1433, 1449–1450, 1456, 1457, and 1472. It has also been suggested that the work *Della prospettiva*, usually included among the popular works of Alberti, is also his.

Toscanelli studied medicine at Padua between 1417 and 1424. In this fecund environment, he also took up the study of astrology. It was research into the relationships between medicine and astrology that led him to later encounter Marsilio Ficino, who was engaged in the same study. At Padua, Toscanelli had as a companion in his studies another great humanistic thinker, Nicolas of Cusa (Cusanus), who in 1450 dedicated to Toscanelli his *De transmutationibus geometricis* and in 1457 made him an interlocutor in his *De quadratura circuli*.

When he returned to Florence, Toscanelli formed friendships and profitable intellectual relationships with the architects Filippo Brunelleschi — who, as Vasari reports, "learned geometry" from him — and Leon Battista Alberti, who dedicated to him the satiric *Intercenales* and the regrettably lost *Epistolae ad Paulum Physicum*.

Toscanelli was very interested in natural phenomena, and it was precisely because of this interest that Matteo Palmieri wrote him from Volterra in 1474 to inform him of the birth of a *monstrum horribile*. His interests in geometry were so broad and so profound that in 1464 Johann Müller — known as Regiomontanus to his fellow

Opposite: The archipelagoes of the Atlantic, the Canaries, Madeira, and the Azores in the ship's log of Grazioso Benincasa (1482). He relates the perhaps legendary episode of Columbus's stop at Porto Santo (Madeira), when a demasted ship approached with only the helmsman still alive; driven by the winds, the ship had touched islands with "naked people" from the other side of the ocean. Gonzalo Fernández de Oviedo y Valdés

writes about this in the Historia general y natural de las Indias *(1535): "They also say that this helmsman was a close friend of Christopher Columbus and that he understood much about the high seas [or rather about the navigation of the high seas] towards that land which was found, as it is told, and that he secretly gave part of his knowledge to Columbus." Oviedo concludes: "For myself, I think this is false."*

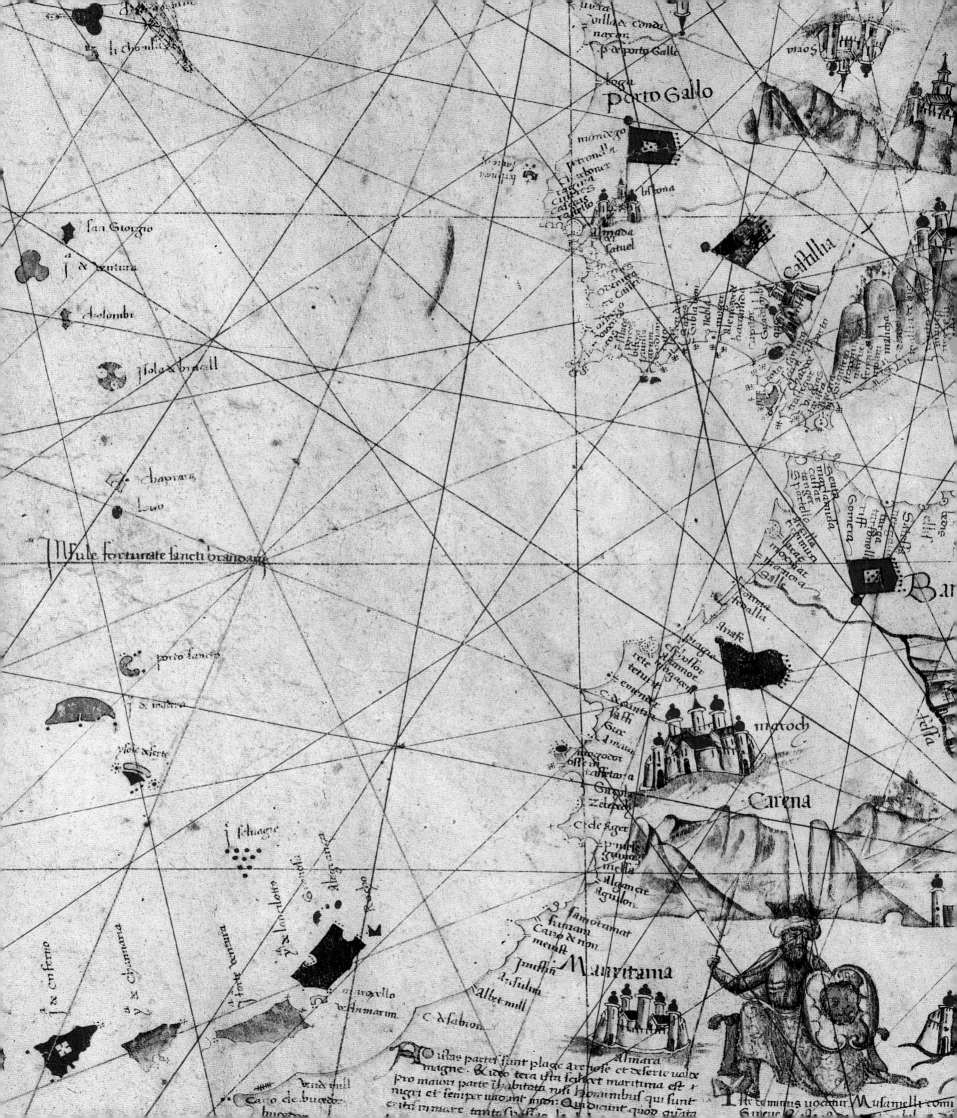

humanists — turned to Toscanelli as the outstanding authority on Cusanus's geometry. Sternly and ferociously anti-Cusanus, Regiomontanus professed great admiration for Toscanelli, whose mathematical ideas, he claimed, were far superior. One surviving letter allegedly written by Regiomontanus to Toscanelli deals with the interest that the Florentine mathematician and astrologer had shown in Archimedes, the classical author who was then the subject of many studies and who offered much material for research on the connection between science and technology.

For Toscanelli, geography and cosmography were not subjects of secondary importance. Cristoforo Landino — who left a detailed account of Toscanelli in his *Disputationes Camaldulenses* — portrayed him anxiously interviewing travelers from distant lands. Nor should it be forgotten that Landino was the author, in "vernacular" Italian, of the encyclopedic work of Pliny the Elder, a work much used by Leonardo da Vinci, and a thickly annotated copy of which belonged to Columbus.

Thus we can see the strong intellectual bonds and lines of communication connecting Cusanus, Brunelleschi, Alberti, Ficino, Columbus, Leonardo, and many of the other leading humanists of the day. Paolo dal Pozzo Toscanelli appears as the knot firmly joining all these threads.

It is particularly significant that the Florentine Toscanelli and the Lisbon canon Fernão Martins came together, elbow to elbow, in the archbishop's palace in Todi at the deathbed of Cusanus; both signed the philosopher priest's testament in August 1464, about a month after the severe attack of Regiomontanus on Cusanus's geometric theories.

Ten years after their encounter at Cusanus's deathbed, on June 25, 1474, Toscanelli sent Martins — "friend and companion" of the Portuguese sovereign — a letter detailing his belief that the ocean route between Portugal and the Indies was much shorter than anyone suspected. Included with this letter was the Florentine geographer's "map made with my own hands, in which are presented our shores, and the islands from which the voyage should begin, always towards the west, and the areas

The city of Genoa and its port, 1481. At this time, Columbus was 30 years old and had already left the city to move to Lisbon. He had gone to sea even as a boy, perhaps at 13. In 1501 he affirmed, with some exaggeration, that he had "had the habit of sailing for more than forty years, having traveled everywhere that has up to now been navigated."

"The Admiral was a well-formed man of greater than average height, with a long face and cheeks a little high but without becoming either fat or lean. He had an aquiline nose and pale eyes; he was pale but glowed with color. In his youth he had fair hair, but when he reached thirty it turned white." This is how Ferdinand Columbus describes his father in the Historie. *It is doubtful that any of the known portraits (as many as 71 were gathered together and evaluated by a team of experts for the Universal Exhibition in Chicago in 1893) shows the discoverer's real features. This version, known as the "Talleyrand portrait," is attributed to Sebastiano del Piombo. It does not lack a certain inner warmth.*

where one would arrive, with the declinations from the pole and the equatorial line, and how much distance, that is, how many miles would have to be covered to reach those areas so fertile of every sort of spice and jem. And do not be surprised that I call western ports those that have the spices, while they are usually called eastern, for those who continually navigate in a westerly direction, using for navigation the antipodes, will reach those regions." Toscanelli's description of the wonders of this distant Orient shines with the colors of the ideal cities described in hermetic philosophy by Filarete and Francesco di Giorgio Martini. At the same time, it gives off the scent of the spices noted in the Florentine "market records" and evoked by the many pages written by travelers and narrators of the chivalric novels of the time.

In drawing up his map, Toscanelli had studied a map of the world loaned him by Francesco Castellani. Christopher Columbus copied onto the flyleaf of his copy of the *Historia rerum ubique gestarum*, by Pius II, the text of the letter from Toscanelli to Martins. The circle was closing. Toscanelli had earlier witnessed the hotly contested birth of Santa Maria del Fiore, a supposedly impossible structure erected with the calculations, ability, stubbornness, and plain good luck of Brunelleschi, an architect-artisan who struggled against the opinions of many so-called solemn experts; with his letter and his map Toscanelli provided the impetus for the supposedly ill-conceived voyage to a new continent by a sailor-artisan in his own way as capable, stubborn, and lucky as Brunelleschi.

Ferdinan Columbus and Bartolomé de Las Casas have handed down to us the texts of two letters from Toscanelli to Columbus. The originals of these letters have been lost, and there are doubts as to the authenticity of this correspondence. What is certain is that these men traveled in a similar world of new ideas, goods, and technology, and they shared similar dreams and hopes — for glory, power, and money. It was a world of new nautical maps, new systems for mounting sails or making rudders or planking ships, new diplomatic encounters and new reports from travelers, new architectural experiments and new ways of distributing books or knocking down the walls of a fortress by means of artillery. This was the 15th century; this was the background for the voyage of Christopher Columbus.

The Florentines who opposed the building of Brunelleschi's cupola — "big enough," said Alberti, "to cover with its shadow all the people of Tuscany" — were not at all timid, unintelligent traditionalists. They were, instead, practical and prudent, and they knew quite a bit about architecture. Like the learned men of Salamanca, they were not obtuse and dogmatic opponents on principle of all that seemed new and audacious but were, rather, cautious and discerning custodians of a well-established

A page from the Imago mundi, *by the French prelate and theologian Pierre d'Ailly, with notes by Columbus. The navigator's convictions are revealed. One note reads: "The end of Spain and the beginning of India are not far distant, but close, and it is evident that this sea is navigable in a few days with a fair wind."*

knowledge, faithful royal counsellors who understood as part of their service the protection of the crown from crazy adventurers and financial losses.

King John II of Portugal, visited by Columbus between 1483 and 1484, was also not without intelligence and daring. By then, Columbus had been traveling without interruption for nearly 20 years, from his early days as a captain of coastal vessels to journeys to Scio, Tunisia, Iceland, Madeira, Porto Santo — where he got married — to the Canaries, the Azores, Guinea, and Cape

213

The most celebrated of ships

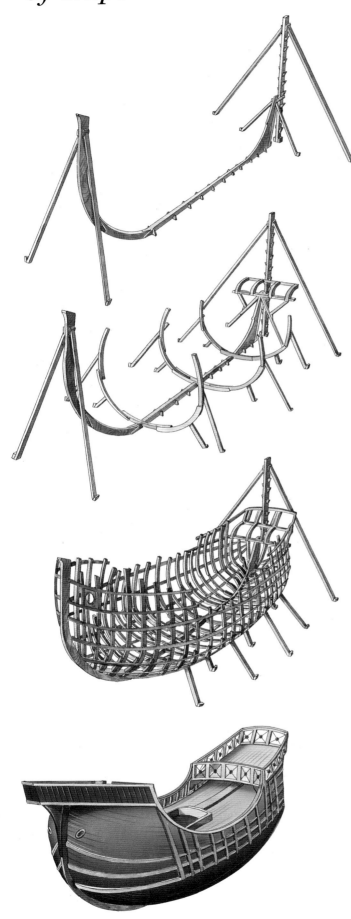

Little is known for certain of the *Santa Maria*, and the various reconstructions that have been made are hypothetical. Columbus referred to his flagship as a *nao*, which means "ship," and the other two ships in his fleet as caravels: This seems to indicate that the *Santa Maria* was not a caravel, and it seems most probable that it was a carrack. It was probably constructed in Galicia, a northern province of Spain on the Atlantic, for its name (before Columbus rebaptized it) was *La Gallega*, "the Galician." A reconstruction of the ship for the fourth centenary of the voyage of discovery at the Chicago exposition of 1893 made use of two drawings of ships with Spanish flags that appear in the nautical charts of Juan de La Cosa, owner of the *Santa Maria* and its first officer during the 1492 trip. However, these drawings are summary. That the ship had a tonnage of 100 tons and a length of around 26 meters are no more than probable conjectures.

Although little can be said of the actual details, a certain degree of certainty can be found in relation to the fundamental elements of the ship's rigging. The mainmast—the largest mast—carried a large square sail. Since reef sails—which reduced the sail surface under a fresh wind—had probably not yet been invented or were used only in northern Europe, the mainmast sail was, in a sense, too small; it could be enlarged by adding to its lower edges one or two bonnet sails. Above the sail on the mainmast, on a second yard, could be unfurled a topsail; that this was trapezoidal in shape is only a guess. In front of the mainmast, on the forecastle, was the foremast, with another square sail. The last square sail, the spritsail, was attached to a yard beneath the bowsprit. The mizzenmast, on the poop, had a triangular sail—called a lateen—used most often for maneuvering. A curious detail is that the helmsman steered blindly; the tiller of the rudder entered the hull at the arch of the stern and extended into the interior of the poop deck, where the helmsman stood. The helmsman moved the rudder following a compass or, more likely, obeying directions from the pilot. A hundred years would pass before the position of the helm

214

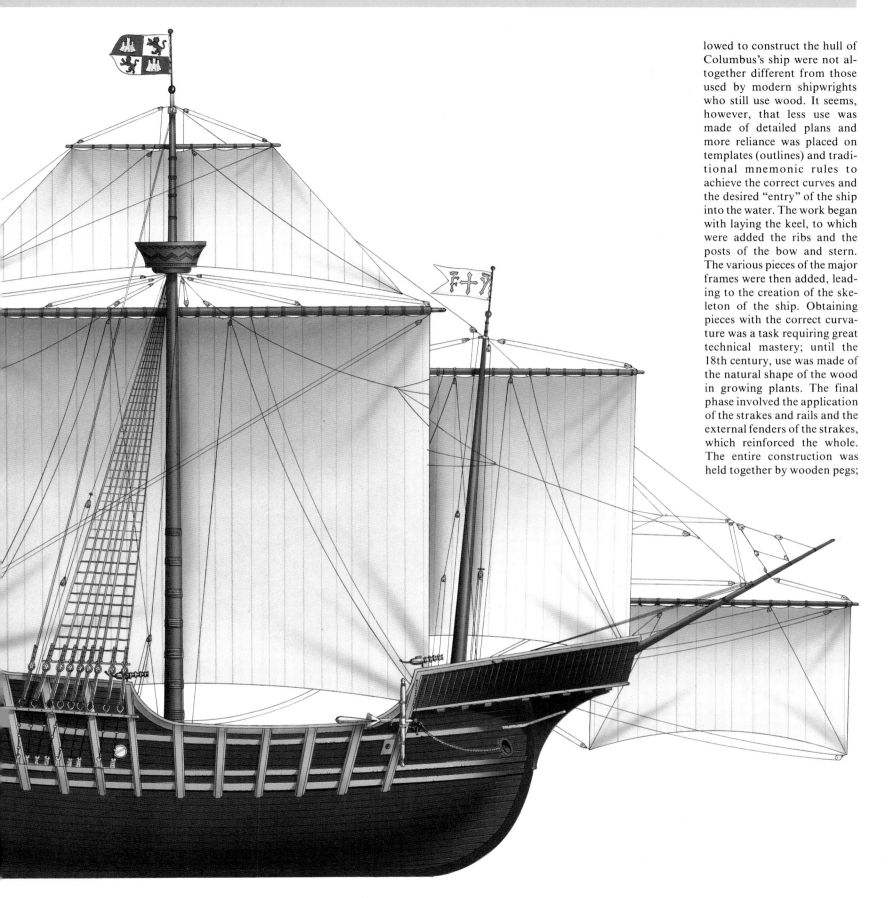

lowed to construct the hull of Columbus's ship were not altogether different from those used by modern shipwrights who still use wood. It seems, however, that less use was made of detailed plans and more reliance was placed on templates (outlines) and traditional mnemonic rules to achieve the correct curves and the desired "entry" of the ship into the water. The work began with laying the keel, to which were added the ribs and the posts of the bow and stern. The various pieces of the major frames were then added, leading to the creation of the skeleton of the ship. Obtaining pieces with the correct curvature was a task requiring great technical mastery; until the 18th century, use was made of the natural shape of the wood in growing plants. The final phase involved the application of the strakes and rails and the external fenders of the strakes, which reinforced the whole. The entire construction was held together by wooden pegs;

was moved into the open, on the deck of the ship, where the hinged rudder could be controlled via a tiller with a vertical shaft that passed through the boards of the deck. Still later came the round helm, which moved the bar via cables. Much information is available on how 15th-century ships were built, and at left opposite are shown phases in the construction of a ship similar to the *Santa Maria*. Naval carpentry has seen a slow evolution, and the procedures followed to construct the hull of iron was used sparingly. The area beneath the waterline was smeared with pitch to protect the wood from shipworms.

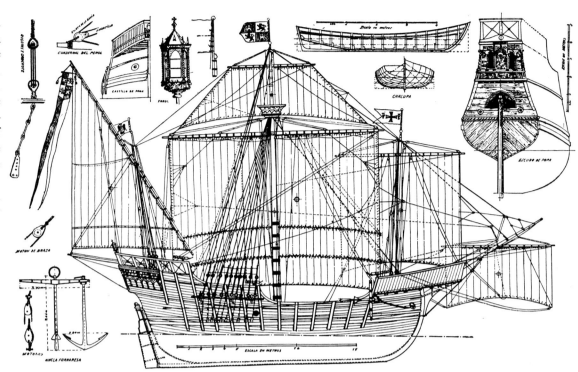

Verde. In 1481–1482 he had corresponded with the 85-year-old Toscanelli, by then near the end of his earthly experience. He had eagerly spoken with sailors, merchants, and privateers, with survivors of shipwrecks, with the tellers of tall tales well versed in the stories recounted in seaside inns, with broken-down men corroded by the saltiness of the sea air and driven crazy by the sun of the tropics or by the fear of high waves or the fear of pirates.

He had gathered evidence — often fleeting and just as often insubstantial or misunderstood — of the existence of a land on the other side of the dark ocean. He had sketched improbable maps and performed dramatically erroneous calculations, confusing the Arabian mile used by Alfragano with the much shorter Italian mile and amassing, in confusion and sometimes desperation, all the proof he could find to support his theory. Anything was acceptable as long as it might serve to convince some-

The trade winds

During the 33 days of the ocean crossing in 1492, Columbus was driven west by eastern winds, except for a brief period of variable winds and rain, ten days after passing the Canary Island of Hierro, and an intense storm during the final phase. In October the small fleet ran for 142 miles on each of 5 consecutive days, equal to a speed of a little less than 6 knots. One day they made 182 miles (a speed of almost 8 knots), and the last day of the journey the three ships went ahead at 9 knots. In effect, Columbus navigated near the northern limit of the stream of the northeast trade winds, a little beneath their annual minimum.

The trade winds are regular winds in the tropics, the result of the circulation of masses of air as a result of variations in the heating of the surface of the planet, between the temperate zones and the equator. Tending to move from the north to the south in the northern hemisphere and from south to north in the southern, this circulation turns "right" due to the rotation of the earth.

In reality, the trade winds come from northeast in the northern hemisphere and from the southeast in the southern. The phenomenon is global but is regular only over the oceans; over the continents it is more difficult to recognize because of the influence of certain local thermal or dynamic factors.

The conditions of the winds has, of course, been the object of much observation by sailors. On the basis of their records, the English astronomer Halley, in 1686, published a map of the trade winds, giving a theory of their formation. The trade wind of the northeast is separated from that of the southeast by an equatorial strip of weak, calm winds, and a similar zone of calm tropical winds divides the trade winds from the winds of the temperate zones. In the Atlantic, more than in the other oceans, winds and calms are distributed with regularity.

The strip of the trade winds, however, moves during the course of the year due to seasonal changes in the distribution of warmth. In March the trade winds of the northeast occupy the area betweeen 3° and 26° north latitude, and in September they move more north, to between 10° and 35°.

one, somewhere, to provide him with the ships with which he would sail behind the sun towards the west, in search of Oriental jewels and spices; in search of fame, wealth, and power; in search of a meeting with the Great Khan and the organization of a new crusade to extend to every corner of the globe the name of Christ, the Cross, and the Word. Christopher Columbus was a man from the race of both Ulysses and Sinbad; and he was also a contemporary of Girolamo Savonarola.

Although he was the leader of a seafaring nation — or perhaps exactly for that reason — the king of Portugal kept his feet firmly planted on the ground. He assembled a *junta dos mathematicos*, an advisory panel presided over by Diego Ortiz de Villegas, archbishop of Ceuta, and including among its members two Jewish masters renowned for their knowledge of nautical astronomy: Rodrigo and José Vizinho. The verdict of the *junta* was unequivocal: All of the brash sailor's calculations were wrong. Greater confidence was put in the plan of the governor of one of the Azores, the Fleming Ferdinand van Olmen (Fernão Dulmo, to the Portuguese). He proposed to discover, to the west of the great dark sea, the island of the Seven Cities, of which many legends were then in circulation. Van Olmen estimated his journey would require 40 days at sea (Columbus was to spend exactly 36 days between the Canaries and the Bahamas). His two caravels set sail in the spring of 1487; they never returned. By exercising caution and backing van Olmen, the king of Portugal had lost the opportunity to join the New World to his name and his crown.

In 1488, Columbus tried again to press his case with the king of Portugal and received a polite, perhaps even provisional response. But in the meantime, although it was clear that van Olmen's expedition had failed, Bartolomeu Dias was returning from his fortunate adventure to the Cape of Good Hope. The way to the east was now open, and Columbus was well aware that no one in Lisbon was interested in the way west. He decided to return to the discussions begun in 1485 when, after the death of his wife, Felipa, he had moved with his son Diego to the Andalusian seaport of Palos de la Frontera. With the help of a fellow visitor to the Franciscan friary of La Rábida, the geographer Antonio de Marchena, Columbus had been introduced to the duke of Medina Sidonia and then to the duke of Medina Celi. Columbus hoped to receive from either one a naval squadron with which to attempt his adventure to Cipangu.

Thanks to assistance from duke of Medina Celi, the mariner was granted an audience with the Catholic kings at Alcala de Henares in January 1486. After the verdict from the group of experts united in Salamanca between 1486 and 1487, a verdict that very much resembled that reached by the experts assembled by the king of Portugal, he was granted another audience, this time near the city of Malaga. Meanwhile, Columbus had been living at Cordoba, where he had met Beatriz de Harana, who in 1488 gave birth to their son Ferdinand.

Columbus slowly gave up on the Portuguese and concentrated on the Spanish. Although Ferdinand and Isabella had already communicated to him at Malaga the negative verdict of the assembled jury, the royal treasury had given him, in several allotments, three or four thousand maravedis. After another audience, at Jaen in August of 1489, the queen had promised that his plans would be taken into consideration as soon as Granada had been conquered. Columbus hung painfully to that promise. More than two years passed, however, and the mariner saw his hopes slowly crumble. Luis de la Cerda, the duke of Medina Celi, generously put him up for a year and repeated his own earlier promises, but nothing came of it. In the autumn of 1491, Columbus returned to La Rábida to pick up his eldest son, Diego, and with him

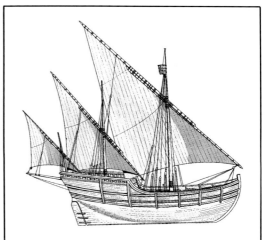

The Niña

The *Niña* was the smallest of the ships that discovered America and also the one Columbus liked most. Its true name was *Santa Clara*; *Niña* was a nickname from the name of the Palos family that owned it. Unlike the *Santa Maria*, it was a caravel; unlike the *Piñta*, the other caravel of the voyage, it had lateen sails, like those used by the Portuguese during the first voyages of exploration along the African coasts. With three lateen sails — the largest on the main mast near the middle of the ship, the median on the second mast on the poop deck, the smallest on a small mast at the stern of the ship — it sailed from Palos to the Canary Islands, where Columbus "changed the lateen sails to square sails . . . so that with more calm and less danger the other ships might follow it." As experts have noted, the rigging with square sails was more efficient for taking advantage of a carrying wind, such as the trade winds on the trip across the Atlantic. Having lost the *Santa Maria*, Columbus embarked on the *Niña* for the return voyage. The *Niña* took part in the second of Columbus's voyages (and his return) and even made a third visit to the Americas in 1498. The size of the *Niña* is a matter of dispute; Samuel E. Morison claims it was 17 meters in length; Captain Enrico Alberto D'Algertis says 24. On board in 1492 when it left for America were 20 or 22 men. The Captain was Vicente Yáñez Pinzón, the first officer was the owner, Juan Niño.

The western sea was no longer a barrier: The ocean could be sailed. Francesco Guicciardini, in his History of Italy *(written in 1537–1540), defines Spanish navigation as "marvelous" thanks to the "inventiveness of Christopher Columbus from Genoa. He, having many times sailed the ocean and conjecturing by his observations of certain winds that which actually happened to him, entreated certain types of ships*

from the king of Spain and sailed towards the west, where, within thirty-three days, he discovered at the ultimate extremity of our hemisphere some islands of which we had never before had any knowledge; these islands are fortunate in their position under the sky and in the fertility of their lands" and in "the inhabitants, very simple in their ways and happy with what the benevolence of nature produces."

On the ocean

On his return, Columbus gave the original manuscript of the ship's log of his voyage of discovery to Ferdinand and Isabella at Barcelona. Its fate is uncertain. The version that has survived is a summary related by the Dominican Bartolomé de Las Casas. Even so, the document is moving:

Saturday, September 8. At three at night on Saturday, the wind began to blow from the northeast, and the admiral plotted a course west. He was taking on water over the prow, and making headway was difficult.

Saturday, September 15. Day and night, the admiral followed the course west for 26 leagues and more. At the beginning of the night they witnessed a wonderful sight, a strip of fire that fell from the sky to the sea at a distance of four or five leagues.

Monday, September 17. They saw a lot of algae, which seemed to come from a river, and found a live crab, which the admiral examined. He said it was a certain sign of land, for such animals never went farther than thirty leagues [in reality, they were in the Sargasso Sea]. They noticed that the water of the sea was less salty than when they had left the Canaries, and the breeze was always sweeter. All followed the voyage with great happiness.

Sunday, September 23. The sea was so calm and smooth that the crew began to grumble, saying that since the sea was so calm there would be no wind to carry them back to Spain. But then the sea grew so swollen that they were amazed.

Thursday, October 11. The admiral navigated west-southwest; they then experienced the stormiest sea they had known during the entire voyage. They saw seabirds and a green branch near the ship. Those on the caravel *Pinta* saw a reed and a stick and grabbed out of the sea another stick that had been carved, it seemed, with iron, and another piece of reed, and other things that grew on land, and a small tablet. Those, too, of the caravel *Niña* saw signs of land and a branch with berries. At these signs, they all took hope.

The next day they stepped ashore on the New World.

leave Spain. The prior Juan Pérez encouraged him to give the queen another chance, and he was once again admitted to the court.

The Christian victory at Granada on February 2, 1492, reawakened Columbus's hopes based on the promise made to him at Jaen. During the following April, the Spanish sovereigns approved the funding for the enterprise to the Indies and gave the necessary privileges, on the basis of which, at the end of May, Columbus returned to Palos to order the construction of two caravels in the small port at the mouth of the Rio Tinto. Payment for these ships was to come from fines that the people of Palos had to pay to the royal chamber for certain instances of smuggling. The ships had a storage capacity of about 60 to 70 tons — the *Pinta* was a bit larger than the *Niña* — and they were both fitted out, although at different times, with square sails. For his flagship, Columbus chose to engage a somewhat larger ship that was already in port, a *nao* of Galician

construction that could hold about one hundred tons.

Columbus's dealings with the court had not always been smooth. He wished to make up for the humiliations he had suffered and for the long time he had been forced to wait. Although protesting that he wanted nothing for himself, in reality he wished for honor, recognition, and financial rewards. The final resistance to Columbus's undertaking at the court had been overcome with help from the royal treasurer, Luis de Santangel. If the undertaking were to fail, the sovereigns would lose only the lives of Columbus and a few sailors, along with the money invested; but if it were successful, argued the treasurer, their earnings would be immense. And after the taking of Granada, there was no longer the danger that the failure of a naval expedition might dim the glory of the Catholic kings.

The two million or so maravedis needed to finance the undertaking were gathered through the banking community — most of

In May 1493, a Latin version of a letter from Columbus to King Ferdinand was printed in Rome, "written on the caravel near the Canary Islands [this is a slight error: He was, in fact, near the Azores] on the fifteenth day of February in the year 1493," in which he describes the results of his voyage. The letter was illustrated with a beautiful ship with the caption Oceanica classis *("oceanic fleet"). This was not, however,*

a reproduction of one of Columbus's ships but more or less the same picture that is found in a xylograph from the Sanctae peregrinationes, *by Bernhard von Breydenbach, published at Mainz in 1486, representing a ship in the Venetian base at Modon in the Peloponnesus.*

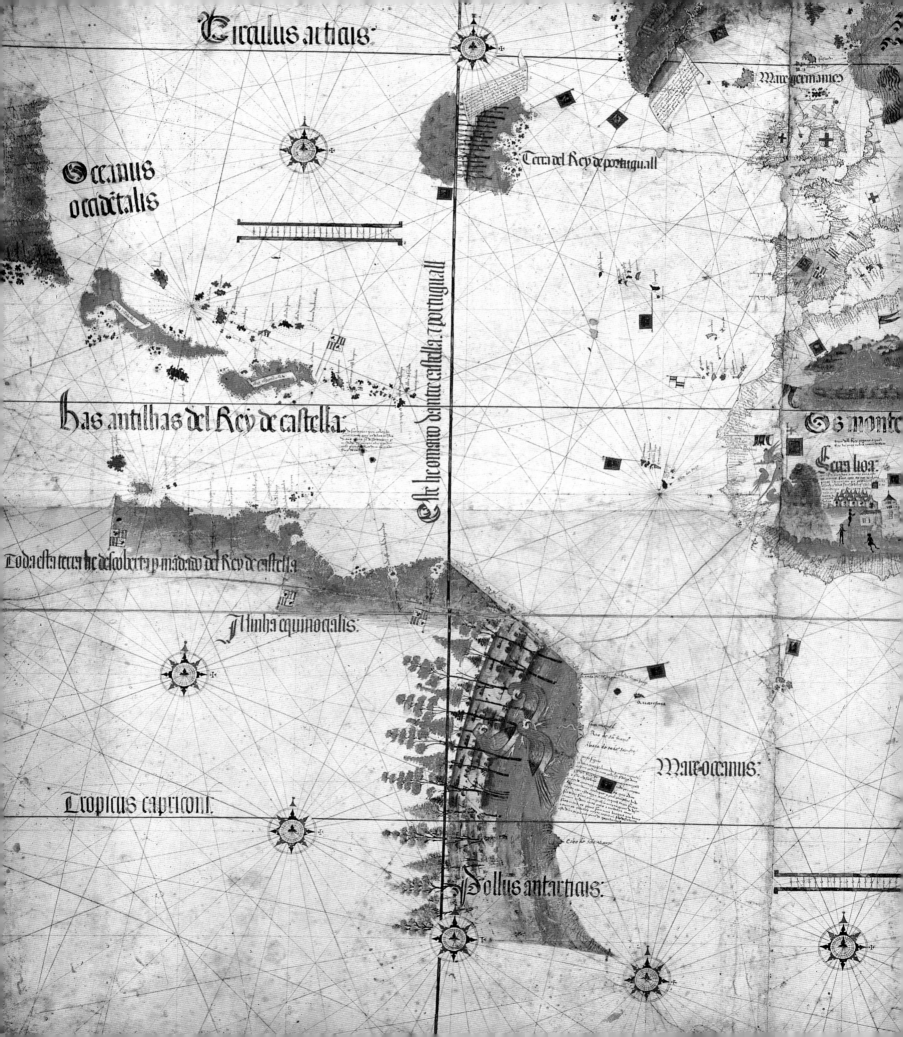

Circulus articus·

Oceanus
occidentalis

Terra del Rey de portuguall

Mare germanies

Has antilhas del Rey de castella·

Este he o mar de entre castella e portuguall

Os monte

Terra boa·

Toda esta terra he descoberta p mādato del Rey de castella·

Illinha equinocialis·

Mare oceanus·

Tropicus capricorni·

Pollus antarticus·

all Genoese, but also Florentine, Castilian,
and Jewish. Isabella and Ferdinand proceeded to name the oftimes refused mariner
an admiral: Now Don Cristobal Colon
would take his place among the nobles of
the realm with the titles of admiral, viceroy,
and governor of all the islands and continents that he might discover. He was to
receive one-tenth of the products of these
new lands and, against payment of one-
eighth of the costs, the same percentage was
due him from any eventual commercial
profits. The title of admiral was to be
hereditary.

The rest of the story is well known: the
boredom, the anxiousness, the fear during
the long voyage, then the commotion of the
landing, the triumphal return to Spain, the
new voyages in search of Cathay and the
Great Khan, the growing awareness that the
discovered land was not, in fact, the continent of Asia but a new continent. And
finally, what had begun in a blaze of glory
ended in shame and humiliation. Charges
of mismanagement plagued his administration in Hispaniola, and in 1500 Columbus
was returned to Spain in chains.

The Middle Ages ended, the modern age
dawned, and the world became suddenly
larger. The legacy of the year 1492 is reflected in the quivering, exhilarating light ashore,
distant and triumphant, observed by Columbus on the night of October 11-12, 1492.
"Like a little wax candle rising and falling,"
it was reflected over the surface of those
unknown waters, over the ancient legends,
over the tales of whirlpools and monsters,
over the distant glow, never again glimpsed,
of Cipangu with its golden roofs. That
distant light, that simple flame lit by the
Indians to keep away the autumn insects,
changed both the color of the ocean and the
course of history. Homage is due the admiral, and together with him all the adventurers and paupers, dreamers and villains, who
threw themselves on the waves of that dark,
frightening, and marvelous epic that was
the conquest of the New World. Of the
impulses that led them on that quest, we will
never know which was stronger — the love
of Christ or the love of adventure and the
thirst for gold. To all of them, founders of
the New World as we know it and of a new
history that began with themselves, is due
the homage of Manuel Machado:

How they believed only in incredible success
going beyond the limits of dreams
of the sea and of the impossible.
Captains of dreams and of chimeras
forever crossing the horizon
following the sun in its course.

221

History, Life, Culture

Chronology of the second half of the 15th century

1450

In this year, Nicholas V is pope; the emperor in the West is Frederick III, elected but not yet crowned, while the Eastern emperor is Constantine XI (Constantine Palaeologus); the king of France is Charles VII, the dauphin crowned by Joan of Arc; the king of England is Henry VI, son of the great Henry V and Catherine of Valois; James II is king of Scotland; the duke of Burgundy is Philip the Good; the king of Portugal is Alfonso V (Alfonso the African); the king of Aragon, Sicily, and Naples is Alfonso V; the king of Castile is John II; the titular king of Bohemia and Hungary is the young Ladislaus of Hapsburg; the king of Poland is Kasimir IV; the king of Denmark and Norway is Christian I; the sultan of the Ottoman Turks is Murad II; the grand duke of Moscovy is Basil II; the doge of Venice is Francesco Foscari; the ruler, though lacking a title, of Florence is Cosimo de' Medici.

Charles VII of France wrests from the English all of Normandy. Francesco Sforza takes over Milan and becomes duke, ending that city's short-lived republic.

Nicolas of Cusa, made bishop of Brixen, travels as papal legate through the imperial territories, preaching renewal of the church.

Leon Battista Alberti begins outlining his influential architectural treatise *De re aedificatoria*. Jean Fouquet paints the *Diptych of Melun* using Agnès Sorel, the favorite of Charles VII, as model for the Madonna.

Three foreign artists make celebrated journeys to Italy during or around this year: Rogier van der Weyden to Ferrara, Petrus Christus to Milan, and Jean Fouquet to Rome.

1451

Philip the Good of Burgundy joins Luxembourg to his dominions.

Led by Dunois, the French take Bordeaux and Bayonne from the English.

Twenty-two-year-old Mohammed II succeeds his father, Murad II, on the throne of the Ottoman Turks.

Rogier van der Weyden paints the *Universal Judgment.*

1452

Nicholas V crowns Frederick III emperor at Rome, the last imperial coronation to take place in that city.

George of Podebrad is elected "administrator" of the kingdom of Bohemia by a diet at Prague.

John Hunyadi, elected regent of Hungary by the Hungarian states in 1446, lays down his power, which passes to the 12-year-old Ladislaus

(posthumous son of the emperor Albert II and thus known as Ladislaus Posthumus, he was duke of Austria and titular king of Hungary and Bohemia; the emperor Frederick III was his uncle).

At Mainz, Johann Gutenberg begins printing a Bible (the 42-line Bible, so-called because of the number of lines per page); he probably printed a calender in 1448, the first instance of printing with movable type.

Lorenzo Ghiberti completes the third bronze door of the Florentine baptistery, called by Michelangelo the "gates of paradise."

Piero della Francesca works on the frescoes of the *Story of the True Cross* in the Church of San Francesco in Arezzo.

1453

Mohammed II besieges and conquers Constantinople; the last Eastern emperor, Constantine Palaeologus, dies in the defense of the city.

The French defeat the English under Talbot at Castillon, ending the Hundred Years War. The city of Calais is the only English possession left on French soil.

Ladislaus is crowned king at Prague, but the true ruler of Bohemia is still the regent, George of Podebrad.

Seventy-three-year-old Poggio Bracciolini becomes chancelor of Florence and begins to write the history of the city.

Nicolas of Cusa writes *De pace fidei.*

Padua is the scene of a celebrated marriage that joins two families of artists: Andrea Mantegna marries Nicolosia, sister of Gentile and Giovanni Bellini and daughter of Jacopo.

1454

The peace of Lodi between Milan and Venice, to which Florence is also a signatory, ends the wars in Lombardy and Tuscany and begins a period of political balance among the Italian states.

The city of San Gallo joins the confederation of Swiss cantons.

The Prussian League recognizes the sovereignty of Kasimir IV, king of Poland; thus begins the long war between the Polish ruler and the order of the Teutonic Knights, which dominates the southeastern Baltic coasts.

1455

Nicholas V dies, and the Spanish cardinal Alfonso Borgia is elected pope as Calixtus III.

Richard of York, protector of Henry VI, takes the place of Edmund Beaufort, duke of Somerset. Thus begins the Wars of the Roses between the houses of York (white rose) and

Lancaster (red rose). Somerset, head of the Lancastrians, is defeated and killed at St. Albans.

An incident from the chronicles: Two middle-class men of Valenciennes take part in a trial by combat, witnessed by Philip the Good. The two battle with cudgels and bucklers; the loser is hanged.

Roberto Valturio completes *De re militari*, the first technical treatise of military arts to be printed (1472).

1456

A Christian army commanded by the elderly John Hunyadi defeats the Turks at Belgrade.

Calixtus III issues a bull calling for a crusade against the Turks.

On Christmas night, a 25-year-old student, together with other rogues, enters the College of Navarre in Paris and steals 500 golden scudos. The student, whose criminal record already includes the fatal wounding of a man in a fight, is the poet François Villon.

Various chronicles note the passage of an exceptionally large comet, covering one-third of the visible sky; Paolo dal Pozzo Toscanelli makes a precise description, including drawings, of what would later be known as Halley's Comet from his observatory in Florence.

Paolo Uccello finishes the three-panel *Battle of San Romano.*

The final work on the façade of Santa Maria Novella in Florence, based on plans by Leon Battista Alberti, begins.

1457

Kasimir IV of Poland occupies Marienburg, capital of the Teutonic Knights; the seat of the grand master of the order is transferred to Königsberg.

Christian I of Denmark is crowned king of Sweden at Uppsala; the defeated Charles VIII Knutsson leaves Sweden.

The Genoese Usodimare reaches the Cape Verde Islands in a Portuguese caravel.

An unknown master paints the *Pietà* of Avignon.

1458

Eighty-year-old Calixtus III dies, and the conclave elects Cardinal Enea Silvio Piccolomini as Pope Pius II.

Alfonso V, king of Aragon, Sicily, and Naples, dies; his brother John II, king of Navarre, succeeds him in Aragon and Sicily, while Naples goes to his son Ferdinand I.

The last Christian dominions in Greece fall into the hands of Mohammed II; Venice manages to hold onto its coastal bases.

Following the death (1457) of Ladislaus Posthumus, the young Matthias Corvinus, son of John Hunyadi, becomes king of Hungary, George of Podebrad is elected king of Bohemia, and the emperor Frederick III and his brother Albert VI divide Austria (Frederick takes lower Austria and Vienna).

1459

Pius II assembles the princes of Europe in a congress at Mantua to organize a crusade against the Turks as Mohammed II conquers Serbia.

The emperor Frederick III succeeds in having himself elected king of Hungary by part of the Magyar nobility but fails to get the upper hand against Matthias Corvinus.

Nicolas of Cusa draws the first modern map of Germany.

Michelozzo di Bartolomeo completes the Medici palace in Via Larga (later the Medici-Riccardi palace), home of Cosimo il Vecchio.

Under the guidance of Pope Pius II, Bernardo Rossellino begins restructuring the pope's village birthplace of Corsignano (today Pienza).

1460

Portugal's Henry the Navigator dies; under his guidance Portuguese explorations along the African coast have rounded Cape Verde and reached Sierra Leone.

In the English Wars of the Roses, the Yorkists defeat the Lancastrians at Northampton, but the Lancastrians gain a victory at Warwick, where Richard of York dies. Richard Neville, duke of Warwick, sides with the house of York and the young Edward, son of Richard.

Mohammed II overcomes the last pockets of resistance in Morea (Peloponnesus).

Following the death of their ruler, the states of Schleswig and Holstein select as successor Christian I, king of Denmark.

1461

Louis XI succeeds his father, Charles VII, as king of France.

The Yorkists proclaim Edward IV king and defeat the Lancastrians at Towton; Henry IV and Queen Margaret flee the kingdom.

Donatello begins work on the bronze pulpits in Florence's church of San Lorenzo; he will die in 1466 without completing the project.

1462

Ivan III, 22 years old, succeeds Basil II as great duke of Muscovy.

Mohammed continues his campaign of conquest, taking Lesbo from the Genoese and conquering the Greek empire of Trebizond.

Under the orders of Louis XI, the city of Lyons is given the privilege to hold four annual fairs.

Driven out by the Turks, Thomas Palaeologus, despot of Morea, arrives at Ancona with the blessed head of the apostle Andrew; Pope Pius II travels to Narni to receive the reliquary, with which he then makes a processional entry in Rome, on foot and accompanied by seven cardinals.

Benozzo Gozzoli completes the fresco of the *Procession of the Magi* in the Medici palace in Florence.

After the donation by Cosimo de' Medici of a villa at Careggi, Marsilio Ficino begins the direction of Florence's Platonic Academy, where he will teach for 20 years.

François Villon, the most important 15th-century French poet, begins composing his *Testament*.

1463

Matthias Corvinus, recognized king of Hungary by Frederick III in exchange for the promise that a Hapsburg will succeed him if he dies without heir, reconquers Moldavia from the Turks.

With the fall to the Turks of the coastal stronghold of Argos, Venice declares war on the Ottoman empire (the war will last until 1479).

Mohammed II occupies Bosnia.

Louis XI of France acquires the cities of the Somme, which were given as security to Burgundy about 30 years earlier.

Ivan III of Muscovy joins the grand duchy of Yaroslavl to his territory.

1464

Pius II dies at Ancona, where he had gone to begin a crusade against the Turks. He is succeeded by the Venetian Pietro Barbo (Paul II).

The celebrated farce *Pathelin* is composed in France.

Antonio Averulino, known as Filarete, dedicates his *Trattato di Architettura* to Piero de' Medici.

1465

The Ligue du Bien Public (League of the Public Weal), of which Charles, duke of Berry (brother of Louis XI) and Charles, count of Charolais (later Charles the Bold, duke of Burgundy), are part, meet the king of France in a battle at Montlery that has an uncertain outcome but forces the king to restore the cities of the Somme

to Burgundy and cede Normandy to the duke of Berry.

Charles of Orléans dies. Son of a brother of the king of France Charles VI, he had been captured by the English at Agincourt (1415) and passed 25 years in prison in England, where he composed a collection of verses (*Libre de la prison*).

Luciano Laurana plans and directs the enlargement of the ducal palace at Urbino; he will be followed, in 1477, by Francesco di Giorgio Martini.

1466

The Second Peace of Torun, made at a city on the banks of the Vistula between Poland and the Teutonic Knights, confirms the political decline of the order. Some of its territory becomes property of the king of Poland; the rest is recognized as falling under the sovereignty of the Polish crown.

Pope Paul II excommunicates for heresy and declares deposed George of Podebrad, king of Bohemia, for being favorable to the Hussites.

The first bible in German is published at Strasbourg.

1467

Mohammed II is unsuccessful in his attack on the Albanian cities tenaciously defended by George Castriota Scanderbeg.

Charles the Bold succeeds his father, Philip the Good (who died at the age of 71), as duke of Burgundy.

Charles VIII Knutsson returns to Sweden to regain power.

Arnold Pennartz and Conrad Schweinheim, the two Germans who brought the art of printing to Italy, publish Cicero's *Epistulae familiares*.

1468

Charles the Bold forces on France's Louis XI the Treaty of Peronne, with which the king of France is forced to assist in the repression of the revolt in Liège that Louis himself had stirred up and supported. The duke of Burgundy marries Margaret of York, daughter of Edward IV of England, with whom he forms an alliance.

Denmark's Christian I gives his 12-year-old daughter, Margaret, as a wife to James III of Scotland; the Orkney and Shetland archipelagoes are part of her dowry.

With the death of Scanderbeg, the Turks overcome Albanian resistance.

Following the death of Sigismondo Malatesta, work on the Malatesta temple at Rimini, planned by Leon Battista Alberti, is suspended.

Cardinal Bessarion donates his library to Venice (it forms the nucleus of the Marciana Library).

1469

Isabella, daughter and heir of Henry IV of Castile, weds Ferdinand, son and heir of John II of Aragon; the ages of the spouses are 18 and 17.

Twenty-year-old Lorenzo de' Medici succeeds his father, Piero, in the informal but actual rulership of Florence.

Burgundy's Charles the Bold gives aid to Sigismund of Hapsburg, duke of Tyrol, against the Swiss Confederates in exchange for territories in Upper Saxony and on the right bank of the Rhine (Treaty of Saint Omer).

Matthias Corvinus, champion of the crusade against George of Podebrad called by Paul II, has himself proclaimed king of Bohemia by the Catholic nobility at Brno. He will be forced out by Podebrad with the aid of the Hussites.

The merchant Niccolò dei Conti dies at Chioggia. Converted to Islam, between 1415 and 1439 he traveled through the Orient with his family. He obtained a pardon from Pope Eugenius IV upon his return and, at the pope's request, dictated a narration his voyages and a description of the countries visited to the papal chancellor Poggio Bracciolini, and the humanist had inserted his story in his *De varietate fortunae* (*On the vicissitudes of fortune*).

1470

The Turks take Negroponte (Euboea), the major Venetian base in the Aegean.

In the Wars of the Roses, the Lancastrians (now backed by Warwick), with the aid of the French, force Edward IV to flee to his brother-in-law Charles the Bold in Burgundy. Henry VI returns to the English throne.

Charles VIII Knutsson, king of Sweden, dies, and Sten Sture the Elder becomes regent.

About this time, Piero della Francesca assembles *De prospectiva pingendi*, the first treatise on perspective, which will remain unpublished (although well known) until 1899.

Leonardo da Vinci, son of the notary Piero di Antonio, is in the Florence workshop of Andrea del Verrocchio.

Work begins on the decoration of the Salone dei Mesi (Hall of Months) at the Schifanoia palace in Ferrara; this will be the most important astrological cycle in Italian art.

1471

Paul II gives the Este family, feudatory nobles of the empire, the rank of dukes of Ferrara.

Succeeding Paul II, the cardinal Francesco della Rovere becomes pope (as Sixtus IV).

At the diet of Ratisbon, Frederick III promulgates a law for the "peace of the empire" that outlaws feuds.

With the help of the Burgundians and the Hanseatic cities, Edward IV returns to England; Warwick is defeated and killed at Barnet, and at Tewkesbury Queen Margaret (of Anjou, wife of Henry VI) is killed; Henry VI is locked in the Tower of London where he soon dies, almost certainly murdered.

Ivan III conquers Novgorod, large and free mercantile city.

Portuguese navigators reach the Gold Coast (Ghana).

Near Stockholm, Sten Sture defeats the invading Christian I of Denmark and forces him to leave Sweden.

The death of George of Podebrad opens the Bohemian succession; elected as king is the 15-year-old Ladislaus, son of Kasimir IV, king of Poland, but another pretender to the throne, Matthias Corvinus of Hungary, goes to war against him.

The 28-year-old Giuliano della Rovere (the future Julius II) is made a cardinal by his uncle Sixtus IV.

Thomas à Kempis, author of the *Imitation of Christ*, dies.

A museum is begun in Rome based on the ancient sculptures donated by Sixtus IV, including the *She-Wolf of the Capitol*.

1472

Ivan III, great duke of Muscovy, marries Zoe Palaeologus, niece of the last Eastern emperor.

The aging John II of Aragon conquers Barcelona and is recognized king by the Catalans.

The first printed edition of Dante's *Divine Comedy* is published in Italy.

The chancel of the church of Saint Lawrence at Nuremberg is completed.

Philippe de Comines, godson of the duke of Burgundy, Philip the Good, and courtier of Charles the Bold, goes into the service of the king of France, Louis XI. His *Mémoires* will become a work of fundamental importance on the reigns of Louis XI and Charles VIII.

1473

A meeting at Trier between Charles the Bold and the emperor Frederick III ends without the hoped for result: Burgundy does not obtain the royal title.

Nicholas Copernicus is born in Torun in Poland.

1474

In an accord at Utrecht, the German Hanseatic cities obtain a guarantee of their mercantile privileges in England in return for the help given Edward IV to retake the throne.

At Constance, Duke Sigismund of Tyrol and the Swiss Confederated cantons exchange recognition of their respective territories and unite in league with the Rhine enemies of Burgundy to oppose Charles the Bold.

Ivan III of Muscovy absorbs the duchy of Rostov.

With the death of Henry IV of Castile, Isabella, wife of the heir of Aragon, becomes queen.

Marsilio Ficino completes the *Theologia platonica*.

Andrea Mantegna completes the decoration of the Camera degli Sposi (Bridal Chamber) for the Gonzagas of Mantua.

Bartolomé Bermejo, leading representative of 15th-century Spanish painting, is commissioned to make a polyptych for the church of San Domenico of Daroca (the central portion of the work is *The Blessing of Saint Dominic of Silos*).

1475

Edward IV of England lands at Calais and negotiates with Louis XI the Peace of Picquigny; in exchange for cash, Edward agrees to relinquish all English claims to the French throne.

The Turks conquer the great commercial center of Caffa in the Crimea, the reputed home of the coffee plant.

The emperor Frederick III goes to war against Charles the Bold; the Burgundian promises his 18-year-old daughter Mary in marriage to the 16-year-old son of the emperor, Maximilian. Charles the Bold drives René II (nephew of the *bon roi* René) from Lorraine and enters Nancy.

The Jews of Trent are accused of the ritual murder of a Christian baby (Simone, later Saint Simonino) on Holy Saturday and are expelled from the city.

The future great humanist Johann Reuchlin of Pforzheim becomes a student in the university of Basel.

Aristotele Fieravanti begins construction of the Cathedral of the Assumption in the Kremlin at Moscow.

1476

The duke of Burgundy, Charles the Bold, attacks the Swiss Confederates but is ruinously defeated by the pike-wielding infantry at Grandson and at Morat (Murten). The spoils of war taken by the

224

victors—tapestries, jewels, illuminated manuscripts, and other artistic treasures that customarily traveled with the dukes of Burgundy even on military campaigns—is one of the richest of all times.

Ferdinand of Aragon defeats Alfonso V of Portugal. The Portuguese monarch claims Castile because of his marriage—never sanctioned by the Church—to Juana la Beltraneja, officially daughter and heiress of Henry IV of Castile.

In Florence, Verrocchio executes his *David*.

In Venice, Antonello da Messina paints the celebrated *San Cassiano Altarpiece*.

Johann Müller—known as Regiomontanus from the name of the city of his birth, Königsberg—dies of the plague in Rome, where he had been called by Sixtus IV to work on the reform of the calendar; in 1472 he had published *Ephemerides astronomicae ab anno 1475 ad annum 1506*, used by the first great maritime explorers, including Columbus.

1477

The duke of Burgundy, Charles the Bold, falls in battle near Nancy, defeated by a coalition of Swiss, the duke of Tyrol, Alsatians, and the forces of René II of Lorraine. This is the end of Burgundy as an independent duchy; Charles's daughter and heiress, Mary of Burgundy, is forced to cede to the cities of the Low Countries the "great privilege" that ends Burgundy's centralizing force. In August Mary marries Maximilian, son of the emperor Frederick III, and the contest begins with the king of France, Louis XI, for control of Burgundy.

Hugo van der Goes completes the altarpiece for Tommaso Portinari, which is brought to Florence in 1485.

In Rome, Melozzo da Forlì depicts Pope Sixtus IV giving custody of the Vatican Library to Platina in a fresco for the dedication of the library.

1478

Ivan III, great duke of Muscovy, annexes the republic of Novgorod.

Edward IV of England has his brother George of Clarence put to death for having joined Warwick and the Lancastrians in restoring Henry VI to the throne in 1470.

In Florence, the Pazzi conspiracy against the Medici fails. Giuliano de' Medici is murdered, but Lorenzo escapes. Because of the death of Giuliano de' Medici, Angelo Poliziano (Politian) leaves unfinished his *Stanze per la giostra*, a verse description of a tournament in which Giuliano was victorious.

Sandro Botticelli paints *Primavera* for the Medici of Castello (the cadet branch of the Florentine family).

Thomas More, author of *Utopia* (1516), is born.

It is probably in this year that Giorgione is born at Castelfranco.

In one of the most prodigious technical undertakings of the period, construction is begun on a tunnel through Monte Viso to connect Delfinato and the Marchesato of Saluzzo; the tunnel is excavated at more than 2000 meters above sea level and is two meters high and two and one-half meters wide.

1479

John II of Aragon dies and is succeeded by his son Ferdinand, husband of Isabella, who had inherited Castile; Aragon and Castile are thus joined, beginning the history of united Spain.

The war between Venice and the Ottoman Turks ends with an onerous peace for Venice, which must accept the loss of various territories and bases in Albania, Greece, and the Aegean islands and pay an annual tribute for the maintenance of its commercial privileges. Following the peace between Venice and the Ottomans, the Venetian painter Gentile Bellini is invited to Constantinople to paint the portrait of Mohammed II.

In the contest for the Burgundian succession, Archduke Maximilian (later Emperor Maximilian I) defeats Louis XI at Guinegate.

At Olmutz, the dispute for Bohemia between Ladislaus and Matthias Corvinus of Hungary ends; both will bear the title king of Bohemia, Ladislaus for Bohemia, Matthias for Moravia, Silesia, and Lusatia.

Hans Memling paints the triptych *Adoration of the Magi* for the Hospital of Saint John in Bruges.

1480

René of Anjou, the *bon roi* René, dies. He had been duke of Lorraine (1431-1453) as part of his wife's inheritance and had then ceded to his son the Kingdom of Naples; however, this had been taken from him by Alfonso of Aragon; but for a long time he had been count of Provence (since 1434). He was known as a poet (*Le livre du cuer d'amours éspris*, 1457). His daughter Margaret of Anjou was wife of Henry VI of England.

Lodovico Sforza, known as il Moro, assumes power in Milan. He is the son of the second Sforza duke of Milan, Galeazzo Maria, and thus uncle of the direct successor, the 9-year-old Giangaleazzo, whom he confines in the castle of Pavia.

The Turks take Otranto (they will remain there until the following year).

The Knights of Saint John (the Knights Hospitalers; later known as the Knights of Rhodes and then Malta) repulse a Turkish attack

on their stronghold on the island of Rhodes.

The final attack on Moscow by the Tartars of the Golden Horde aided by Lithuania fails; the great duke of Moscovy thus frees himself from the yoke of the heirs of Ghengis Khan.

An ancient statue of Apollo is found in the vineyard of Cardinal della Rovere at Grottaferrata; it is then put on display at Belvedere (and thus it is known today as the *Apollo Belvedere*).

1481

Ferdinand and Isabella go to war against the kingdom of Granada, the last Muslim stronghold in Spain.

Alfonso V of Portugal dies and is succeeded by John II.

Christopher I dies and his son John II becomes king of Denmark and Norway.

Mohammed II, conqueror of Constantinople, dies and is succeeded as Turkish sultan by his son Bayazid II.

Charles, duke of Maine, whose uncle René of Anjou had been made heir of Provence, dies; thus, like Anjou, both Maine and Provence become dominions of the French king. The Anjou rights to Naples also become property of the crown.

Sixtus IV calls the best-known Florentine painters—Sandro Botticelli, Domenico Ghirlandaio, Piero di Cosimo, and Cosimo Rosselli—to Rome for the decoration of the Sistine Chapel.

The Tyrolean painter-sculptor Michael Pacher executes the altarpiece in the village church of Sankt Wolfgang in Austria.

1482

Concerned with agitation in the cities of Flanders, Maximilan, ruler of the Low Countries (since in this year his wife, Mary of Burgundy, has died), reaches an agreement with the king of France, Louis XI (the Treaty of Arras). France retains Burgundy—properly speaking, the cities of the Somme and Artois and Franche-Comté—since these were part of the dowry of Margaret of Austria (daughter of Maximilian and Mary, born only two years earlier), the promised bride to the future Charles VIII, son of Louis XI.

James III of Scotland goes to war against Edward IV of England.

For the third time, Matthias Corvinus attacks the hereditary Austrian dominions of the emperor Frederick III.

Led by Diogo Cão, the Portuguese reach the mouth of the Congo River.

Francesco di Giorgio Martini writes his *Trattato d'Architettura*.

Jean Colombe begins work for Charles I of Savoy; he will complete the *Trés riches heures* of the duke of Berry, an illuminated manuscript later inherited by the House of Savoy.

1483

Sixtus IV approves the nomination of the Dominican Tomás de Torquemada as the grand inquisitor in Spain.

In Portugal, the duke of Braganza, brother-in-law of the queen, becomes leader of a conspiracy of nobles that has the support of the Spanish kings Ferdinand and Isabella; John II of Portugal will condemn him (and kill with his own hand the queen's brother, the duke of Viseu, implicated in the revolt).

The Turks occupy Herzegovina.

The 13-year-old Charles VIII, son of Louis XI, assumes the throne of France; his sister Anne of Beaujeu acts as regent.

With the death of Edward IV of England, his sons, Edward V, age 13, and Richard, 10, are entrusted to their uncle Richard of Gloucester, who has them declared illegitimate and then imprisoned in the Tower of London, where they were presumably murdered. Gloucester is proclaimed king as Richard III.

In the service of Lodovico Sforza in Milan, Leonardo da Vinci paints the *Virgin of the Rocks*.

After working in Urbino for Federico da Montefeltro, the painter Pedro Berruguete returns to Spain.

The first two volumes of the chivalric epic *Orlando innamorato*, by Matteo Maria Boiardo, are published; the poem was begun in 1476, and the author will work on it until his death (1494). Ariosto's *Orlando furioso* will take up the tale.

Raphael, son of the painter Giovanni Santi, is born in Urbino.

Martin Luther, son of a miner, is born in Eisleben.

1484

Cardinal Giovanni Battista Cybo is elected pope (as Innocent VIII) following the death of Sixtus IV.

The papal bull *Summis desiderantes affectibus* authorizes the Dominicans Heinrich Kramer and Jakob Sprenger to carry out investigations into the phenomenon of witches in Germany; on the basis of their experience the two inquisitors will publish (Strasbourg, 1487) the celebrated treatise *Malleus maleficarum (Hammer of witches)*.

After passing two years as a lector in the convent of San Marco in Florence, the Dominican Girolamo Savonarola becomes an itinerant preacher in various cities of northern Italy.

Ulrich Zwingli, the future Protestant reformer, is born in Wildhaus, Switzerland.

According to astrological prognostications, 1484 is a *magnus annus*.

1485

Henry Tudor, duke of Richmond and Lancastrian heir, lands in England; at Bosworth Field he defeats the forces of Richard III, who is killed in the battle. Tudor becomes king of England as Henry VII and weds Elizabeth, daughter of Edward IV, uniting the houses of Lancaster and York and thus ending the Wars of the Roses.

Ivan III of Moscovy annexes to his dominions the principality of Tver.

The king of Hungary, Matthias Corvinus, seizes the city of Vienna and makes it his personal residence.

In Naples, a conspiracy of nobles against Ferdinand I fails.

William Caxton, England's first printer, publishes the *Morte d'Arthur*, written by the adventurer Sir Thomas Malory during his long years of imprisonment.

The Venetian Giovanni Bellini paints *Saint Job*.

The Neapolitan pastoral poet Jacopo Sannazaro, courtier of the duke of Calabria, completes the *Arcadia*, which is not published, however, until 1504.

An incident from the chronicles: In Orléans, people climb onto roofs to listen to the Lenten sermons of Olivier Maillard; 64 working days are needed to repair the damage.

1486

Maximilian is elected and crowned king of the Romans. His father, the emperor Frederick III, issues the *Reichlandsfriedengesetz*, a law for the peace of the empire.

Work is begun on the façade of the church of Saint Paul in Valladolid.

Tiziano Vecellio (Titian), aged 9, of Pieve di Cadore, is brought to Venice to learn art in the workshop of Sebastiano Zuccato.

Hieronymus van Aeken (the painter Hieronymus Bosch, believed to have been born around 1460) enrolls in the Brotherhood of Our Lady, a confraternity of the cathedral of s'Hertogenbosch.

In the courtyard of the Ferrara castle, members of the Este court perform an Italian translation of *Menaechmi*, by Plautus, in one of the first examples of the revival of classical theater.

1487

The Portuguese Bartolomeu Dias rounds the southern extremity of Africa, known as the Cape of Storms (later the Cape of Good Hope).

An 11-year-old boy who will later be

known as Erasmus enters an Augustinian monastery in Rotterdam.

1488

James III of Scotland dies in battle against rebellious nobles; he is succeeded by his 15-year-old son James IV.

Maximilian is made a prisoner by the rebellious citizens of Bruges. He will be freed when his father, Frederick III, and German princes attack the city.

Nobles and the cities of the Swabian League gather at Esslingen in response to intrusions by neighbors, particularly Bavaria. The duke of Württemberg, the margrave of Baden, and the duke Sigismund of Tyrol also side with the league.

In Milan, Donato Bramante completes the sacristy of the church of San Satiro.

Verrocchio dies without completing his last work, the equestrian statue of the condottiere Bartolomeo Colleoni, which will be finished in 1496 by Leopardi.

The 13-year-old Michelangelo Buonarroti enters the Florentine workshop of Domenico Ghirlandaio.

Following his father's wishes, the 15-year-old Lodovico Ariosto begins the study of law at the university of Ferrara.

1489

The Venetian Caterina Cornaro, widow and heiress of James II of Lusignan, king of Cyprus, agrees to cede the island to the republic of Venice in return for the domain of Asolo, to which she retires. Her court at Asolo will gain a reputation of literary and artistic distinction.

Ferdinand of Aragon conquers Malaga.

Muscovy continues to expand, acquiring the republic of Vjatka.

In Florence, Benedetto da Maiano begins construction of the Strozzi Palace.

Veit Stoss, a German painter, sculptor, and engraver, completes the large polychrome wood altar in the church of Saint Mary in Krakow, one of the major examples of gothic art in the German region.

Giovanni Pico della Mirandola dedicates to Lorenzo de' Medici the *Heptaplus*, a sevenfold interpretation of Genesis derived from knowledge of the cabbala.

Antonio Allegri is born in a town near Parma; because of the place of his birth he will later be known as Correggio.

1490

Matthias Corvinus, king of Hungary, dies;

Maximilian immediately takes back the lost Austrian lands and enters Vienna. Ladislaus, king of Bohemia, is elected king of Hungary. In the same year Maximilian receives the lands of duke Sigismund of Tyrol and weds by proxy the 14-year-old Ann, duchess of Brittany.

In Spain, Bermejo paints the *Pietà* for the canon Lluis Desplà.

In Venice, Vittore Carpaccio begins to paint the large canvases with the *Legend of Saint Ursula*.

Leonardo designs the scenic astrological apparatus known as the "Festa del paradiso" (known from literary sources) for the wedding of Giangaleazzo Sforza and Isabella of Aragon.

Michelangelo is welcomed to the Medici court by Lorenzo the Magnificent.

On August 1, Girolamo Savonarola holds his first sermon in Florence in the church of San Marco.

Pope Innocent VIII makes Prince Djem, brother of the Ottoman sultan, Bayazid, his prisoner.

1491

The union of the crowns of Bohemia and Hungary by Ladislaus is formally accepted by Maximilian, who receives in exchange the right of succession should Ladislaus die without male heirs (the two crowns will eventually pass to the Hapsburgs with dynastic marriages between the heirs of Maximilian and those of Ladislaus).

Having annulled her matrimonial contract to Maximilian, Charles VIII of France marries Ann of Brittany and thus acquires the Breton duchy.

In Guipuzcoa is born the last of thirteen children, Ignatius de Loyola, who will later found the Jesuits.

1492

Cardinal Rodrigo Borgia is elected pope (as Alexander VI) by a conclave following the death of Innocent VIII.

With the death of Poland's Kasimir IV, his sons John I and Alexander become, respectively, king of Poland and great duke of Lithuania.

Veit Stoss carves the tomb of King Kasimir in the church of Saint Mary at Krakow.

Ivan III of Muscovy builds the fortress of Ivangorod in front of Narva, the commercial city founded by the Danes and then passed to the Hansa, which blocks access to the Baltic.

Lorenzo de' Medici dies at 43 years of age; his son Piero becomes head of the family and ruler of Florence.

For 745,000 scudos, Charles VIII of France buys peace from Henry VII of England (by the Treaty of Etaples), in preparation for his planned undertaking in Italy.

Granada, last Islamic city on the Spanish peninsula, falls to Ferdinand and Isabella. Following this Muslim defeat, the Jews are expelled from Spain.

The German navigator and cosmographer Martin Behaim constructs the first known world map in the form of a globe.

On behalf of the king of Spain, Christopher Columbus sets sail from Palos to reach the Indies by heading west. Having crossed the Atlantic Ocean he arrives at Guanahani in the Bahamas and later discovers Cuba and Haiti.

In one of the first instances of modern town planning the architect Biagio Rossetti designs, on behalf of Ercole I d'Este, the enlargement of Ferrara (the so-called Herculean addition).

1493

Defeated at Salins, Charles VIII of France concludes the peace of Senlis with Maximilian, ending the question of the Burgundian succession; Burgundy and Piccardy remain with France, which gives back Artois, Charolais, and Franche-Comtè to the Hapsburgs (who also retain the Low Countries, the wealthiest area of the former dominions of Burgundy).

With the Peace of Barcelona, Charles VIII gives to Spain the counties of Roussillon and Cerdagne.

The Emperor Ferdinand III dies; Maximilian succeeds him in the empire in the hereditary lands of the Hapsburgs.

Having returned to announce his discovery, Columbus leaves on his second oceanic voyage.

With the papal bull *Inter caetera*, Alexander VI divides all the lands not already owned by Christian princes between Spain and Portugal following a line established to the west of the Azores.

The German doctor and humanist Hartman Schedel publishes at Nuremberg the *Liber chronicorum*.

Antonio del Pollaiuolo carves the tomb of Sixtus IV in Saint Peter's.

Hartmann Schedel's *Liber chronicorum* is illustrated in the workshop of Michael Wolgemut; known as the *Nuremberg Chronicle* and decorated with xylographs, it is one of the most precious German books; the young Dürer collaborates on the work.

1494

The Treaty of Tordesillas between Spain and Portugal relocates farther west the demarcation line in the ocean drawn by Alexander VI.

Bianca Maria Sforza, niece of Lodovico il Moro, weds the emperor Maximilian I.

Charles VIII enters Italy with a large army and powerful artillery to reclaim the Angevin reign of Naples.

Piero de' Medici is driven from Florence by the democratic faction and the city is given to Savonarola.

The 25-year-old Niccolò Machiavelli begins his bureaucratic career as an assistant in the Florentine chancellery.

Sebastian Brant publishes *Das Narrenschiff* (*The Ship of Fools*).

Albrecht Dürer begins his first trip to Venice.

The Succession of Power

Popes, Emperors, Kings, and Princes in 1492

These pages present the people who occupied the seats of political power during the last 50 years of the Middle Ages. Dynastic information is provided for each, as in many circumstances marriages and family rank had great historical importance.

Following the popes and the emperors are the rulers of England, France, Burgundy, Portugal, Castile, Aragon, the Italian states (Milan, Venice, Florence, Naples), Bohemia, Hungary, Denmark and Norway, Poland and Lithuania, Muscovy, and the empire of the Ottoman Turks.

The Popes

Nicholas V (1447-1455)
Italian named Tommaso Parentucelli; born in Sarzana (Liguria) in 1397; bishop of Bologna in 1444; made cardinal by Eugenius IV in 1446.

Calixtus III (1455-1458)
Spaniard named Alfonso Borgia; born in Jativa (province of Valencia) in 1378; archbishop of Valencia.

Pius II (1458-1464)
Italian named Enea Silvio Piccolomini; born in Corsignano (Siena) in 1405; scholar and secretary to Antipope Felix V and then Emperor Frederick III; ordained priest in 1446; made cardinal by Calixtus III in 1456.

Paul II (1464-1471)
Italian named Pietro Barbo; born in Venice in 1417; made cardinal by his uncle Eugenius IV in 1440.

Sixtus IV (1471-1484)
Italian named Francesco della Rovere; born in Celle Ligure (Savoy) in 1414; a Franciscan, he was made a general of the order in 1464; made cardinal by Paul II in 1467.

Innocent VIII (1484-1492)
Italian named Giovanni Battista Cybo; born in Genoa in 1432; made cardinal by Sixtus IV in 1473.

Alexander VI (1492-1503)
Spaniard named Rodrigo Lancol y Borja (or Rodrigo Borgia in Italian); born in Jativa (province of Valencia) in 1431; made cardinal by his uncle Calixtus III in 1455.

The Empire

Frederick III
Born in Innsbruck in 1415, died in Linz in 1493; son of Ernst I (Ernst the Iron, a Hapsburg of the Leopoldine line); on the death of his father (1424) he became duke of Styria and Carinthia; on the death (1439) of his distant cousin Albert II (a Hapsburg of the Albertine line; the division of the house into two branches took place with the two sons, Albert and Leopold, of Albert II, duke of Austria, Styria, and Carinthia, who died in 1358), he was elected king of Germany (1440); married Eleanor of Portugal (1452); was crowned emperor at Rome (1452); he inherited upper and lower Austria in 1457 on the death of Ladislaus Posthumus (son of Albert II).

Maximilian I
Born in Wiener-Neustadt in 1459, died in Wels in 1519; son of Frederick III; married (1477) Mary of Burgundy, daughter and heiress of Charles the Bold (by this marriage the Low Countries passed to the Hapsburgs); elected king of Germany (1486); married by proxy Anne of Brittany (1490; this marriage was annulled, and Anne married Charles VIII of France in 1491); succeeded his father as emperor (1493); married Bianca Maria Sforza, niece of Lodovico Sforza (1494); his son Philip I (Philip the Handsome) married Joanna the Mad, heiress of Ferdinand of Aragon and Isabella of Castile (their son, Charles V, heir to the Spanish crown and the Hapsburg dominions, was elected emperor in 1519).

England

Henry VI
Born in Windsor in 1421, died in London in 1471; son of Henry V and Catherine of Valois; became king when not yet nine months old under the regency of his uncles, Humphrey, duke of Gloucester, and John of Lancaster, duke of Bedford; married Margaret of Anjou (1445); the dynastic battle between the houses of Lancaster and York known as the Wars of the Roses began (1455); he fled (1461) when Edward IV was proclaimed king; restored by Warwick (1470), he was later imprisoned in the Tower of London, where he died.

Edward IV
Born in Rouen in 1442, died in Westminster in 1483; son of Richard, duke of York; was proclaimed king (1461) in place of Henry VI with the support of the earl of Warwick; Warwick then sided with Henry VI and put him back on the throne (1470), but Warwick died at Barnet (a victory for Edward with the help of his brother-in-law, Charles the Bold); Margaret of Anjou was captured at the battle of Tewkesbury, where the Lancastrian party was again defeated, and like her husband she was put in the Tower of London; Edward IV reigned the next 12 years in peace.

Richard III
Born in Fotheringhay Castle in 1452, died at Bosworth Field in 1485; younger brother of King Edward IV; on the death (1483) of Edward IV, Richard proclaimed himself regent and protector of his nephew, the young king Edward V, whom he put in the Tower of London, together with Edward V's brother, Richard, duke of York; Parliament declared his brother's children illegitimate and had Richard crowned king (1483); rumor has it that the two young princes were murdered; Henry Tudor (later Henry VII) landed in Wales and defeated and killed Richard at Bosworth Field (1485).

Henry VII
Born in Pembroke Castle in 1457, died in Richmond in 1509; son of Edmund Tudor, earl of Richmond, and Margaret Beaufort; on the death of the imprisoned Henry VI he became head of the house of Lancaster (the red rose) by maternal inheritance; forced to flee England under Edward IV (house of York, the white rose); he returned to England (1485), defeated Richard III at Bosworth Field, and became king; married (1486) Elizabeth of York (white rose), daughter of Edward IV, thus uniting the factions of the Wars of the Roses; his daughter Margaret Tudor married James IV of Scotland, a marriage that led ultimately to the Stuart line.

France

Charles VII (Charles the Victorious)
Born in Paris in 1403, died in Mehun-sur-Yevre in 1461; fifth son of Charles VI and Isabel of Bavaria; dauphin in 1417 following the deaths of all his older brothers; the Treaty of Troyes (1420) disinherited him from the throne in favor of Henry V of England; be became nominal king of France on the death of his father (1422); married Mary of Anjou (1422); he was crowned at Reims (1429) by Joan of Arc.

Louis XI
Born in Bruges in 1423, died in Plessis-les-Tours in 1483; son of Charles VII, whom he succeeded in 1461.

Charles VIII
Born in Amboise in 1470, died in Amboise in 1498; son of Louis XI, whom he succeeded (1483) under the regency of his sister Anne of Beaujeu; married Anne of Brittany (1491); having left no male heir, he was succeeded by his cousin Louis XII, of the Valois-Orléans branch, the head of which was Louis duke of Orléans, brother of King Charles V and husband of Valentina Visconti.

Burgundy

Philip the Good
Born in Dijon in 1396, died in Bruges in 1467; son of John the Fearless and Margaret of Bavaria and grandson of Philip the Bold (the Valois-Burgundy line began with Philip the Bold, younger son of King John II of France); duke of Burgundy after the death of his father (1419); married (1409) Michela, daughter of Charles VI, king of France, Bona d'Artois (1424), and Isabella of Portugal (1429).

Charles the Bold
Born in Dijon in 1433, died in Nancy in 1477; son of Philip the Good and Isabella of Portugal; married Catherine, daughter of Charles VII, king of France (1440), Isabella of Bourbon (1454), and Margaret of York, sister of Edward IV of England (1468); became duke of Burgundy on the death (1467) of his father.

Mary of Burgundy
Born in Brussels in 1457, died in Bruges in 1482; daughter of Charles the Bold and Isabella of Bourbon, heiress of Burgundy and the Burgundy territories; she married Emperor Maximilian of Hapsburg (1477).

Portugal

Alfonso V (Alfonso the African)
Born in Cintra in 1432, died in Cintra in 1481; son of Duarte and Queen Leonor; succeeded to the throne (1438) at the age of six in the care of his uncle, Dom Pedro, the duke of Coimbra, who was killed in 1449; married (1475) Juana la Beltraneja, daughter of Henry IV of Castile; his reign saw the efforts of Henry the Navigator, duke of Viseu, another uncle.

John II (John the Perfect)
Born in Lisbon in 1455, died in Alvor in 1495; son of Alfonso V, whom he succeeded in 1481.

Manuel I
Born in Alcochete in 1469, died in Lisbon in 1521; son of Ferdinand, duke of Viseu; succeeded (1495) his cousin John II, who left no heirs.

Castile

John II
Born in Toro in 1405, died in Valladolid in 1454; son of Henry III, whom he succeeded at the age of 22 months (1406) under the regency of his uncle Ferdinand.

Henry IV
Born in Valladolid in 1423, died in Madrid in 1474; son of John II, whom he succeeded in 1454; because the paternity of his daughter Juana la Beltraneja was in doubt (her mother, Juana of Portugal, was Henry IV's wife, but her father was reputed to be Beltran de la Cueva), Henry first made his brother Alfonso heir (he died in 1468) and then his sister Isabella.

Isabella I (Isabella the Catholic)
Born in Madrigal de la Altas Torres in 1451, died in Medina del Campo in 1504; daughter of John II; married (1469) Ferdinand, heir of Aragon; succeeded (1474) her brother Henry IV on the throne of Castile; her heiress was her daughter Joanna the Mad.

Aragon

Alfonso V (Alfonso the Magnanimous)
Born ca. 1396, died in Naples in 1458; son and successor of Ferdinand I as king of Aragon and Sicily; adopted and made heir by Joanna II of Naples (they quarreled, and the throne went to Louis III of Anjou and then to René of Anjou); at her death (1435) he was recognized as king of Naples (1442) after a long war; he left Naples to his son Ferdinand I and the rest of his kingdom to his brother John II.

John II
Born in Medina del Campo in 1398, died in Barcelona in 1479; son of Ferdinand I; king of Navarre beginning in 1425 through his marriage with Blanche, daughter of Charles III of Navarre; succeeded his brother Alfonso V as king of Aragon and Sicily.

Ferdinand II (Ferdinand the Catholic)
Born in Sos in 1452, died in Madrigalejo in 1516; son of John II of Aragon; married (1469) Isabella of Castile; succeeded his father as king of Aragon and Sicily (1479); since his wife was already queen of Castile (1474), their marriage brought about the union of the two Iberian crowns; on the death of Isabella (1504), Philip the Handsome (Philip I), son of Holy Roman Emperor Maximilian I and husband of Joanna the Mad (daughter of Ferdinand and Isabella), refused to recognize Isabella's will, which made Ferdinand ruler of Castile; Philip's death (1506) and Joanna's madness allowed Ferdinand to maintain his power in Castile; Ferdinand married (1506) Germaine de Foix, niece of Louis XII; this marriage was without issue, so the crown of Aragon and Castile passed to his grandson, Charles of Hapsburg (later Holy Roman Emperor Charles V), son of Philip I and Joanna.

Milan

Francesco Sforza
1401-1466; natural son of the condottiere Muzio Attendolo, called lo Sforza ("the forcer"); married Bianca Maria (1441), daughter of the duke of Milan Filippo Maria Visconti, and after Filippo's death (1447) made himself master of Milan and was proclaimed duke (1450).

Galeazzo Maria Sforza
Born in 1444, died in Milan in 1476; son of Francesco Sforza, whom he succeeded as duke (1466); married Bona of Savoy; his daughter Bianca Maria married the emperor Maximilian I.

Giangaleazzo Sforza
1469-1494; son of Galeazzo Maria Sforza, whom he succeeded as duke (1476) at the age of seven under the care of his mother, Bona of Savoy; he was deprived of power by his uncle Lodovico Sforza; his daughter Bona Sforza married Sigismund I of Poland.

Lodovico Sforza (Lodovico Il Moro)
Born in 1451, died in Loches in 1508; son of Francesco Sforza, he seized power in Milan, unseating his nephew Giangaleazzo (1479) and with Giangaleazzo's death (1494) assumed the title; married Beatrice d'Este; was first expelled from Milan in 1495 and then again in 1500 by Louis XII of France, who had a hereditary claim to the duchy of Milan because he was the grandson of Valentina Visconti, wife of his grandfather Louis of Orléans.

Venice, the Doges

Francesco Foscari (1423-1457)
Pasquale Malipiero (1457-1462)
Cristoforo Moro (1462-1471)
Niccolò Tron (1471-1473)
Niccolò Marcello (1473-1474)
Pietro Mocenigo (1474-1476)
Andrea Vendramin (1476-1478)
Giovanni Mocenigo (1478-1485)
Marco Barbarigo (1485-1486)
Agostino Barbarigo (1486-1501)

Florence and the Medici

Cosimo de' Medici (il Vecchio)
Born in Florence in 1389, died in Careggi in 1464; son of Giovanni di Bicci de' Medici and older brother of Lorenzo (head of the Castello line of the Medici family, from which came the condottiere Giovanni dalle Bande Nere and his son Cosimo I); virtual ruler of Florence, he succeeded his father (1429); exiled in 1433 but recalled the following year, he ruled with formal respect for republican institutions.

Piero de' Medici (il Gottoso)
Born in Florence in 1414, died in Florence in 1469; son of Cosimo, he succeeded his father as leader of the Florentine state (1464).

Lorenzo de' Medici (the Magnificent)
Born in Florence in 1449, died in Careggi in 1492; on the death of his father (1469) he governed, at first together with his brother Giuliano, who was assassinated during the Pazzi conspiracy (1478); married Clarice Orsini; his son Giovanni became Pope Leo X.

Piero II de' Medici
Born in Florence in 1471, died in Cassino in 1503; eldest son and successor of Lorenzo the Magnificent; was expelled (1494) because of his alliance with France's Charles VIII, in Italy to claim the crown of Naples; power in Florence passed to the democratic party, inspired by Girolamo Savonarola.

Naples

Alfonso I (V) of Aragon
Born ca. 1396, died in Naples in 1458; king of Aragon and Sicily; took Naples (1442) after a long war as the adopted heir (later revoked) of Joanna II.

Ferdinand I (Ferrante) of Aragon
Born in Valenza in 1423, died in 1494; son and successor in Naples of Alfonso of Aragon.

Alfonso II of Aragon
Born in 1448, died in 1495; son of Ferdinand I; Charles VIII of France invaded Naples (1495) during the period of Alfonso II's succession, and Alfonso abdicated in favor of his son and withdrew to Sicily, where he soon died.

Ferrante II (Ferdinand II) of Aragon
Born in Naples in 1467, died in Naples in 1496; son of Alfonso II; inherited the reign from his father, who abdicated following the French invasion; he took refuge at Messina and returned to Naples during the summer of 1495; he then became king of Naples as Ferdinand II.

Bohemia

Ladislaus V (Ladislaus Posthumus)
Born in Komarom in 1440, died in Prague in 1457; posthumous son of the German king Albert II, who was also king of Bohemia and Hungary; proclaimed king of Bohemia (1440, as Ladislaus I) and elected king of Hungary (1444); was under the guardianship of his uncle, the emperor Frederick III; was crowned (1453) king of Bohemia at Prague.

George of Podebrad
Born in Podebrad in 1420, died in Prague in 1471; Hussite nobleman, administrator during the minority of Ladislaus Posthumus; elected king of Bohemia (1458) after the death of Ladislaus; excommunicated by Pope Paul II (1466), who organized a crusade against him; Matthias Corvinus, in aid of the pope, attacked him and had himself proclaimed king by the Catholic nobility (1469) but was then driven out; at his death his supporters elected Uladislaus of Bohemia (as Ladislaus II).

Matthias Corvinus
Born in Cluj in 1440, died in Vienna in 1490; elected king of Hungary on the death of Ladislaus V (1458); persuaded by Pope Pius II to take up arms against George of Podebrad; took the title king of Bohemia (1469); the conflict continued until 1479, when Ladislaus II ceded to him Silesia, Lusatia, and Moravia.

Uladislaus II
Born in 1456, died in Buda in 1516; son of Kasimir IV of Poland; elected king of Bohemia (1471, as Ladislaus II) as successor to George of Podebrad and thus found himself in conflict with Matthias Corvinus, king of Hungary; after the death of Matthias Corvinus, Uladislaus II also had himself elected king of Hungary (1492).

Hungary

Ladislaus III
Born in Cracow in 1424, died at Varna in 1444; king of Poland (1434-1444); at the death of the emperor Albert II of Germany, who was also king of Bohemia and Hungary, he was elected king of Hungary (1440, as Uladislaus I) against the rights of Albert's son, Ladislaus Posthumus; died in battle against the Turks.

Ladislaus V (Ladislaus Posthumus)
Born in Komarom in 1440, died in Prague in 1457; posthumous son of the German king Albert II; proclaimed king of Bohemia at his birth; elected king of Hungary (1444, as Ladislaus V); Hungary was, however, ruled by John Hunyadi; after the death of John Hunyadi, he had Hunyadi's son Ladislaus decapitated (1457); hated for this act, he was forced to flee Hungary and go to Prague, where he died the same year, perhaps poisoned, perhaps of the plague.

Matthias Corvinus
Born in Cluj in 1440, died in Vienna in 1490; second son of John Hunyadi; elected king of Hungary (1458) after the death of Ladislaus V.

Uladislaus II
Born in 1456, died in Buda in 1516; son of Kasimir IV, king of Poland; already king of Bohemia in 1471, he was elected king of Hungary (1492, as Ladislaus VI) after the death of Matthias Corvinus.

Denmark and Norway

Christian I
Born in 1426, died in Copenhagen in 1481; son of Count Dietrich of Oldenburg, elected king of Denmark (1448), of Norway (1450), of Sweden (1457; he lost Sweden in 1471); inherited Schleswig and Holstein (1460).

John I
Born in Aalborg in 1455, died in Aalborg in 1513; son of Christian I; at his father's death (1481) he inherited Denmark and Norway; took the throne of Sweden in 1497, but the country rebelled.

Poland and Lithuania

Kasimir IV
Born in 1427, died in 1492; ruler of Poland and Lithuania (1447-1492), he took the throne of Poland after the death of his brother Ladislaus III.

John I
Born in Cracow in 1459, died in Torun in 1501; son and successor (1492) of Kasimir IV.

Muscovy

Vasily II
Born in 1415, died in 1462; grand duke of Moscow; son and successor of Vasily I, great prince of Vladimir and Moscow; his claim was contested by his uncle Iuri; he battled against his uncle and his two sons for 20 years (one of the sons of Iuri succeeded at a certain point in taking the throne temporarily and had Vasily blinded); he finally (1453) triumphed against his enemies.

Ivan III (Ivan the Great)
Born in Moscow in 1440, died in Moscow in 1505; great duke of Moscow and all Russia; son and successor (1462) of Vasily II; his second marriage was to Zoe Paleologa, niece of the last Byzantine emperor.

The Ottoman Turks

Murad II
Born ca. 1401, died in Edirne in 1451; son and successor of Mohammed I (1421).

Mohammed II
Born in Edirne in 1432, died in Tekfur Cayiri in 1481; son of Murad II, he first became sultan in 1445, when his father abdicated (only to immediately retake power), then definitely in 1451, on his father's death.

Bayazid II
Born ca. 1447, died in Demotika in 1512; son of Mohammed II, at the death of his father (1481) he was called to power by the janissaries, the elite arm of the Ottoman army, preferred to his brother Djem, who took refuge in the west; the janissaries forced him to abdicate (1512) in favor of his son Selim; he died a month later.

Selected Bibliography

For background material on the events, personalities, and ideas that predate the 15th century but that helped shape the world of the Renaissance, the reader is directed to the excellent text by Brian Tierney and Sidney Painter, *Western Europe in the Middle Ages, 1300-1475* (New York: Alfred A. Knopf, Inc., 1978). A good general introduction may also be found in the *Atlas of Medieval Europe* (New York: Facts On File Publications, 1983), by Donald Matthew.

One of the best overall texts on the 15th century itself is Will Durant's *Renaissance: A History of Civilization in Italy from 1304-1576 A.D.* (New York: Simon and Schuster, 1953); like its companion volumes in the Story of Civilization series, this one is thorough enough for the serious student of history while remaining understandable and interesting for the average reader. Somewhat more complex is Johan Huizinga's classic *Waning of the Middle Ages* (New York: Doubleday, 1954) or his *Men and Ideas: A Study of the Forms of Life, Thought and Art in the 14th and 15th Centuries* (New York: St. Martin's, 1984).

Other in-depth texts include the first volume in the Cambridge New Modern History, *The Renaissance, 1493-1520* (1957), edited by G. R. Potter, and John Rigby Hale's *Renaissance Europe: The Individual and Society, 1480-1520* (University of California Press, 1978). Shorter but very good overviews are found in Myron P. Gilmore's *World of Humanism: 1453-1517* (New York: Harper & Row, 1952) and *The Foundations of Early Modern Europe, 1460-1559* (New York: W. W. Norton & Company, Inc., 1970), by Eugene F. Rice, Jr. See also *The Fifteenth Century: The Prospect of Europe*, by Margaret Aston (New York: Harcourt Brace, 1968).

For more information on specific topics, one may begin by looking up a particular entry in the *Encyclopedia of the Renaissance* (New York: Facts On File Publications, 1987), edited by Thomas Bergin, Jennifer Speake, and others, or John Rigby Hale's *Concise Encyclopaedia of the Italian Renaissance* (New York: Oxford University Press, 1981).

Fernand Braudel is a distinguished economic historian whose work on the subject of 15th-century finance has become the acknowledged starting point for any further investigation; see in particular the first three volumes in the Civilization and Capitalism series: *The Structures of Everyday Life* (1985), *The Wheels of Commerce* (1986), and *The Perspective of the World* (1984), all published by Harper & Row. See also his two-volume work, *The Mediterranean and the Mediterranean World in the Age of Phillip II* (New York: Harper & Row, 1978). In recent years, a remarkable group of French historians has begun to reconstruct history by focusing on the details of everyday life rather than political events. The second volume in the History of Private Life series, *Revelations of the Medieval World*, by Georges Duby (Cambridge, Mass.: Harvard University Press, 1988), *Montaillou*, by Emmanuel Le Roy Ladurie (New York: George Braziller, 1978), and *The Civilization of Medieval Europe*, by Jacques Le Goff (New York: Basil Blackwell, 1988) are particularly revealing.

For an account of the role of women in this period, *Marriage and Family in the Middle Ages*, by Frances and Joseph Gies (New York: Harper & Row, 1987), is a good introduction, while the recent discovery of *The Book of the City of Ladies*, by Christina de Pizan (New York: Persea, 1982, originally written in 1402), provides an extraordinary perspective.

A lively account of the Italian peninsula in the 15th century—the power struggles among autonomous city-states, the colorful political and artistic characters in each, and the loss of independence following the French and Spanish invasions—is told by Lauro Martines in *Power and Imagination: City-States in Renaissance Italy* (New York: Alfred A. Knopf, 1979), as well as in *History of Italy*, by Franco Guicciardini (London: Collier Macmillan, 1969).

Any discussion of the Italian Renaissance will lead to the great masters of the period: Botticelli, Michelangelo, Leonardo, Titian, and a host of others. Detailed accounts of each artist's work are widely available, but the layman would do well to begin with briefer articles that integrate each master into the wider spectrum of art history as a whole; two standard reference works for this purpose are H. W. Janson's *History of Art: A Survey of the Major Visual Arts from the Dawn of History to the Present Day* (New York: Harry N. Abrams, Inc., 1962) and *Art through the Ages* (New York: Harcourt, Brace and World, Inc., 1970), a thorough revision of Helen Gardner's original work (1926) by Horst de la Croix and Richard G. Tansey. See also E. H. Gombrich's classic work, *The Story of Art* (Oxford: Phaidon, 1950).

On the age of exploration in general and the voyages of Columbus in particular, see *The European Discovery of America: The Southern Voyages, 1492-1616* (New York: Oxford University Press, 1974), by Samuel Eliot Morison, a distinguished historian whose knowledge of his subject is matched by his joy in writing about it. And for more information about the ships on which Columbus and his fellows sailed and how they were constructed, see James Dodds's *Building the Wooden Fighting Ship* (New York: Facts On File Publications, 1984) and Frederic C. Lane's *Venetian Ships and Shipbuilders of the Renaissance* (New York: Ayer Co. Publishers, 1979).

Arms and Armor of the Medieval Knight: An Illustrated History of Weaponry in the Middle Ages (New York: Crescent Book, 1988), by David Edge and John Miles Paddock, is a good introduction, and its full-color photographs portray 15th-century armor as the work of art it had become. Contrast this with John Keegan's description of the battle of Agincourt (1415) in his unsurpassed *Face of Battle* (New York: Viking Press, 1976), which captures the brutal realities of hand-to-hand combat.

A recognized authority in its field and the first place to go for more information on its subject is the *Encyclopedia of Witchcraft and Demonology* (New York: Crown Publishers, Inc., 1959), by Rossel Hope Robbins; for the 15th and 16th centuries in particular, see Brian P. Levack's *Witch-Hunt in Early Modern Europe* (New York: Longman, 1987) and William Monter's *Ritual, Myth and Magic in Early Modern Europe* (Athens, Ohio: Ohio University Press, 1980).

Savonarola and 15th-century evangelism are covered in Norman Cohn's *Pursuit of the Millennium* (New York: Oxford University Press, 1970). For more on the philosophy the period, Ernst Cassirer and Paul Oskar Kristeller are experts in the field, and the two (with John Herman Randall, Jr.) have collaborated on *The Renaissance Philosophy of Man* (University of Chicago Press, 1948).

An excellent look at the spectacle and pageantry of 15th-century life is provided in *The Courts of the Italian Renaissance* (New York: Facts On File Publications, 1986), by Sergio Bertelli, Franco Cardini, and Elvira Garberzorz. For the more commonplace but often just as ritualized daily experience, see E. R. Chamberlain's *Everyday Life in Renaissance Times* (New York: G. P. Putnam's Sons, 1980) and, finally, *Medieval Households* (Harvard University Press, 1985), by David Herlihy.

Index

233

235

237

Acknowledgments

The paintings, illuminations, drawings, and engravings reproduced in this book are almost all from the second half of the 15th century or beginning of the 16th. The contemporary landscape photographs are by Toni Nicolini.

The following abbreviations are used in the credits: **a** (above); **b** (bottom); **c** (center); **l** (left); **r** (right).

AISA, Madrid: 20l
Graphische Sammlung Albertina, Vienna: 40**a**, 49,186, 187**r**
Archiv für Kunst und Geschichte, Berlin: 104**a**, 104**b**, 105**r**
Artothek, Kunstdia-Archiv Jürgen Hinrichs, Planegg bei München, Munich: 9, 74l
Ashmolean Museum, Oxford: 188
Cathedral of Barcelona: 62l, 126**r**
Biblioteca Apostolica Vaticana, Vatican City: 41**a**, 48, 82**r**, 183
Bibliothèque Nationale, Paris: 20**r**, 21**b**, 22l, 23, 30, 31, 43l, 84**a**, 103, 104-105**c**, 107l, 143, 170**r**, 177**r**, 178, 181l, 193, 207
Bibliothèque Publique et Universitaire, Geneva: 18
Bibliothèque Royale Albert 1er, Brussels (manuscripts): 16, 52, 63**r**, 131, 149
Bodleian Library, Oxford: 144l
British Library, London: 14, 21**a**, 35, 42**a**, 99, 102l, 128**r**, 129l
British Museum, London: 56l, 102**r**
Ets. J.E. Bulloz, Paris: 62**r**
Giancarlo Costa, Milan: 20**b**, 73, 87**a**, 93**a**, 96**r**, 97, 101, 112**a**, 133**r**, 138, 157**r**, 158l, 163**b**, 197**r**, 200, 208, 209
Photo Services, Gruppo Editoriale Fabbri, Milan: 32**b**, 42**b**, 44**b**, 56**r**, 60l, 68l, 75, 77, 84**b**, 85, 86l, 87**b**, 107**r**, 109l, 112**r**, 117**r**, 120, 122l, 123, 127, 140, 142l, 146**c**, 158**r**, 161**r**, 165, 167, 173, 179, 192, 195, 205
Germanisches Nationalmuseum, Nuremberg: 64**b**, 64**r**-65, 78-79, 86**r**, 109**r**, 113l
Giovetti Fotografia & Comunicazioni Visive, Mantua: 184
Photographie Giraudon, Paris: 98, 145l, 148**a**, 162, 166, 199**r**
Historia Photo, Bad Sachsa: 139
Historisches Archiv der Stadt Köln, Cologne: 28**r**
Duca dell'Infantado Collection, Madrid: 114

Janusz Podleki, Krakow: 94**a**, 95, 116l
Kunsthistorisches Museum, Vienna: 59**c**, 128l
MAS, Madrid: 170l
Memlingmuseum-Sint-Janshospitaal, Bruges: 58**c**
Metropolitan Museum of Art, New York: 32l (detail), 58**r** (detail), 93**r** (detail), 213**r** (detail)
Musée des Beaux-Arts, Lille: 54**r**
Museo Civico, Turin: 115
Národní Muzeum V Praze, Prague: 130l
National Gallery, London: 46, 116**r**, 146**a**
National Gallery of Art, Washington, D.C.: 10
National Portrait Gallery, London: 34
Toni Nicolini, Milan: 6, 26**b**, 36, 37l, 54**b**, 55**b**, 76, 160, 219
Österreichische Nationalbibliothek, Vienna: 17, 28**a**, 40**b**, 91
Pierpont Morgan Library, New York: 37**r**, 137**r**, 194
Laboratorio Fotografico Donato Pineider, Florence: 134, 199l
Prado Museum, Madrid: 39, 125**r**, 156l
Fotostudio Quattrone Mario, Florence: 59l
John & Mable Ringling Museum of Art Foundation, Sarasota, Florida: 69
Rosgartenmuseum, Constance: 93**b**
Royal Library, Windsor Castle, Berkshire: 151
Sansoni, Florence: 41**b**
Istituto Fotografico Editoriale Scala, Florence: 2, 8, 11, 12 (cover illustration), 19, 22**r**, 26**a**, 27, 29l, 33l, 44**a**, 45, 51, 55**a**, 56**a**, 57, 60**r**, 61**b**, 64**a**, 66l, 66**r**, 67, 82l, 83, 85**b**, 89, 90, 95**b**, 99, 100l, 101, 106**r**, 108, 116l, 118l, 124, 129l, 135**r**, 136**a**, 137, 141, 146, 150l, 150**r**, 154, 156, 157l, 159**r**, 163**a**, 164l, 171, 180l, 181, 187l, 189, 190, 196, 196-197, 198, 201, 203**a**, 204, 211, 212, 220
Otto Shafer Collection, Schweinfurt: 118**r**
Staatliche Graphische Sammlung, Munich: 28l, 74**a**
Staatliche Museen Preussischer Kulturbesitz, Berlin: 58l, 59**r**, 61**a**, 80l, 112**s**, 119, 133**b**, 137l, 186-187
Staatsarchiv, Hamburg: 87**r**
Städelsches Kunstinstitut, Frankfurt: 113**r**
Stadt Ulm, Stadtarchiv, Ulm: 143**r**
Studio Lourmel 77, Paris: 81
Szépmüvészeti Múzeum, Budapest: 133**c**
Uffizi Gallery, Florence: 130**r**
Wallace Collection, London: 43**r**, 132**c**
Worchester Art Museum, Worcester, Massachusetts: 29**r**